WRITING IN THE VICINITY OF ART

WRITING IN THE VICINITY OF ART

VOLUME 1

TRACEY WARR

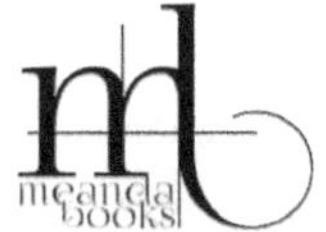

Published by Meanda Books

https://meandabooks.com

Copyright © 2023 by Tracey Warr

ISBN 978-1-7392700-9-4

A CIP catalogue record for this book is available from the British Library.

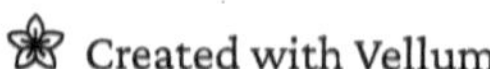 Created with Vellum

CONTENTS

INTRODUCTION: WRITING IN THE VICINITY OF ART

From 1982–1984 I was part of the exhibitions team at the Institute of Contemporary Arts (ICA), London, working alongside Sandy Nairne, Iwona Blazwick, Declan McGonagle and Steve White. I worked on exhibitions and catalogues by artists including Robert Mapplethorpe, Laurie Anderson and Derek Jarman. I then worked as Combined Arts Officer at the Arts Council of Great Britain, focusing on performance art (1985–1987). From 1986 onwards, I worked as an independent curator with a wide range of artists, including Helen Chadwick, Isaac Julien, London Fieldworks, Hayley Newman, Cornelia Parker, James Turrell and Urbonas Studio.

Alongside my work as a curator, I produced many texts on contemporary artists. I published my first piece of 'art writing' in 1987. It was a slender book co-edited with Jeni Walwin and Gray Watson, entitled *Live Art Now*. I generated exhibition catalogue essays, book chapters, journal articles, online publications, conference papers, interviews with artists, exhibition and art book reviews and creative writing pieces made in the context of art exhibitions and residencies. This book is the first of two volumes presenting a selection of my writing on contemporary art.

WRITING WITH ARTISTS

I have been inspired by two key sources: James Joyce's circumlocutory vision in *Finnegans Wake* of everything in the world endlessly moving and recycling—'a commodius vicus of recirculation' (1939, p. 3); and Marcel Duchamp's thesis of the co-production of the work of art by context, artist and audience in 'The Creative Act' (Duchamp, 1957, pp. 138–140).

Duchamp argued that the creative act is a complex process of co-creation. He described the artist as drawing from their context like a medium, working with conscious and unconscious intentions and with materials and then putting the art object or act back out into the context where it continues to be diversely co-created again and again through the readings of generations of spectators.

In contemporary practice, it is a familiar idea that artists and audiences co-produce art. Duchamp's other point, that the artist is a kind of medium, drawing from a context and then giving back out to a context, is still in contention with an ingrained notion of the artist as self-expressing innate genius (see, for instance, 'the Van Gogh myth' (Pollock, 1980) and 'the Jackson Pollock myth' (Orton and Pollock, 1996)).

The point of negotiation in contemporary art is the artwork and not the artist. There is more than the artist's making involved in the creative act. The artist's creative act is of course essential, but the artwork consists also of the context the work is coming from and presented in, the reception of the work by diverse audiences and the modes of presentation of the work. With this notion of 'the open work' (Eco, 1989), I argue that a curator or writer may sometimes be part of the creative act.

My PhD was entitled *The Creative Act: Curating and Writing with Artists*. Historical artworks have passed through the filter of 'posterity', as Duchamp points out. Their worth has been weighed by generations of commentators and viewers. Contemporary artworks, on the other hand, appear to us raw and naked, unaccompanied by this blizzard of valuing by critics, curators and viewers. It is, therefore, particularly important and challenging to carefully look at and write about contemporary artworks. They are vulnerable, teetering on the potential to sink into obscurity. I had curated the work of many of the artists I wrote about. I had witnessed their work from inception to presentation and reception. Curatorial commentaries on projects including the Edge biennales, which are extracts from my PhD, are included in *Writing in the Vicinity of Art*, Volume 2.

In my writing and curated projects, I challenged traditional binaries between artists and curators and artists and institutions, but also between mind and body, body and world, spiritual and social. I also challenged traditional modes of writing and logocentric modes of engaging with experience. I focused on the complex of co-creation in relation to creative acts of dialogue between the practices of artists, curators and writers; creative acts of experiencing the world; and creative acts of making art about experiencing (see Warr, 2006).

I developed a mode of writing with (rather than about) artists and was often 'embedded' in the artists' making processes. I generated writing from dialogue with artists, collaborations with artists and witnessing of the making of artworks. The book's title, *Writing in the Vicinity of Art*, is derived from Smithson's phrase, 'Language in the Vicinity of Art' (1968; and see Weiss, 2004; and see Smithson's 1966 artwork, *A Heap of Language*, which influenced my *Ecology of Words* workshop at HIAP, Finland in 2017 (Warr, 2018b)).

An example of my 'writing with artists' is 'Measuring Beauty in the Upper Ice World' on London Fieldworks' art project *Little Earth* (included in this book; Warr, 2005, pp. 11–19). This text was the result of my long-term engagement, as both a curator and writer, with these artists and their work. The project was about Victorian weather observatories on Ben Nevis mountain in Scotland and on Haldde mountain in Norway. I went to Fort William with the artists and spent time on and around Ben Nevis. I researched the history of the weather observatory and the two scientists London Fieldworks were focusing on. I found out about extreme weather events the two scientists might have witnessed and incorporated that into the text. It is a text creating an analogy between weather and consciousness. Being an embedded writer may take away a critical layer, but it adds a layer in which the writer can enter into an engagement with the artists' processes.

In another example of writing with artists, I went to Brazil with the performance group Optik—but in my *Performance Research* article (included in this volume), I did not so much write about their practice as write provoked by what they were doing—moving and not moving. The text responds to their work but is also about my own interest in the peripatetic consciousness and the nature of experience.

My writing projects were often iterative, where I worked repeatedly with certain artists, such as Allenheads Contemporary Arts (ACA), Tine Bech, Marcus Coates, London Fieldworks, Christian Thompson and Urbonas Studio.

My texts range through scholarly historical and interpretative writing to more subjective modes of writing. I took my embodied consciousness on research trips and kept stream of consciousness journals. Marcel Mauss writes of the body as our first instrument, our first technology (1934, p. 461) and Francisco Varela describes the body as a mobile laboratory (1999, np). Rather than the interpretative stance of the external commentator, I was developing a form of writing about art that incorporated subjective responses in a body-based writing practice drawing on physicality.

Throughout my work, a direct engagement with artworks in situ —field research—has played an important role. I undertook research trips for my work on land art—to the Netherlands in 1999, when I visited Turrell's *Skyspace* in sanddunes near Den Haag, Smithson's *Broken Circle/Spiral Hill* in Emmen and Robert Morris'

Observatory in Flevoland. In 2000, I travelled to Arizona and New Mexico and visited Turrell's *Roden Crater*. A subjective mode of writing is evident in my *Contemporary* article on Turrell (included in this book), which is part critical account of an artwork and part experiential travelogue.

My ideas about writing and streams of consciousness were informed by my early literary study of Joyce, Dorothy Richardson and D.H. Lawrence. I was trying to use writing in a fluid mode, inspired by the stream of consciousness, through an inclusion of external and internal data and connecting writing with the physicality of walking and swimming.

There was always an issue of creative collaborating with artists in my practice—but, in some of my more recent work, I was explicitly taking on the role of artist or creative writer. I have not included, in this book, the creative writing I generated in art residencies, such as *Exoplanet Lot* with Maison des Arts Georges et Claude Pompidou, Cajarc, where I wrote a future fiction novella, *Meanda*, or in *Microhabitable* with Matadero and Inland, where I wrote a story. These texts are published and available elsewhere. (See 'Texts Not Included' at the back of this book.)

THEMES

Most artists and writers find they are dealing with recurring themes and drawing repeatedly on the same sources. Recurring themes in my writing include collaboration, embodied consciousness, site, water, mortality.

During the 1980s and the early 1990s, I started a practice of site-based curating and writing about the work of performance and installation artists. In the 1990s, I was engaging with theories around body art, land art and consciousness. In 1995 Phaidon Press invited me to edit *The Artist's Body* survey book as part of their 'Contemporary Art Themes and Movements' series (Warr, 2000a). I engaged in four years of research for the book, which was the art historical and theoretical grounding for much of my continuing work. In addition to researching artists' work for the book, I undertook a very wide-ranging review of the interdisciplinary context in which the artists were making work, which included texts relating to anthropology, history, literature, philosophy and psychology, as well as art theory.

In curating and editing, there is always the unavoidable dilemma of canonising practice. You are always making a selection, an extract, and committing exclusion. It is important to find strategies to avoid being reductive. I hoped that with *The Artist's Body*, while unable to avoid the canonising process of a survey book, I was opening up new ideas with the way that I had put together the material, what I had put in proximity or sequence with what, the demonstration of the dialogue between artists' work and between artworks, texts and ideas.

My readings of body art developed in directions that were contrary to a lot of other critical writings. The contemporaneous critique of body art in the 1960s and 1970s was mostly bewildered and resorted to interpretations ranging from psychosis, anti-feminism, exhibitionism or masochism. These interpretations of body art as 'sick' or 'masochistic' are still the starting points of the arguments that Linda Kauffman (1998) and Kathy O'Dell (1998) bring to this work in their books. (See my review of these books Warr, 2001a.) Other recent revisionist analyses of body art, such as Amelia Jones' work (1998), have focused on identity politics. My own writing placed an emphasis on artists' engagements with mortality and consciousness. In addition to exploring the human body and identity as social construct many of the artists are, I feel, discussing conditions that are shared by all bodies and not constructed—transient and visceral life, intense consciousness and death.

From 1998 on, the focus of my research shifted to land art and consciousness and a recognition of the connections between theory and practice around body-based and site-based art. There was a shift away from the urban site curating I initially undertook toward an increasing emphasis on rural curatorial projects, an exploration of artists' engagements with the natural environment and the development of my work around consciousness.

After *The Artist's Body* had gone to press, I was feeling oppressed by being confined to a discourse of the body for so long and wanted a different area of research, which became land art. I had discovered, through writing reviews for the *Times Literary Supplement* in the 1980s, that it is relatively easy to be critical and cynical and to write 'good copy' but it is much harder to write positively, to say why something is good or moving, to write about beauty, the numinous, what Joyce described as 'epiphanies'. I decided to attempt it. I became particularly interested in our awed responses to the natural environment and wanted to examine the notion of the sublime—especially in relation to Romantic painting and literature and the revisiting of Romanticism in contemporary art. I was interested in how this might relate to what is unlanguaged and resistant to logocentric interpretation and articulation.

My publications and projects addressed embodied consciousness, experience and the natural environment. The two-year period I spent working as a curator with Turrell was a significant influence on this area of my research. Turrell's own writings address these concerns, as do Robert Smithson's (Turrell, 1993; Smithson, 1979).

Water emerged as another obsessive theme in my work, particularly in my collaborations with Urbonas Studio in *The Culture of Rowing and Swimming*, *River Runs* and *The Wet Symposium* (see 'Writing with Water' in this book; also see Urbonas, Lui and Freeman, 2017).

An all-encompassing research question was posed by Polish performance artist, Jerzy Beres, in a performance in *Edge 88* in London. Standing with a large white question mark painted on his naked body, Beres appeared to be asking what is the body? what is embodied consciousness? what am I? what are you? The body can articulate in ways that are unlanguaged and not polarised or fixed but instead fluxional, pulsional and perpetually maintaining potentials (see 'A Hysterical Sense of Leaking' in *Writing in the Vicinity of Art*, Volume 2).

> The unknown is a provocation that propels us on a journey, a route of unknowing in which we experience many of the ways that we do not know something. (Buckingham, 2003, p. 94)

How are immaterial ideas made manifest in the world? Elaine Scarry writes eloquently about the relationship between ideas and ideology and the physical, manifest world and the role of making and unmaking,

> The referential fluidity or instability of the body allows it to confer its reality onto other things .... A disembodied idea that has no basis in the material world ... can borrow the appearance of reality from the realm that from the very start has compelling reality to the human mind, the physical body itself .... The absolute intention of all human making [is] to distribute the facts of sentience outward onto the created realm of artifice, and it is only by doing so that men and women are themselves relieved of the privacy and problems of that sentience. (1985, pp. 42–45)

In my writing, I was often engaging in a polemic against binaries and exploring a vision of the circumfluent, dynamic, creative natures of world and consciousness in interaction with each other.

WRITING IN THE VICINITY OF ART, VOLUME 1

In recent years, the pandemic, arts funding cuts and other changes have led to the closure of key arts organisations, which means that areas of recent art history are at risk of sinking into obscurity. I hope some of the texts included here, and especially the account of site-specific art and performance art from my PhD (coming in Volume 2), contribute to ensuring that important artists, artworks and exhibitions made in the last few decades are recorded and accessible.

The texts are ordered A–Z by artist or title. Where a text primarily deals with one artist, they are listed A–Z under the artist's surname. Where the text deals with multiple artists, they are listed under the text title. There is no thematic or chronological ordering. *Writing in the Vicinity of Art* Volume 2 is also organised A–Z and there is no chronological division between the two volumes (which is, rather, arbitrary).

Where my texts were published by mainstream publishers and are still readily available in book form, I have not included them in this book. (See 'Texts Not Included' at the back of this book.)

I took a decision not to include images of artists' works, hoping the writing would, instead, conjure images in the readers' minds. A Google search should turn up images for most of the artists and works mentioned.

Most of the texts included in this volume were commissioned as catalogue essays or exhibition or book reviews. 'On the Tip of my Tongue' is a journal article based on my teaching and writing practice. 'Silent Running' is a text I wrote after participating in Alan Smith's *Parameter* in a disused lead mine in Cumbria. 'Writing in Water' charts the collaborative research process for my project with Urbonas Studio, *River Runs* at Modern Art Oxford in 2012 and *The Wet Symposium*, which I organised.

A second volume of *Writing in the Vicinity of Art*, coming soon, has texts on artists including Cyril Lepetit, NVA, Carolee Schneemann and Urbonas Studio and on projects, including the *Edge* biennales, *Frontiers in Retreat*, *Outlandia*, *A Study Room Guide to Remoteness*, *Wanderlust*, *Women's Body Art Now* and *Zooetics*.

The overall research journey I have been on has taken me from an initial interest in stream of consciousness in literature, to an engagement with contemporary artists' practice exploring the embodied consciousness in dynamic and creative interaction with the natural environment. Research is often described as a process of moving knowledge forward but perhaps we are simply moving knowledge around and making knowledge moving.

> As soon as we follow one line … a journey emerges … and of course that journey unavoidably becomes a story. (Buckingham, 2003, p. 94)

Tracey Warr, Laguépie, August 2023

1

MARINA ABRAMOVIĆ: TO RUPTURE IS TO FIND

1995. First published in *Women's Art Magazine*, May/June, pp. 11–13.

The Museum of Modern Art in Oxford recently organised the first solo touring show survey of Marina Abramović's work. Abramović will be working shortly at the Henry Moore Sculpture Trust Studio in Halifax and two books on her work will be published this year (Abramović, 1995a, 1995b).

Abramović's 1970s performance work can be seen alongside 'body art' by Chris Burden, Vito Acconci, Gina Pane, the Viennese Actionists, Paul McCarthy and others, all of which is currently subject to a revival of interest and reappraisal in shows such as *Hors Limites* at the Pompidou Centre in Paris and *Endurance* held earlier this year at Exit Arts in New York. Abramović's work, however, has a second context with her origins in Eastern Europe in Tito's Yugoslavia.

In the communist and socialist regimes of Eastern Europe, the body, on the one hand, was your only property: the place of freedom and, as in the West, for many women artists, it was, of course, also a political site. On the other hand, the body was colonised by state language and imagery, by the representation of the body of power practised by Tito and Stalin and the use of the Lenin cult (the statues and the embalmed body of Lenin). Conceptual and abstract artists had fewer direct problems with state censorship than representative painters and sculptors. At the same time as Abramović was beginning her performance work, other women artists in ex-Yugoslavia, such as Sanja Iveković were exploring the body.

Between 1973 and 1975, Abramović's work relentlessly and systematically tested the limits of the body. *Rhythm 2* was a seven-hour performance in which she took the usual medication for acute catatonia and for schizophrenia. 'I put my body in an unpredictable state' (Meschede, 1993). In *Rhythm 0*, she announced, 'I am the object', and, for six hours, she allowed the audience to do whatever they liked with her. Her clothes were cut from her with razor blades, her skin was cut, various minor sexual assaults were carried out on her body. She offered no resistance. The audience response was extreme. Some worshipped the artist-like object as one would a beautiful statue, and others humiliated 'it'. Occasionally, there were human and humane interventions: a woman wipes paint (or tears?) from the artist's face, and another intervenes at the end of the performance to remove a loaded gun held to her head.

In a series of performances, *Freeing the Voice*, *Freeing the Body* and *Freeing the Memory*, Abramović screamed for three hours until she lost her voice, moved to African drumming for eight hours until she collapsed from exhaustion and recited words for 90 minutes until she could remember no more. In the two-hour performance, *The Lips of Thomas*, Abramović ate a kilo of honey, drank a litre of red wine, cut a five-point star on her stomach with a razor blade, whipped herself for as long as she could, then lay naked, slowly freezing on an ice cross until the audience removed her. 'When she grapples with the limits of her physical and mental consciousness, she is concerned with opening up ... areas of perception which lie outside of rational conventions' (von Drathen, 1993).

In 1975, Abramović left Yugoslavia and based herself in Amsterdam and in 1976 she met the German artist, Ulay, with whom she began a 12-year collaboration. They continued to explore the parameters of the body and also the parameters of their relationship and gender in works, such as *Relation in Space*, where they ran naked in space constantly colliding; *Imponderabilia*, where they stood naked in the narrow entrance to a museum and visitors were forced to slide between the artists, choosing which artist to face; and in *Light/Dark* where they alternately slapped each other's faces for twenty minutes.

After spending time in the desert with nomadic Aborigines, Abramović and Ulay's work began to deal more with the cosmic and the spiritual in *Nightsea Crossing* (1982–1986) and later in *Modus Vivendi* and *Anima Mundi*. In *Nightsea Crossing*, the artists sat at a table, motionless, silent and fasting for a total of 90 non-consecutive days, completed at various venues around the world. It was a journey into the self, into the consciousness. Their final work together was in 1998 when, in *The Lovers*, they each walked 2,000 km from opposite ends of the Great Wall of China to meet in the middle.

Working on her own again in the nineties, Abramović turned to lapidary. A series of works made in Brazil in 1991, entitled *Waiting for an Idea*, used mined rock crystals. She also began to make a series of copper and quartz objects.

Her work broke out of a 'purist' visual art performance genre to explore theatre, comedy and baroque. It draws on her lurid personal background, including a grandfather who was poisoned with crushed diamonds and parents who were both high-ranking officers in the partisan army and met while saving each other's lives (*The Body in Communism*, 1995). She started to perform *Biography* in 1992, a mixture of theatrical autobiographical monologue and extracts from her 'real' performance works, including the five-point star cut on her stomach from *The Lips of Thomas*. She intends to continue performing *Biography*, constantly updated, until the end of her life.

In her most recent work, a video installation entitled *Cleaning the Mirror* (commissioned by the Museum of Modern Art, Oxford and the Ruskin School of Drawing), the artist's hands are held over 'power-objects' selected from the Pitt Rivers collection. They include a mummified ibis, an albatross, a Greek mirror and an African medicine box. A video narrative includes a skeleton lying on top of the artist's naked body, which moves up and down as she breathes. The sound of her breathing fills the room and the camera pans in until all that is seen are the mouths of the skeleton and the artist. There is also a stack of five video monitors showing an over-sized image of the skeleton being energetically cleaned with deter-gent and a broom. (Talking at *The Body in Communism* symposium in Berlin, (1995), Abramović revealed that her mother was obsessed with cleaning and 'germs'. As a teenager, she smeared brown shoe polish over her bedroom walls to create her own space and exclude her intrusive mother.)

In her crystal objects, instructions for spectators are concise: 'Sit down. Put your head under the helmet. Eyes closed. Motionless. Depart.' These instructions are echoed in *Chairs for Departure* (1991) and other works, such as *Shoes for Departure*, where immovable amethyst clogs urge the visitor to step into them and depart. In this exhibition surveying her work, the consistency with which her work since 1972 has envisaged journeys of the spirit can be discerned.

> I left Yugoslavia in 1975 and have travelled ever since, leading an essentially nomadic existence where waiting in rooms and airport lounges and the space in between have become my artist's studio, the place where I can work and have ideas, where I am completely open to my destiny and my perception is stronger. (Warr, 1995b, np)

An early installation in a Belgrade hotel foyer surprised the public with airport style announcements, telling them to board their planes to various destinations, provoking them to undertake imaginary trips. At the same time, amplified birdsong was played through loudspeakers in the trees outside. While, on one level, this work may be read as wishful longings to escape to the West or youthful *wanderlust*, it is also an early summons to the soul to journey and to migrate, and this occurs throughout Abramović's work.

Her 'furniture' objects, such as beds and chairs, tables, quartz pillows and immovable clogs are domestic but not comfortable or homely. Instead, they are doors through which the spirit can escape. 'Breaks with conventional understanding are important to me. I want to produce a "mental jump", want to lead people to a point where rational thinking fails, where the brain has to give up' (von Drathen, 1993). The material used in her work, whether it be the body, rock crystals, power objects, or video and sound, is literally that: the material as opposed to the spiritual, a means to gain access to the non-rational. Abramović' remarks, 'Rational understanding is only a tiny part of our perceptive faculties; the rest, dreaming, imagination, contemplation and meditation, visions or telepathy, has been completely buried' (Warr, 1995b, np).

Her work obsessively probes the parameters of the material: of the body, of fear and of pain. 'If an idea frightens me, then I do it' (Warr, 1995b, np). In the performance, *Dragon Heads* (1995) she sat for an hour in a ring of ice, with five pythons moving around her head, face and body. In the audience, you could see and smell her fear.

She sets up tensions between precise ritualistic requirements and abandonment and lack of control. The ritualistic requirements may be time—90 days, so many hours—or space, colour or physical obligations, such as fasting. A vivid example of this is the 1973 performance, *Rhythm 10*, where she had 12 knives, and performed a knife trick with her hand splayed on a table while she rapidly stabbed between her fingers. A tape recorded when she cut herself. Each time she cut herself, she changed knives. When she had used up all the knives, she listened to the tape and then repeated the exercise, trying to cut herself again at precisely the same moment, in the same place and with the same knife as the first time round. The ritual creates and shapes a pathway out of the material to the spiritual.

Abramović regards the body as a receiver of ideas, of instinctive knowledge. 'What do we do to prepare to make art? Nothing. Cennini advised three months' preparation: one month without wine, two without meat, one without sex and one week with the right hand in plaster' (Broeke, 2015). Her work is about thinking through the body, proving 'axioms in philosophy … upon our puls-es', as Keats wrote. Bojana Pejić succinctly describes what the body is in Abramović's work:

> If one conceives of the body as a 'site of activity', the 'minor narra-tive of the body [itself] avoids the pitfalls of thinking, which is essentially monological, logocentric and Eurocentric. The body as site not only means that the body is not divorced from its mind, neither does it mean that the body and mind are in a state of static 'harmony'. It is the site where, in a dynamic process of mutual making (and un-making), the body continuously forms the mind while at the same time the mind shapes the body. (1993)

Abramović sees our reliance on technology, the visual, the rational and the intellect as obscuring all our other perceptive abili-ties and knowledge. Recently, we have begun to be aware of the more holistic and less anthropocentric world views held by the world's surviving indigenous peoples. The South African Dogan tribes know that Pluto has a second satellite although it is invisible to the naked eye. The Ancient Egyptians' extraordinary knowledge of astronomy is just starting to come to light. An Amazonian tribe's dreams of a 'cosmic serpent' have recently been linked by an anthropologist and biologists to the structure of DNA (Narby, 1999). Abramović's body and objects are amplifiers and transformers of emotional and physical knowledge.

2

HEATHER ACKROYD AND DAN HARVEY: PASSING PRESENCE

2002. First published in H. Ackroyd and D. Harvey (eds) *Afterlife*. London: Beaconsfield/Arts Admin, np.

For the last ten years Heather Ackroyd and Dan Harvey have been using grass as a living photographic medium. Conventional photography captures a present moment and, in an instant, turns it into the past. Photography sets up, in effect, not a perception of the being-there of an object... but a perception of its having-been-there (Barthes, 1964, p. 47). Ackroyd and Harvey's photography, on the other hand, is without closure.

Exploiting the light-sensitivity of young growing grass, they imprint photographic images on to grass grown vertically, so that the image is on the length of the blade, rather than dispersed over the tips. As the grass grows, the image becomes sharper. The further away you stand from the image, the higher the resolution—the more distinct it is. But time is, of course, embedded in the fragility of these chlorophyll apparitions. We know that the image will fade, the grass will yellow and die. The gradual disappearance of the image from vision, memory, life, is implicit in what we are looking at. Ackroyd and Harvey are giving photography a performative charge. As Peggy Phelan has pointed out, performance is about disappearance rather than preservation. Performance plunges momentarily into visibility in a maniacally charged present and disappears into memory (Phelan, 1993, p. 147). Ackroyd and Harvey's work is a potent evocation of presence and presentness. It briefly delays the passing present but eventually both medium and representation mimic their subject and fade away.

Alongside their photographic work with grass, Ackroyd and Harvey have also been making architectural and spatial interventions with grass. *The Other Side*, made in Italy in 1990, was the first of a series of architectural interventions altering and engulfing structures with grass. In this work they grew the grass up the interior walls of a vaulted room. *Grass House*, 1991, in Hull, was a derelict house covered with a green skin. Their environment, *The Undertaking*, 1992, was made underneath The National Theatre of the Palais du Chaillot in Paris, where a labyrinth of tunnels leads to the city's ancient catacombs and cemeteries. Here, they lined the walls, floors and ceilings of passages and stairways with grass, evoking both the claustrophobia of the open turf-lined grave and a sense of life renewing and springing up again. Footsteps worn in the grassy stairwells bore witness to time and memory.

In Theaterhaus Gessnerallee, Zurich, 1993, grass was grown over the entire exterior facade of a building, emphasising the outlines of its classical proportions through the blanket of grass. In *The Divide* (Wellington, New Zealand, 1996), they split and separated a derelict building and grassed the vertiginous walls of the narrow divide. Like Gordon Matta-Clark's split buildings or Rachel Whiteread's *House*, Ackroyd and Harvey bring these buildings into the consciousness of the viewer in the form of ghosts—their pasts temporally remote. But they are also given new life through becoming verdant abstract sculptures.

In 1996, Ackroyd and Harvey collaborated with Pierre d'Avoine Architects on the *Host* interventions in Venice. The fact that the city is relentlessly undermined year by year by its canals, prompted them to create and exhibit lumps of plaster—pummelled under a dripping tap for ten days or holed like cheese in a stream for four days—which displayed the effects of water over time. In their work, nature becomes a performer. And this performance by nature is even more pronounced in Ackroyd and Harvey's photographic grass work. It began as an accidental discovery in their first architectural intervention.

Having left a ladder leaning against the growing grass wall, they found that its image had been imprinted. They began to explore the capacity of grass to record either simple shadows or complex photographic images. 'The haunting presence of the emergent organic image was and still is quite revelatory to us' (Ackroyd, Harvey and Thomas, 2000).

In 1997, with support from a Wellcome Trust Sci-Art Award and subsequently a NESTA grant, Ackroyd and Harvey started working with scientists at the Institute of Grassland and Environmental Research in Aberystwyth to explore the possibility of preserving the image longer. Professor Howard Thomas and Dr Helen Ougham were working on a stay-green grass, studying leaf ageing and developing techniques for controlling the enzyme that degrades chlorophyll as a leaf dies. During the course of their collaboration with the artists they have advanced hyperspectral imaging, which allows them to study minute colour changes in grass and a prototype stay-green grass seed, which is growing in trials at the moment. In 1998 Ackroyd and Harvey made *Mother and Child* using staygreen grass and then dried it for exhibition in Santa Barbara, California. This process lasts longer than their earlier grass photography but still fades eventually, maintaining the concern with transience and presentness in their work.

These grass photographs recall the strange magic of early

images made by photography pioneer William Henry Fox Talbot. He placed an object on paper sensitised with silver salts and then placed both in the sun. When the object was removed, the exposed paper retained the silhouette of the object. The frustration of capturing and then losing the image as it faded led him to seek ways to fix the image. In the 1920s, Man Ray adopted a similar technique with his rayographs or photograms and in 1950, Robert Rauschenberg and Susan Weil made *Blueprints*, in which Weil's nude body was placed directly onto light sensitive paper (Molesworth, 1993).

> Every photograph is the result of a physical imprint transferred by light reflections onto a sensitive surface... the physical transposition of an object from the continuum of reality into the fixed condition of the art-image by a moment of isolation, or selection. (Krauss, 1985)

In the fixed photograph there is a predatory, acquisitive instinct at work—an appropriation, a commodification, a stealing of souls. The fixed photographic image evinces a desire to hold on to things, an attachment to visibility. The camera has been theorised as a tomb, the photograph as a form of death. Things in process become images of frozen moments, artefacts of the past.

Ackroyd and Harvey have developed a deviant form of photography, without closure. Their works briefly stabilise the elusive and transient, and then let it fade away. Instead of the impression of having been there, in their grass photography we experience presence as fleeting present. Imprinting the human image on the living medium of grass they succeed in conjuring presence and presentness in a celebration of the living moment. At the same time, they remind us of the inevitability of grass, image and subject fading away.

Ackroyd and Harvey's grass photography makes literal the idea that pervades Thomas Hardy's writing that Nature is both a mute witness and an inexorable contributor to the tragedy of human transience. And verdant Nature rolls on, recycling, regenerating while we must imagine a world eventually without us in it. Confrontation with our own mortality emphasises the intensity and vitality of the present lived moment. Ackroyd and Harvey's choice of subjects is celebratory rather than morbid—the lined faces of the elderly who have lived long, a family picnic, mother and child. In *Sunbathers*, 2000, exhibited at Exit Art, New York, both subject and medium are soaking up light. In their imprints of the human face and body on grass, Ackroyd and Harvey collide the surface of the material with the subject, mutability with the indexical.

Lush, green grass, saturated with light and water, is a symbol of life, fertility, abundance. The vegetable resurrection myths of the Green Man, Osiris and Balder celebrate the regenerating cycle of life. Plant photosynthesis gives us life by producing oxygen, but grass grows lushly too on our graves. Like the skull, grass is a *memento mori*—all flesh is grass (*The Bible*, Isaiah, 40: 6–8)—an image of the inevitable corruption and decay of all living matter.

Ackroyd and Harvey's use of grass as a photographic medium is an indexical practice, rather than a representational methodology. In their grass works there is a continued physical relationship with the subject. Physical traces—stains, footprints, body casts, shadows have all been identified as indexes rather than symbols (Didi-Huberman, 1984; Krauss, 1985). In Duchamp's ten-foot-wide painting *Tu m'* (*You/Me*), 1918, cast shadows of his readymades, including the bicycle wheel and the hatrack, were projected onto the surface of the canvas. In other indexical works, Piero Manzoni marked his inky thumbprint on eggs (*To Devour Art*, 1960). Gilchrist's enlarged thumbprint was tattooed on his own arm (*Transmutations*, 1996) and relayed to an audience both as visual performance and as the sound of his pain, through the use of a galvanic skin resistance meter.

In her essay, 'Notes on the Index: Part 2', Rosalind E. Krauss

(1977) describes a performance by dancer Deborah Hay in which she did not dance but instead delivered a monologue to the audience, insisting that she was there. In their performance, *Nightsea Crossing* (1981–1986), Abramović and Ulay sat in immobile silence, over a total of 90 days, making the same mute point. These are all indexical documents of presence, to which can be added Ackroyd and Harvey's grass photography where presence and presentness is momentarily slowed.

For their new work, *Afterlife*, at Beaconsfield, Ackroyd and Harvey have captured their human subjects on a nearby zebra crossing in Vauxhall. The portraits of these passers-by are imprinted larger than life onto screens of growing grass but are not just pictures of other people in an unusual medium. Looking at these green images striding through the gallery and life, we see our own reflections caught briefly in the act of passing on.

3
ALLENHEADS CONTEMPORARY ARTS: ECOTAXOLOGY

2009. First published in T. Warr, H. Ratcliffe, A. Smith, and E. Carpenter (eds) *Setting the Fell on Fire: Allenheads Contemporary Arts: Art in a Rural Context*. Sunderland: Editions North, pp. 13–15 and pp. 29–34.

PLACE

Wading down the Allen river in the North Pennines from its source with ecotaxologist, Alan Donaldson, and a group of artists, I can see where the water runs down off the hills to the watershed turning the ground into a raft that bounces when you jump on it, bending the reeds out of its path before it has even become a river, then carving, cutting and meandering its way through the land dragging shards of fluorspar, limestone and ancient pottery downriver and depositing them elsewhere. Ankle-deep in the cold, clear river, like a group of eager David Bellamys, we can taste the watermint growing mid-stream and observe the tiny plant ergot near the bank that it would not be so good to taste. Its toxin causes hallucination and has been blamed for historical bouts of witch-burning. You see how the river has drawn human settlement and industry to it through the centuries, and the legacies of that human and river interaction are visible in the landscape.

The following day, we spent four hours underground in a disused lead mine at Nenthead, wading thigh deep in watery tunnels hand-chiselled by miners through the limestone, marvelling at deposits of galena glittering in the rock like the milky way, hauling myself on hands and knees and sliding flat on my stomach through tight holes in the rock until we emerged into a vast cavern where thousands of tons of lead had been mined out. With our helmet lights out, we sampled just how dark dark is when you are hundreds of feet underground. How sound reverberates when you are encased in solid rock.

We weren't on an outward-bound course. These immersions in geology, atmosphere and landscape were part of a week-long artists' workshop organised by ACA. The week's activities took us beyond our romantic or urbanite preconceptions of landscape and weather and beyond our previous conceptions of ourselves, expanding our sense of relationship with the environment. 'The city gives the illusion that the earth does not exist' (Smithson, 1979, p. 83). Instead of observing that it was raining outside, we felt on our faces that it was raining and that the wind was whipping cold across the fells with clouds streaming past fast and their shadows pursuing them on the grass.

Allenheads School House is 1,400 feet above sea level, the highest point of England's highest village, on a near vertical hairpin bend, near the border between Cumbria and Northumberland. In 1747, nearby Cross Fell was described as 'generally ten months buried in snow and eleven in clouds' (*The Gentlemen's Weekly* cited in Hopkins, 1989, p. 65). On a clear day, Allenheads looks and feels like the top of the world. The eye is awash with sky and moor, the wind feels like it might blow you off the planet. In the winter, the sky closes into the land and the guide poles are the only way of knowing where the road out and in once was, now buried under several feet of snow. To the north, are Hadrian's Wall, Kielder Forest and the Cheviot Hills and the 'disputed lands' adjoining the Scottish border.

Some mornings the school is in the clouds, the village below invisible, sounds wafting up from the bowl of the River Allen valley beneath. The nearest towns are Allendale and Hexham to the north. It is an hour's drive to the nearest cities—Newcastle and Durham to the east and Carlisle to the west. If you go due south or due north, it is many miles before you reach any major urban area. Artists and curators working here must inevitably engage with the place, with its rural community, the contemporary economics and politics of the countryside, cultural assumptions about the country, the human geography, the dialogue and, sometimes, confrontation between the urban and the rural. Britain's 'green and pleasant land' is an essential reference point for a sense of national identity. Yet it is as much the result of centuries of agricultural husbandry and early industry as it is 'natural' or produced by more recent conservation and green tourism.

When students and artists arrive at Allenheads, the project directors—Helen Ratcliffe and Alan Smith—devise ways to swiftly immerse their visitors in a sense of where they are. Sitting in a shooting butt on the windswept moor-top alone for an hour will do it. Spending four hours underground in the old lead mine tunnels confronted with dark and silence will do it. Spending two hours watching the technicolour performance of the sky as it changes from blue to red to dark, at sunset, in Turrell's *Skyspace* will do it. Wading down the icy River Allen. That will make you feel on your pulses where you are. Spending an evening chatting to 'locals' in the Allenheads Inn will do it too. One's sense of self is different here from the city. Morris wrote of 'a place in which the perceiving self might take measure of certain aspects of its own physical existence ... the terms of this interaction are temporal as well as spatial. .. existence is process' (Morris, 1970, cited in Tiberghien, 1993, p. 83). Every artist who has spent time at Allenheads has in some way, and in very diverse ways, made a portrait of the place.

THE GREEN ROAD

The Carrier's Way, Black Way and Broad Way, near the village of Allenheads in Northumberland, are old Green Roads. They were thoroughfares for travellers on foot and horseback, going from countryside to market or places of pilgrimage before the advent of the car and tarmac. Walking up a Green Road, you are immersed in a combination of contemporary, historical and mythical 'country'. The entrances to the Green Roads attract like the back of the wardrobe to Narnia or the rabbit hole down to Alice's Wonderland. They beckon the walker back into a nostalgic world preceding the car and the cut-up of the countryside by the profusion of roads and pylons. All journeys involve the allure of the unknown and the imagined.

Around the tops of the green valley bowl that Allenheads sits in, the surrounding moors roll into distances as far as the eye can see. The 360-degree bend of the horizon gives a sense of being on the planet, rotating in space. Trees, sheep and ruined farm buildings dot the landscape. Our ancestry as hunter-gatherers in forested land-scapes has left the contemporary eye especially attuned to the colour green. Just as there are hundreds of different words for snow and ice in Scandinavian languages, there are hundreds of words for greenness in the English language. The eye evolved with spectral tuning to light reflecting off green leaves, which were the dominant feature of the colour environment of our primate and prehistoric ancestors. Professor Howard Thomas, biologist at the Institute of Grassland and Environmental Research in Aberystwyth writes that 'something special happens when the human eye and green leaves meet' (IGER, 2000, np).

Most of the time people are looking at the green countryside of Britain from a car, a train or (more rarely) a bus window. The peripatetic or walking consciousness has a different experience of being immersed in the landscape it is moving through. In walking, there is a heightened awareness of the fine membrane, the permeable border, between self and world. All journeys are simultaneously travels into the exterior and into our own interiors. Moving stirs up the contents of consciousness so that as a writer you can find sentences and paragraphs by literally taking your consciousness for a walk. When we live in a city our navigation of other people, obstacles, routes and traffic becomes a bodily habituation. After practice, this moving sinks out of consciously directed action and into the body, into reflex. In the city, the body runs on its own well-worn grooves and ruts. In the country, the kind of self-location experienced differs from the experience of self in the city.

The rural environment of Allenheads can be Eden or it can be Hell. Nature here can appear a wondrous and sublime gift or red in tooth and claw. Depending on your mood or perspective it can appear as paradise and Cockaigne or as a bleak reminder of human transient insignificance. Contemporary anthropocentric ecology casts a kindly mother nature as victimised and damaged by rapacious, consumerist humanity. Hurricanes, earthquakes, floods and tsunami, however, remind us that nature is itself an immensely destructive force and we are not the authors or controllers of it. The sensed presence of a sentient nature can be fearful or wondrous.

Romantic artists, such as J.M.W. Turner, Frederic Church and Caspar David Friedrich, painted the awesome spectacle of nature. Many of the landscapes in John Martin's apocalyptic paintings were based on the Allen Valley around Allenheads. For these painters, the humbled, human observer is looking on, outside of nature. For many contemporary artists, however, we are not outside observers looking at nature. Instead, the human embodied consciousness is co-creating what it is looking at. Human and nature are connected, contingent, mutually impacting one on the other. Jackson Pollock declared, 'I am not painting *inspired* by nature, I *am* nature'.

Contemporary art is often an instrument with which to see, think, feel and be our dynamic connectedness with the natural environment. This emphasis on a dynamic and creative immersion in nature reflects shifting understandings in the science and philosophy of the relationships between human body, consciousness and the environments we are moving through and perceiving. Contemporary art is increasingly revisiting the Romantic themes of subjectivity, emotion, nature. Tacita Dean's *Fernsehturm* film of sunset from the revolving top of Berlin's television tower; Marielle Neudecker's real-time films of sunrise and sunset, *Over and Over, Again and Again*, shown at the Tate Britain in the Turner rooms in 2005; Olafur Eliasson's recreation of a sun-drenched day in the Tate Modern's Turbine Hall; or Susan Derges' photographic 'portraits' of rivers and her images of the moon through trees inspired by the nineteenth-century painter Samuel Palmer, are all examples of a contemporary Romantic enquiry. Several of the artists who have worked at ACA, including Turrell, London Fieldworks, Alan Smith and Coates, are also treading this ground.

There is often a chasm between experiences of nature and the articulation of those experiences. Much of our experience is received and processed bodily, somatically without language. We are aware of epiphanies defeating language—sunset, moonshine, the numinous and the ineffable.

Technology fails to capture the full timbre of human embodied experience. A camera or minidisk gaffer-taped to my body as I walk around does not capture anything like my experience. It captures its own experience. It does not possess and cannot be fully directed to achieve my ability to simultaneously sense, receive and interpret data. It does not have my peripheral vision. It does not have my bodily—as opposed to merely visual or aural—capacity to engage with an environment.

In Turrell's *Skyspace* in Kielder, to the north of Allenheads, you must sit patiently for two hours or so at dusk waiting for the transformation of the sky visible though the circular aperture in the roof (see *Cat Cairn—The Kielder Skyspace*, no date). On a clear day you will see the sky go from blues to pinks to reds to purples to blacks. On a cloudy day you will see the pale grey light, diffused through damp clouds, shaft into the space and appear so tangible that you think you can hold it. One of the chief effects produced by Turrell's work is an experiential blurring of boundaries, a correlation of inner and outer space. Turrell addresses an experience beyond language, the ineffable—the gap between experience and interpretation (Rugoff, 1999, pp. 23–29).

There is a dynamic relationship between the perceiving consciousness or subjectivity and the environment or 'reality' it is bodily moving through. The environment is both produced by us and really there and received by us. In the city, it seems as it if it entirely produced. In the country, without the human clutter of the city, we can see the sky and sense the given stuff surrounding us more clearly. We become more aware of the reception of the environment, instead of its production or construction.

We are living in a material culture where the visual and the tangible dominate. You don't have to be a mystic to know that there are substantial parts of what is out there in the world that we cannot see. Force, mass, gravitational attraction, electrical charge are phenomena that exist. They are not constructed or co-created by our perception. Our sensory systems provide us with dimensions of experience that model the energies surrounding our bodies. Sensory systems are committed to specific modalities of experience. The given stuff, this world of gravity, energy, magnetic force is variously perceived by different human individuals and by different species through diverse sensory and cultural systems so that we are all modelling differently this same given stuff. These experiences represent rather than accurately report what is going on in the world. The act of perceiving the world is itself creative. Confined within our own species-specific sensory modality we can only conjecture at what a frog or a cat sees, what a dolphin or a bat hears or what it feels like to be a homing pigeon experiencing changes in the magnetic field (Nagel, 1974, pp. 435–450).

A poetic conflation might be made—as London Fieldworks' art suggests—between human consciousness and meteorology. Consciousness resembles the cooperative processes of weather, such as fire, lightning, waves, tornadoes. Consciousness is emergent. Existence is process. Consciousness has evanescent qualities rather than the stable properties of material objects. But even matter as apparently stable as rock is in slow flux.

One's mind and the earth are in a constant state of erosion, mental rivers wear away abstract banks, brain waves undermine cliffs of thought ... Vast geological movement crushes the landscape of logic under glacial reveries. This slow flowage makes one conscious of the turbidity of thinking. Slump, debris slides, avalanches all take place within the cracking limits of the brain (Smithson, 1979, p. 82).

Consciousness is embodied but the body is also situated and immersed in and permeated by the world. 'The mind is not in the head since its roots are in the body as a whole and also in the extended environment where the organism finds itself' (Varela, 1999, np). The body is a process rather than an entity and something that is immersed in and open to its environment rather than self-contained. The situated and immersed body is constantly perceiving and sensing its context, its environment and co-creating it. Max Velmans writes,

I find it useful to think of consciousness as the creator of 'subjective realities' ... we participate in a process whereby the universe observes itself – and the universe becomes both the subject and the object of experience. Consciousness and matter are intertwined (2000, p. 280).

Gilchrist and Joelson's residencies in Allenheads have contributed to their experiments with light and the body and their elaboration of the body as a mobile laboratory—a complex sensory probe and recorder and a near-simultaneous analyser and interpreter. Mauss described the body as,

man's first and most natural instrument. Or more accurately, not to speak of instruments, man's first and most natural technical object, and at the same time his first technical means, is his body. (1934, p. 461)

Western culture and language is based on taxonomy—separation, labelling and categorising—and this allows us to communicate and manipulate concepts. It is necessary but also reductive. Because Western culture is logocentric, it is easy to forget that linguistic labels are approximations and fictional boxes. These taxonomies and definitions are dependent on a strategy of polarisations—defining something by what it is not—and a range of fictional binaries have developed to aid communication. Spurious oppositional and fixed categories, such as body/mind, body/world, social/metaphysical, country/city, distort understanding of ourselves and the world.

The country is often described as a place of escape and escapism, but the self-location there is a crucial part of metaphysical being. George Grosz attacked abstract painters, such as Wassily Kandinsky and Franz Marc, for being 'wanderers into the void... silent and indifferent, that is, irresponsibly, in relation to social occurrence'. He scoffed at their 'cosmic inspirations', their 'ridiculous useless speculation on eternity' (Harrison and Wood, 1992, p.

452). Kandinsky, on the other hand, argued convincingly that a loss of contact with the metaphysical in a secular and materialist society *is* a social issue (Harrison and Wood, 1992, p. 87–98).

We have a very narrow idea of what the sociopolitical is. We talk about the sociopolitical and the spiritual as if the two could be disaggregated, as if our life aspirations and our conscious and mortal condition are not entirely integrated with our material existence. A re-engagement with the metaphysical, with what Sigmund Freud's friend Romain Rolland described as 'the oceanic' (Freud, 1930, pp. 64–65), is part of a contemporary Romantic focus on natural environments.

The majority of us live with a city/country dichotomy in our heads. I grew up in the Green Belt—the planning exclusion zone around London, so I am an edge of Londoner. My dad is listed on my birth certificate as an agricultural engineer. He specialised in tractors. By the 1970s, the demand for that specialism on the edge of London had near enough died out and been replaced by miles of golf courses. Now my dad is a retired golf fan. The country was not an idealised escape for me—it was really there—the ancient woodland and commons of Hadley on the edge of the city. I had a hybrid existence of megatropolis and muddy walks over stiles in green fields. Again, the dichotomy is misleading. There is an essential inter-dependence between city and country going on with mutually dependent economies at both ends, which impact on the lives of people in both places.

Why do we make art about our experiences of nature? It's not because *I*, for instance, need to show *you* what I saw. Because you can see it yourself or you can see your own version of it. It is about my fear of absence from the world, my knowledge that there will come a time when I will never be here again and my wanting to leave some memorial of my consciousness, of my experience, which can only be articulated in a dynamic engagement with environment.

The embodied consciousness is an enormously temporary and precarious cohesion. The material body along with all matter is in an inexorable state of mutability and is constantly confronted with its own impending caesura.

> The body's vulnerability, isolation and mortality, are the motivations for the constructs of civilisation. The body's visceral, somatic, pulsional and mortal character is reflected in the things we make. (Scarry, 1985)

Thomas Nagel describes the subjective character of experience as 'something it is like to *be*' (Nagel, 1974, p. 436). The body is always becoming itself, in process and always becoming its own death. Our sense of being something is above all defined by our anticipation of eventually not being that something. A large part of our sense of being something is enmeshed in our relationship with the natural environment—how it makes us feel, how it is the stuff we are immersed in, how we will be absent from it in death, and the circumfluence of nature and our circuitous journeys into light and dark.

4
JEAN MICHEL BASQUIAT: READING BASQUIAT

2014. Review of Jordana Moore Saggese, *Reading Basquiat*, first published in *Times Higher Education*, 25 September.

Jean-Michel Basquiat, the American artist hailed by critics as the 'Radiant Child' and the 'Black Picasso', had a short, prolific career: first exhibiting in 1981; appearing barefoot and dreadlocked in an Armani suit on the cover of *New York Times Magazine* in 1985; dying from a heroin overdose in 1988. Art dealer Jeffrey Deitch described his work as 'a knockout combination of de Kooning and subway scribbles'. In this well-researched study, Jordana Moore Saggese unravels the myth of Basquiat as unschooled and naive street artist.

Basquiat left his Brooklyn home as a teenager, couch-surfed in Manhattan and hung out at the Mudd Club. Working under the sobriquet SAMO with Al Diaz, he spray-painted cryptic, poetic texts on to walls, critiquing 'MICROWAVE & VIDEO X-SISTANCE'. He shifted from SAMO to the noise band Gray, and then into a meteoric career as a painter, befriended by Andy Warhol, William Burroughs, Madonna, Debbie Harry and art dealers Annina Nosei and Mary

Boone. Saggese evokes the milieu of 1980s New York: punk and hip hop, 'the overhyped contemporary art market', 'a cultural landscape dominated by media culture like never before' and Basquiat's conflicted position within it. She explores 'his place within an African American art tradition' and the 'syncretic nature of his artistic practice', and the inspiration he took from both black jazz musicians and beat generation writers.

He was concerned with 'all diasporas and the cross-pollination of cultures, histories, and ideas', and Saggese grapples with distinctions between spontaneity, automatism and improvisation, and discusses the role of appropriation and sampling. Basquiat's work is loaded with eclectic references: comic strips, cartoons, Western art history, African spirituality, bebop. As she notes, 'the use of recognizable quotations—sometimes called licks, tricks, patterns, motives, riffs, or cribs by musicians' is a distinctive feature of his work.

As her title suggests, Saggese's emphasis is on 'reading' as opposed to looking at the paintings. Discussion of scale, colour, texture and composition is slight, but the strength of her account is its focus on 'the overwhelming abundance of written words on the canvas' and how 'Basquiat complicates the boundary between text and image'. Drawing on graffiti, hieroglyphics, calligraphy and gestural painters, such as Franz Kline, Basquiat explored the kinship between writing and mark-making. A crudely drawn crown blurs with the letter W; painting the letter A, he 'pushes past its function as a letter and [it] becomes an image instead'. Saggese also weighs his repeated redactions. 'I cross out words so that you will see them more,' he said of work that suggests the complexity and rapidity of thinking dropped on to canvas.

Many of Basquiat's paintings incorporate elements of self-portraiture. *Gold Griot* (1984) shows a fierce, energetic black figure on gold-painted strips of wood. In West Africa, the griot is a storyteller, praise singer, repository of oral tradition, adviser to kings, with a devastatingly honest wit and formidable knowledge of history and current affairs, occupying a position akin to medieval skalds; Basquiat was the griot of 1980s Western culture. *Reading Basquiat* is amply illustrated with colour plates, and Saggese makes good use of them in a lucid account that encourages the reader to look with refreshed eyes at the richnesses of the artist's work.

5

TINE BECH: MATERIALISATION

2002. First published in T. Bech and A. Damgaard, *The Inbetween: Plus & Pulse*. Arhus: Arhus Kunstbygning, np.

Tine Bech and Annette Damgaard are both working with categorical ruptures. They are grafting technology onto textiles and exploring a hybrid of biology and materials in order to examine the notion of materiality. The naked human body is the explicit subject of Damgaard's work. The body is also everywhere suggested and evoked in Bech's work, and in some of her 'action drawings' she has literally used her own body as a tool—jumping on charcoal to make drawings. Through an exploration of materials and materiality, these artists address the body's languageless experience of the world. Their approach is not logocentric. They are addressing the gap between sensuous, bodily experience and its interpretation in words and categories.

Abject bodily fluids are frequently suggested in Bech's work. An example is *Pink Pussy Hair*. The materials she uses, such as tapioca, egg yolk and hair, are vaguely phobic or nauseating. One of her action drawings, titled as a landscape, recalls Duchamp's 'drawing' of his *Sinning Landscape*, made with semen on black velvet.

Bech often presents us with disturbing, disorientating views of something familiar. Is *Space Pussy* for instance derived from an eye, a vagina or neither? These are mysterious objects and images. We feel we should know what they are, but they elude our categorisation, sliding past our full recognition. There is a visceral trace in her work. She renders the familiar unfamiliar, so we are no longer sure what landscape we are looking at. This is a strategy akin to Surrealist photographs by Brassaï or Jacques-André Boiffard and the exploration of fetishistic close-ups by Georges Bataille and Sergei Eisenstein.

Bech's textured sculptures frequently seem organic or uncannily alive: *Fnug* with its expressive open mouth, or *Boundless in Space*, sprouting and shedding duplicate smaller versions of itself in an amoeba-like reproductive process. Her drawing of a *Sea Creature* looks like a cross between a flesh-eating plant and an exotic insect, and her sculpture, *Tumbleweed* could be a nest or a container for an unseen life-form.

Bech's work is a soap-opera of microbes and macrocosms—both referring to the human body. She says that some of her drawings have been inspired by the body's holes or by jellyfish, for instance. Her tactile materials are reminders of physicality—we want to touch her objects, we need to walk around them, to experience them, to meet them and they interact with us, responding to our proximity. But her drawings are also inspired by the forces of nature and by events in the cosmos—by black holes, images of galaxies, landscapes seen from space and rainfall. In *Spacehole* we are flung into a macrocosmic void, a black hole. Bech gestures at both the miniscule world of the microbe and the vasty world of the cosmos.

Bech is concerned with the formless space between categories and Damgaard is concerned with polarities and the communication between those polarities. In Damgaard's work we enter into the body rather than imagining a sometimes-slimy contact with it, as we do in Bech's work. Damgaard's felt tent in *Plus* resembles a breast that we walk into and that encloses us. Her work explores the dichotomies of nature and culture, man and woman, material and immaterial, time and timelessness. She employs a language of oppositions, of black and white, hard and soft, naked and clothed, circle and square, inside and outside, handcrafted textile and digital media, to underscore these dichotomies. Just as the nothing between heartbeats is an essential something along with the beats themselves to construct the on/off of a pulse, so too in Damgaard's *Plus*—the joining or interplay between opposites is as critical as the delineation of the two things opposing each other.

In *Plus*, in a tent, on a PC screen, a computer animation of a naked woman appears as the second hand of a clock. She is ticking her way around the clock face, blinking wryly at us as she circles 360 degrees, holding eye contact with us all the while. She reminds us of the body clock of fertility and the body clock of mortality. We recognise we are trapped in the inevitability of time, just as she is. In the other part of the work, a naked man is projected onto felt capes/hangings in a space. He is shown in a series of poses—frozen in mid-action, doing something purposeful—climbing through an opening, reaching or throwing, thinking, jumping, going somewhere. He recalls Muybridge's photographic studies. The viewer has to consider the contrasts between the two images in *Plus*—male and female, and we also consider the plus between them.

The substancelessness of Damgaard's light projections of a naked man contrasts with the materiality and weight of the felt screens hanging on the wall that they are projected onto. The virtual naked female body on a PC screen contrasts with the materiality and sensuality of the felt tent container housing it. These felt constructions are layered metaphors—her tent is architecture, room, and the body, and her felt capes are clothing, screens, doorways and pictures on the wall, like tapestries or wall hangings.

Women artists have frequently used textiles to subvert the idea of 'high art' and to promote the notion of female craft—in Miriam Schapiro and Faith Ringgold's quilts for instance. But Bech and Damgaard's use of textiles is not simply aligned to this history of women's art. Their textiles refer also to the comedy of sexual, environmental textiles in the works of Yayoi Kusama; to Claes Oldenburg's limp sculptures, such as *Green Beans;* or to Eva Hesse and Morris' use of felt to explore materiality and gravity. Bech's use of materials is sometimes reminiscent of the Surrealists' exploration of visceral and fetishistic materials, of Meret Oppenheim's *Cup and Saucer*, for instance. An examination of abject material continued in the sixties and seventies, in the work of artists, such as Piero Manzoni—with his fake fur balls and *Artist's Shit*, Lucio Fontana with his anthropomorphic but undefined forms, Rauschenberg in his experiments with the abject in *Black Paintings* and Morris' experiments with detritus in *Threadwaste*. Abjection was explored too in the theoretical writings of Bataille, Sartre and Kristeva and associated with the mother and the female. Bech and Damgaard's textiles resemble membranes and skins—they exist on a boundary between animate and inanimate, between human and thing and they articulate the gap between language and experience.

6

TINE BECH: WATERY LOOKS

2009. First published in *Bech/Nacha*. Toronto: Open Studio.

Everything is secretly alive in Bech's work: shoes, bridges, streetlights, balloons and coloured blobs. They hum and react with a playful anthropomorphic life that is liable to take you by surprise. *Boundless in Space* is a pink blob looking a little like a cushion on wheels that moves and clicks when you come close to it. *Echidna* is a black wiry sculpture, emitting sounds in response to your touch, which was inspired by the Australian hedgehog of the same name. Coloured lights are activated as people pass on the bridge beneath in *Tracing Light*. A large red blob accompanies the artist on a bicycle tour of Toronto Island in another work. And in *Mememe*, visitors move around in flamboyant sculptural shoes creating sound compositions in a gallery space. Bech's sculptures and installations are full of bright colours, evoking sunlight and playgrounds. Her drawings, on the other hand, employ the black, white and sepia end of the colour range. In the *Water Trees* series, created for this exhibition at Open Studio, Bech is concerned with the other end of the weather range too—with the rain that falls incessantly against your windowpane some days.

She has created the *Water Trees* drawings by taking an image of a tree out into the rain. 'Big fat drops of rain,' she says, are best to create 'watery looks'. The image of the tree is mirrored by its upside down double, like a tree reflected in the surface of still water. The alchemies of printmaking and lithography allow Bech to extend the range of her visual language so that the process she uses is mimicking her subject. Lithography relies on the porosity of stone to attract water and on a film of water repelling printing ink from a greasy drawing. Between the stone, the grease and the water, Bech's images of drowned or floating trees emerge with their fragile limbs and roots like capillaries. The self-reflection of these delicate traceries of branches and roots suggests the water cycle moving through rain, rivers, sea, trees and all living organisms. Water keeps going around and around. Trees contribute to the continuous movement of water by drawing it up from the ground and then transpiring it out through their leaves. There is no beginning or end to the water cycle and no new water. There is only water recycling endlessly through liquid, vaporous and solid ice states since the beginning of time.

Weather and water are recurring motifs in Bech's work. In *Rain Balloons,* large black balloons float through the gallery and their movement activates the sound of rain. In *Purple Membrane,* swimmers pass slowly through a purple mist hovering above the surface of a public swimming pool. 'Drawing is a way of thinking,' Bech writes, and her thinking is concerned with the body moving through the environment that it is immersed in. In other drawings, she created her images by jumping on charcoal sandwiched between paper.

Most of Bech's drawings look like holes, openings and non-specific round and oval forms. These echo the balls and blobs in many of her sculptural works (such as *Tumbleweed, Fnug, Felt Sphere* and *Everything Round*). Her work draws on a tradition of organic female forms in the work of women artists, including Georgia O'Keefe, Clark and Hesse. 'Life is probably round,' mused Van Gogh (cited in Bachelard, 1969, p. 232). 'We live in the roundness of life, like a walnut that becomes round in its shell ... being is round,' wrote Gaston Bachelard (1969, p. 234).

7

HIERONYMUS BOSCH AND PIETER BRUEGEL THE ELDER: FROM ENEMY PAINTING TO EVERYDAY LIFE

2017. Review of Joseph Koerner, *Bosch and Bruegel*, first published in *Times Higher Education*, 19 January.

'Nothing but devils, buttocks and cod-pieces,' declared seventeenth-century Spanish poet Francisco de Quevedo on the paintings of Hieronymus Bosch. Undaunted, Joseph Leo Koerner pairs Bosch with his fellow Netherlandish artist Pieter Bruegel the Elder in a bid to prove that they were the inaugural masters of secular genre paintings, the paintings of everyday life.

Bosch and Bruegel lived in Brabant when the Low Countries were under Catholic Habsburg rule from Spain. These were dangerous times of developing Reformation and violent Spanish efforts to crush heresy with war and Inquisition. In emerging Protestant iconoclasm, images themselves were physically attacked. It grew safer for artists to tackle secular subjects rather than traditional religious material.

Based on Koerner's 2008 A. W. Mellon Lectures, this book is a lucid and rewarding read, and lavishly illustrated with 325 reproductions (although it would have been useful to have artwork dimensions, a list of illustrations and a bibliography). Ruminating on works including Bosch's *Adoration of the Magi* (c. 1510) and *The Garden of Delights* (1504), Bruegel's *Winter Landscape with Bird Trap* (1565) and *The Peasant and the Bird Thief* (1568), Koerner carefully advances his interpretations. Historical context, other artists' work and the evidence of copies and engravings are utilised as Koerner probes layers of meaning in these complex artworks. His use of illustration details from the paintings is particularly effective.

Both artists use vast planes, with an array of mesmerising details, to captivate and 'overload our sense of sight, entangle our eye, ensnare us in enigmas'. Bosch's ethereality contrasts with Bruegel's stolid down-to-earthness. Bosch depicts a diabolical enemy at war with God, while Bruegel is unremittingly focused on the human. Koerner navigates deftly through fraught attributions and interpretative controversies. He argues convincingly that Bosch's depictions of cosmic hostility between God and Devil, 'enemy paintings', became the unlikely cradle for the painting of everyday life.

Bosch creates 'pictures of a world that never was or ever could be'. Koerner's discussion of Romanesque grotesque sculpture and Bosch's compelling organic monsters is illuminating. Koerner describes how *The Garden of Delights* was commissioned by the Burgundian overlords of Brabant for their pleasure palace in Brussels, and coveted by their enemy, the Spanish Duke of Alba. The painting arrived in Spain in 1593 after Alba had brutally tortured William of Orange's concierge to reveal its hiding place. Bosch's triptych 'stands apart from the entire Netherlandish tradition', Koerner observes. Its jewel-like brilliance, the delectation of the picture, 'draws us like bees to blossom'. Bosch depicts lust as a verdant garden, bursting with seedpods and oversexed humanity. Figures swarm in a vast amorphous space, with birds, fruits and shellfish. We see 'scores of tiny eyes looking at us looking at their cavortings'.

Bruegel creates an atlas of human culture with scenes of peasant revelry and seasonal labour, where village existence appears as an enclave of timelessness. Koerner emphasises the 'marked presentism' of Bruegel's art, how he thrusts us into life's midst, precariously balances us 'on future's fluid brink'. With Koerner, the reader steps into these scenes. The views these paintings offer 'so far exceed our capacity to look that we can never feel finished looking'. Referencing the Low Countries in his metaphor, Koerner compares analysing Bosch and Bruegel to 'looking for a watershed in marshland', and he does an admirable job of it.

8

BROOK & BLACK: MELLOW FRUITFULNESS

2013. First published online in *Plot 16: The Fermenting Room*. IXIA.

One sunny evening in September I answered an invitation from artists brook & black to an event at Plot 16 Allotment in Rose Hill, Oxford. Arriving, I strolled past patches sporting the expected rows of veg, but at the far end of the allotments was the uncommon sight of the Plot 16 hop garden. A white aluminium sculpture resembling a 3D drawing of a small-scale glasshouse from Kew Gardens rose 25 feet into the air and spanned 30 feet across but was barely discernible beneath the fecund heft of a great swathe and swag of hop bines garlanding its frame. Although the sculpture was ostensibly there—made from metal and paint—it had an ethereality and conveyed the quality of a drawing or a thought held down by the swarming bines. Alongside it, yet more hops twisted and tangled up a fretwork of canes and strings, made leafy teepees, arrayed themselves at the top of poles like living Maypoles.

Hop bines are beauteous things. The hops are the female flower clusters and seed cones of the hop vine, *Humulus lupulus*. The pale green and flashes of white of the hops are like oversize pointy Brussel sprouts, dangling in bunches from the darker green leafy stems.

Visitors were invited to help harvest the rampant hops. You could push aside the plant curtain cladding the sculpture and enter the cool, green shadow of its interior, stippled with sunlight. Youthful amorous outdoor escapades concealed in bushes and woods sprang immediately to mind in that hidden fertile space, along with the echoes of centuries of May and Harvest rites.

Things change and they don't.

Inside, a projection showed a sequence shot using time-lapse photography from a static tripod, telescoping the changing seasons on the plot, from the stripped-down foliage of winter, enabling a view of the Norman Church next door, to the long buzzing heydays of summer. The projection moved through the year of the changing plot, from bare soil to fruitful bounty, forced by sun, rain and the nutrients of the soil from nothing to abundance.

The ancient art of horticulture has been practised through time, from monastery and manor gardens to the market gardens, hop fields and fruit orchards that supplied the Victorian cities of the south, through to allotments now. An allotment is an alternative space, an escape, a small kingdom. There is the camaraderie of chatting over the garden fence, and a considerable amount of interest from other allotment holders as to what you are doing, occasionally bordering on competition or surveillance. The other gardeners of the Lenthall Road Allotment Association offered the artists advice and assistance as they laboured in wellington boots and manure.

At the *Hop Fest* event in September 2011, the two artists, Leora Brook and Tiffany Black, wore straw hats garlanded with hops, reminding us of Green Men and stilt-walking hop pickers. They invited the growing group of visitors—artists, curators, allotment gardeners, the neighbours from over the road—to sample bottles of green hop beer made from the hops. The bottle labels showed the green tangle of robust rhizomatic roots, the unseen part of the plant beneath our feet, tangled like hair, like blood vessels, like nerves.

As the first beer caps twanged, the celebrations began: speeches of congratulations and thanks followed by the prancing, hanky swishing, leg-bell jangling, stick-clashing of Morris Men and Women, followed by Matt Black's declamations of vegetable poetry and greenery odes, accompanied by Bruno Guastalla's cello, followed by a processing jazz band named Horns of Plenty, playing and dancing round and through and round the hop-covered sculpture with their ups and downs trill of saxophone and trumpet, celebrating and giving thanks for nature's cornucopia.

Things change and they don't.

Months later, everything on the allotment plot is gone—the hops, the frame, the dancing, drinking, declaiming people. The soil is returned to its plain brown state but the memory of the heavy bines of late summer, loading the white frame, still hangs in the crisp winter air.

From 2010–2011, brook & black's art project, *The Fermenting Room: The Return of the Rhizome,* inhabited Plot 16 of the Rose Hill Allotments on the south-west outskirts of Oxford and forayed too with events and a residency at Modern Art Oxford gallery in the city. The frame that the artists grew the hops around was a scaled-down outline of the Modern Art Oxford building which, in its previous incarnation, had been Hanley's City Brewery, built in 1882. Writing in 1890, Alfred Barnard described the state of the art, steam-powered brewery equipment and processes: 'we never saw a place so well arranged and kept in such exquisite order' (p. 464). David Elliot, the first Director at the Museum of Modern Art Oxford (the gallery's former name) describes how the six-storey tower in the centre of the building was strengthened to accommodate the weights of water and grain used in the brewing process, that the basement had been the malting floor and what is now the upper gallery had been the fermenting room (1978, pp. 57–58). Surrounding place names are redolent of the area's brewing history —the Old Malt House, Brewer Street—and of its reliance on the streams, brooks and wells that riddled the area. Brewing and malting was one of Oxford's leading trades for centuries, serving the thirsty scholars and workers of the city, producing a 'good, nutritious and exhilarating beer' (Barnard, 1890, p. 443). Beer and books were such natural partners for academics that a Trinity College drinking song declares that MA stands for Master of Ale (Barnard, 1890, p. 444).

Things change and they don't.

The Plot 16 sculpture, with its green-loaded frame of the gallery invaded by the unpredictable energy of plant growth, is a vivid image of how nature can and will overgrow culture and reclaim defunct spaces. Years ago, I went inside a derelict and long-closed Edwardian department store. Small trees pushed through the peeling wallpaper, damp and mold climbed the ornate winding staircase, gaggles of pigeons replaced the throng of disappeared customers, and where the salesmen had lent their knuckles on the wooden counters, mounds of pigeon shit clustered like dull cairns.

The artists used the hops to brew two editions of Plot 16 beer with Shotover Brewery. The process of growing is not an easy business. It takes time—nature's time, and the patient time of gardening: mulching and weeding, fertilising and turning over the soil, sowing the seeds, pruning and watering, then harvesting. Long-term collaboration is a feature of brook & black's work—with each other, over more than ten years, and with communities. They were in residence at Plot 16 for one and half years.

The ghosts of the brewing process haunt the Modern Art Oxford building—the malting, milling, mashing, lautering, boiling, fermenting, conditioning and filtering. It is possible to imagine the coppers, kettles and vats occupying each specialist room and floor, as the concoction moved from process to process, conveyed by a steam-powered hoist in the transformative alchemy of fermentation or zymurgy. We can almost see and taste the malted barley steeping in water in the massive oak mash tun, fermenting with yeast, flavoured with hops to offset the sweetness of the malt. The hops add floral or citrus or herbal aromas and flavours and have natural antibiotic and preservative qualities. The brown, earthy, almost sickly pungency of malt mingles with hops, loading the air—impossible to forget once savoured, lodging permanently in your olfactory memory. Outside the building, are the echoes of the cooperage and the horse drays on cobbles in the loading yard, tended by men in white jackets and aprons. 'We were much struck with the tidy and natty appearance of the stablemen and draymen' (Barnard, 1890, p. 444). Compared to the processes of growing and brewing, the process of consuming beer is a much simpler business.

In *The Fermenting Room*, brook & black resurrected the histories of their two sites: Rose Hill, close to the Norman church of Saint Mary the Virgin in Iffley and the Thames, and Modern Art Oxford in the city centre. They conducted archaeology down through the layers of time, through the archive of the soil. They grew not only hops, but a visual history, a manifestation of memory, creating a third imaginary site between the allotment and the gallery.

In the twelfth century, the area now known as Rose Hill was simply Iffley Hill, a low hill of ampthill clay rising from the river meadow (the ley), safe from flooding. There was a bridge, a bridge hermit, a malthouse, a water-mill grinding malt, barley, corn, and a miller constantly arguing with the bargees who wanted to get past the mill. The community living here were farmers, carpenters, masons, shoemakers, servants, labourers and paupers. They caught eels in the river. There was a ferryman to bring coffins across the river to the churchyard because it was bad luck to carry a coffin across the bridge.

Iffley Lock was built in the 17th century and in the 18th century the stocks stood on Church Way opposite the hop garden. (It was probably the effects of beer that put most of the offenders in the stocks.) In the 19th century, the occupants of the area were railway workers, bookbinders, college servants and grocers (*Iffley History Society*).

Aside from its ancient university, Oxford was principally known for brewing and malting, along with publishing, iron foundry and marmalade making. In 1913, Morris Motors was established, and Oxford became a city of car manufacturers, dons and writers. In the beginning of the twentieth century, Iffley was still a village surrounded by fields.

A sturdy village life persisted: there were mummers at Christmas, May Day celebrations, visits of Jack-in-the-Green and travelling bears ... Walking weddings and funerals were still the village custom. (*British History Online*)

The Old English customs of the May Day Maypole and the Harvest Festival band and supper are redolent of times that moved to a different rhythm, a different dependency on the rhythm of the growing year. When I was eleven, I was crowned May Queen at my primary school's May Day. My head and my throne garlanded with flowers, I announced the commencement of the Maypole dancing and the May songs. That is not a forgettable experience.

In the early twentieth century, fritillaries grew by Iffley Lock and communication with the city was by horse-bus and river barge. The Iffley Foresters held a feast and fair, accompanied by a brass band, in early July and September. In 1908, Iffley Mill burnt down after eight centuries of operation. Dig down into the layers of soil and there are the traces and detritus of earlier times, fragments of letters and bills, broken crockery, discarded toys, nails, buttons.

Things change and they don't.

The Rose Hill estate was built in the 1930s to house people from the Jericho slums in central Oxford, many of whom came from old river bargee families. In the fifties and sixties, more homes were built here for the Morris Motor factory workers. The road previously known as Iffley Highway was renamed Rose Hill after an early nineteenth-century house that had stood there belonging to Dr Ireland, a Scottish apothecary, who

> made up [his] own medicines, attended ladies at the most interesting period of their lives, sold Epsom salts, blisters, hair powder... He was a grandiloquent, pompous man ... a dissolute old scamp. (William Tuckwell, *Reminiscences of Oxford*, cited in *Oxford History*, no date)

The archaeology of site and echoes of past structures mapped onto contemporary structures occurs in brook & black's earlier work. Art projects are rarely discrete and entirely self-contained. They spring from the artists' ongoing obsessions. They build on and have a continuity with earlier work. There is a coherent visual language in brook & black's projects. Their work, such as *Behind the Facade* at the Pitt Rivers Museum in 2008, often engages with the highly cultivated spaces of museums—storehouses of memory, packed with fetish objects of other times and other lives. Beds are a recurring trope in their work: beds to sleep in and seed beds: sites of generation. The excitement of space and engagement with themes of the contained and the habitual runs through their art. Their project *Loco Solis* at Greenwich Maritime Museum in 2005, where they installed telescopes capped with mirrors in the courtyard, examined the formal order of the eighteenth century: its measuring, taxonomies, discoveries, and appropriations.

Their work often translates one place, one time, into another and also frequently draws on the work of earlier artists. *Drift* at the Henley River and Rowing Museum in 2009 was an installation created from doors, inspired by Gericault's painting, *The Raft of the Medusa* (1818–1819).

For *Bagatelle Parallel* at the Wallace Collection in London in 2008, they were inspired by Fragonard's *The Swing* (c. 1767). In the painting (also known as *The Happy Accidents of the Swing*), as a young woman is pushed on a swing by her elderly husband, one shoe flies off and her skirts and petticoats rise revealing her legs to a young man hidden in the bushes below. brook & black installed an abstracted sculpture of a swing on top of the museum's entry portico that also suggested a guillotine and on the lawn below a white cast of a seventeenth-century lady's shoe was captured under a bell-jar. Inside the building, video and sound installations reflected the daily routines of cleaning the artefacts, winding the clocks, opening and closing window shutters.

At the Toulouse-Lautrec Museum in Albi, France in 2011, brook & black unpacked Lautrec's visions of the dancer Jane Avril and of his own absinthe-swilling culture (brook & black). Their works reimagine art history and turn the 2D into 3D and back again. Their artworks often invite the viewer to travel imaginatively through windows and doors, or through the looking glass and the back of the wardrobe.

Things change and they don't.

The Fermenting Room project resonates with many alchemies: nature, growth and decay, time and history, the chemistry of the artists' shared imaginations, the transformation of places by people.

9
CIRCUITRY: KNOWHERE

2001. First published in *Performance Research*, 6(3), pp. 8–12, DOI: 10.1080/13528165.2001.10871800. *Performance Research* is published by Taylor & Francis: https://www.tandfonline.com/.

In the winter of 2000–2001, a group of blind, partially sighted and sighted artists came together to work on the *KnoWhere* project, organised by London Fieldworks. This was a series of workshops, a field trip to Lundy Island in the Bristol Channel, and the creation of a mixed media art event addressing sight, site and light.

In the workshops, the group exchanged information on their own artworks and on their sensory modalities. They had demonstrations and discussions led by a range of workshop contributors, including Dr Frances Geesin presenting her research on touch sensitive electro-textiles; Tony Bassett discussing technologies activated by presence; Kuljit Bhamra demonstrating theramin technology—generating music from gesture; Aaron Williamson talking about audio description; Please Imbibe discussing sensory sculptural projects and interactive websites; and Peter Staples and Isabel Maxwell Cade from The Awakened Mind, who demonstrated a range of biofeedback technologies. During the workshops, the group discussed creating artworks and access to art for visually impaired audiences. I joined them for some of the workshops and on the field trip to Lundy Island.

Prior to the Lundy Island field-trip, blind and visually impaired members of the group familiarised themselves with the physical shape of the island, using tactile forms as an aid to 'visualisation'. On Lundy, sculptor Lynn Cox, for instance, referred to the memory of these shapes as a way of roughly orienting herself in the landscape. Having some residual sensitivity to bright light, she could combine the sun's placement with time read from her braille watch, thus, orienting the shape of the island with the cardinal compass points.

On Lundy, the group's remit was to engage with the natural light in this island landscape with their differing sensory capabilities and to develop material for the collaborative artwork. They made video works with audio descriptions, audio and textual works, a live performance work, interactive and tactile sculptures and an experimental website designed with the visually impaired in mind. (See *Sally Booth Projects*, no date; Cox, 2001.) Liz Porter, for example, developed spoken-word material and songs from the Lundy Island fieldwork. The material produced was further processed by sound-artist David Gilchrist and incorporated into the performance soundtrack. David also produced stand-alone sound works for the performance: *Dark Tracker* and *Lost It Found It*, delivered via a surround-sound system. Visually impaired sculptor, Lynn Cox had been introduced to theramin technology. The theramin produces sound modulated by hand movements around an aeriel, through the disruption of the aeriel's electromagnetic field. The theramin equipment was adapted to act as an interface to Cox's responsive sculpture *Echoscape*, activating neon lighting and sound samples. (A selection of some of the artworks produced can be found on the CD accompanying *Performance Research*, 6(3)).

The *KnoWhere* project explored human interaction with the environment, escaping from a traditional dominance of the visual and emphasising an expanded notion of sensory perception. I walked around the island with Liz Porter and Felix Mood—both partially sighted—and they talked to me about their experiences of the landscape. Liz described how she was deriving information about the environment, not only from a heightened aural and olfactory sensitivity, but also from tactile experiences that were coming from her feet and her bodily and facial resistance to wind and weather, as well as from her hands. She was acutely aware of the terrain changing beneath her feet—from granite rock to spongy moss and sucking mud.

Sally Booth used a video camera as a prosthetic, filming the moon when she could not see it, for instance, and then being able to see it close up on the video playback. Felix photographed objects in the landscape, a ruined castle, mossy walls, gnarled rhododendron roots—framing the pictures perfectly without any detailed vision of the things he was photographing. Like Sally, he would see the detail later in the photograph. Felix's explanation for his apparently uncanny ability to beautifully frame his shots was that, unlike sighted people, he did not try to make the camera act as if it were the naked eye. His partial vision had more in common with the camera's abilities itself. He could discern light and shade and in which direction it might be interesting to aim the camera. He was not distracted by a plethora of detailed visual information and could point the camera into the landscape and get it to register something evocative. Sally Booth's exquisite sketches and paintings of the landscape similarly were devoid of the details that she could not see and alight with the brightness of the air.

David Rice and Bruce Gilchrist worked together examining interactions between the environment and David's embodied consciousness, using biofeedback technologies. David, who has been blind for thirty years, sat in various spots on the island, experiencing them and they later represented these experiences in live performance. Lynn Cox created tactile sculptures based on the places that David sat, and he then attempted to recreate his experiences of those places as he felt the sculptures in the performances. Kuljit Bhamra and David Gilchrist's sound works were woven through the collaborative video and web works and they also made independent soundworks recreating aspects of the island—screeching birds, relentless tides, oil barrels echoing in a coastal cave, squelching mud and gravel.

Bruce Gilchrist and Jo Joelson's own work is concerned with exploring the interaction of the embodied consciousness, human physiology and the environment. They contend that the body is a mobile laboratory, a set of instruments and technologies in itself, that can be taken out into the environment and used to record and process data.

The project overall was looking at the possibilities of various technologies to extend and also to interpret sensory experiences. The group went to the island and brought back experiences that they then translated into artworks in an attempt to recreate and share those experiences with audiences who had not been to that place. The participating artists' own experiences of the island were expanded by their communal visit—making it, to some extent, a shared experience—highlighting how we are continually searching for a way to communicate our experiences across that existential divide of the self and other. But, of course, the body is not simply an instrument that records, it is also an embodied consciousness that interprets. An underlying question that this project poses then is: What is 'experience'? We set great store by our experiences. We believe that we need 'experiences', and travelling is often a crucial contributor to our stock of experiences, but what exactly is experience and to what end do we experience?

Looking at prehistoric earthworks and the land and body art of the 1970s in her book, *Overlay*, Lucy Lippard comments; 'Art itself must have begun as nature—not as imitation of nature, nor as formalized representation of it, but simply as the perception of relationships between humans and the natural world' (1983, p. 41). We are immersed in the environment, in constant interaction with it, co-creating it with our sensory and cognitive systems, experiencing it. Lippard contends that art is the perception of the relationship between us and the natural world. We define ourselves through our experiences—what we have done, where we have been, what we have seen or sensed. We distil ourselves in this reciprocal experience in a never-stopping process, the flux of self and consciousness.

Lundy Island is run by The Landmark Trust (see *Lundy Island*, no date). 'When people see an island in the distance they usually want to land on it,' remarks one of the Lundy Island tourist information leaflets, and flying into the island by helicopter I couldn't disagree with this statement. Flying from the Devon mainland toward the island it seemed to approach us while we simply hovered above the sea waiting for it to arrive. We flew through a rainbow, which from the air, appears as a full circle. Raindrops moved up the windscreen.

Touching down, we all set about experiencing the island in our own ways. Jo and Sally set up video cameras, recording the sunset from the top of a lighthouse, filming the full moon, filming the reeds. David R sat for hours on the castle wall or on a damp clifftop, while Bruce recorded his physiological and subjective reactions. David G strode up and down the island with his boom, recording mud, birds, wind, kite strings, the sound of thigh friction in waterproof trousers. Liz correlated her experiences of the island with the research she had done on folktales and traditional songs associated with it. Felix balanced precariously on cliff paths pointing his camera. Kuljit drummed on everything with anything he could find, including extraordinary plants thrown up by the sea. He sat on a rock recording the incoming tide while it rolled in around him. In the church, he coaxed the organ back to life through layers of dust and years, playing the opening cascade of a Hammer Horror theme. Like a baby exploring its new world by putting everything into its mouth, gumming everything it can get hold of, Lynn's hands sampled walls, moss, bones, old unidentified fragments of decaying things that she tripped over. Her sampling was accompanied by a continuous enthusiastic vocal response to the material, the stuff, the thingness of everything she could feel.

So why do we travel and why did we choose the island? Going to a different place, shifting environment is a way of challenging our self anew: 'By changing space, by leaving the space of one's usual sensibilities, one enters into communication with a space that is psychically innovating. . . . For we do not change place, we change our Nature' (Bachelard, 1994, p. 206). The island gave us parameters to define our shared experience, it gave us limits to our experiences —the island's literal edges. It was an immersive experience where we were surrounded by sky, sea, light, weather and had a sense of being in the world. According to James Turrell, islands and volcanoes have a 'terrestrial thingness' about them (1993, p. 26). The island was an extracted experience. It can be reached by boat from the mainland in summer, but in winter the helicopter was more reliable. The previous visitors before us, a group of campanologists, had been stranded an extra week by the weather. Although it has had a colourful history of human occupation—by pirates, buccaneers, naturalists, ghosts and recluses—the island is now uninhabited apart from a skeleton staff running the pub, the shop and looking after the animal occupants: the sheep, goats, ponies and deer. We could study our responses to an environment that was shared, extracted, defined and relatively without distractions. Many journeys that we make are round trips—going nowhere. Odysseus wanders lost in a mythical Aegean but eventually returns home;

Leopold Blood circumnavigates Dublin in a day in James Joyce's *Ulysses*; lone yachtswoman, Ellen McArthur, set sail recently from France and, via a sublime experience of ocean, sky, ice, she went to France. What are we looking for in our circumnavigations? A desire lies behind maps, directions and journeys that is not simply about getting somewhere specific or exploring that place—journeys are self-explorations.

Lundy Island is drawn and quartered by walls and lines on maps —1/4 wall, 1/2 wall, 3/4 wall. Down the central track was the castle. Up the east track was the Old Lighthouse. On our final day on the island, Liz and I got up at dawn, determined to walk the length of the island, to conquer it with our feet. Mapping land and journeying through it is a form of possession and a key for imagination. The map is a stasis laid on motion and the journey is a reanimation of that map and an activation of consciousness. A map is a kind of diagram but unlike other diagrams it does not reduce, it represents and abstracts space but retains coordinates for imaginative engage-ment with a place—through its colours, shapes, place names, repre-sentation of materials and forms.

Travelling in northern Norway a few years ago, I was on a train that crossed the Arctic Circle, and tourists leapt up and photographed the cairns marking the map reference, as if the lines drawn on maps are really there. Robert Smithson remarked that 'the "curved" reality of sense perception operates in and out of the "straight" abstractions of the mind' (1979, p. 113). His artworks probe this relationship between abstracted space and the experien-tial reality of space. He sees the earth as a map undergoing disrup-tion. Nothing and nowhere is stable and fixed. And Tacita Dean's work, often inspired by and referring to Smithson, also examines this gap between maps and the aspirations of journeys, quests and pilgrimages.

Earthworks and artworks in the landscape, such as the land art of the seventies, form landmarks and spaces that can frame and enclose our relationship with the natural environment, manifesting celestial and agrarian cycles, enabling us to temporarily place and acquire that relationship. Robert Morris' *Observatorium* in Flevoland, Netherlands, for instance, is based on neolithic henges; Smithson's now drowned *Spiral Jetty* in the Great Salt Lake in Utah; or Turrell's various sky spaces and his major work, *Roden Crater* in Arizona's Painted Desert (see Tiberghien, 1995 and Kastner, 1998) are all structures and sites focusing our relationship with the environment and with ourselves, enabling 'the placement of ourselves in a dimension of our being' (Dixon, 1982, p. 199). According to Turrell, we are afraid to dissolve ourselves into any sort of human cosmic consciousness—to acknowledge our bond with the stuff that we are immersed in.

Land artist, Charles Ross, is building a naked-eye observatory of the orbit of Polaris in New Mexico, *Star Axis*, where he says he is not trying to insist on any particular interpretation of our relationship with the cosmos, just trying to point out that we are directly plugged into metaphysics, into stars, sky, sea, weather. So there is a possible answer here to my original question about what the end product of our travels, our insistence on our 'experiences' is. Journeying, navigating, we engage in a metaphysical quest to know ourselves. There is a dynamic relationship between our neurophysiology, the wiring of our brains and nerves and the stuff out there. Our sensory systems provide us with dimensions of experience that model the energies surrounding our bodies. These experiences represent, rather than accurately report what is going on in the world.

The act of perceiving the world is itself creative. Many of our most memorable experiences of the natural world are of awesome vastnesses and voids where we experience a sense not only of the immensity of space but also the depth of time and our place within all this. Again, in northern Norway, standing on the edge of Lofoten island where the Vikings set sail into the unknown, hundreds of years ago, I saw the endless girdle of the sea under the midnight sun with no sign of any other landmass. On the very edge of the shore, a mound had been built up by sea eagles shitting in the same place over many years. Our landmarks, like the eagles' mound, are markers in the circumfluence of nature, locators in emptinesses, signposts of our circuitous journeys into light and dark.

10

MARCUS COATES: BEING SOMETHING

2001. First published in M. Coates (ed) *Marcus Coates*. Ambleside: Grizedale, np.

Philosopher Thomas Nagel defines consciousness as 'what it is like to be something' (1974). Coates' art works are frequently concerned with being animal. Working as an artist in residence in Grizedale Forest, Cumbria in 1999, Coates sat for hours up a high tree 'being' a goshawk, he turned his bed-and-breakfast room into an animal den and performed an animal-call karaoke while buried underground. Coates' efforts at being animal are captured in a range of media: video, photography, soundworks, performance, painting, sculpture and text. By trying to become animal, he empathises with the animal's sense of being and he explores how this might differ from human consciousness and the human experience of self and being. He investigates humanness by experimenting with peregrineness, deerness, foxness.

Coates' work is embedded in a dialogue with ornithology, zoology, anthropology and philosophy—the studies of animal and human—but instead of rational or scientific analysis, he explores his subject by doing and imitating, by immersing himself in other modes of being and literally inhabiting their skin. He crawls along the ground on all fours with a deer strapped to his back. In *Sparrowhawk Bait*, he runs through the forest with dead birds tied to his hair. In the video work *Stoat,* he tries to gallop in a pair of stilts that mimic the footprints and stride of a stoat. We see the artist's feet in walking socks with the awkward stoat stilts strapped on. Trying to imitate the stoat's gait he repeatedly twists his ankle and falls over until he eventually manages a spurt of stoat speed. We see him going through a process of learnt embodiment. His work has been informed by the psychology literature on children reared by animals —wolfchildren and gazelle-boys—which reveals an extraordinary degree of physical and psychological adaptation to otherness.

Coates' animals are not slick imitations. Like a child's make-believe, his disguises are incomplete and crude. A red boilersuit denotes a fox. An animal den is constructed from a frilled duvet and pillows. Coates is not simply in disguise. He is being the animal—it is there—and the leftover parts—the human bits that remain outside the disguise are assumed to be invisible. A child is furious with an adult who erroneously perceives that child behind a mask, because they are not simply pretending to be Spiderman. They are Spiderman. We have a long-standing fascination with the inter-species boundary evidenced in our narratives of half-human half-animals: vampires, werewolves, minotaurs, gods in the form of swans and other animals, frog princes and mermaids. These hybrid species are figures of violation, flouting and polluting what is natural and normal, but they are also figures of possibility, escaping the physical and social constraints of the merely human.

We often use our constructions of this interspecies boundary to define ourselves (see Haraway, 1989, for instance). For Descartes there was a clear distinction between the human mind and the non-conscious state of 'brutes'. But for contemporary theorists, while other minds—even other human minds—are unknowable, the balance of evidence supports that there is some sort of consciousness going on in non-human minds, even though it may be quite different and is often fed by a very different array of sensory data. Confined within our own species-specific sensory modality we can only conjecture at what a frog or a cat sees, what a dolphin or a bat hears or what it feels like to be a homing pigeon experiencing changes in the magnetic field. Several artists in the seventies and early eighties explored this boundary between human and animal consciousness. Terry Fox, for instance, tied dying fish to his tongue, penis and hair in *Pisces*, experiencing the vibrations of their death throes; Beuys spent a week in a gallery with a coyote seeking a means of interspecies communication and exploring the mythic dimensions of both human and animal; Bonnie Sherk ate her lunch in public in a San Francisco zoo cage next door to the lions' cage (*Public Lunch*, 1971) and Mark Thompson inserted his head in a beehive (*Live-In Hive*, 1971). Peter Weibel—pulled around Vienna on a lead by Export, and Oleg Kulik—biting the legs of sponsors at exhibition openings, have both tried experiencing life from a dog's perspective. But closer to Coates' endeavours are Rebecca Horn's body extensions mimicking birds or unicorns and Austrian artist Franz West's *Adaptives* which, resembling antlers and facial or head prostheses, lay somewhere between the fantastic and the legible (see Ferguson, 1998; Fox, 1982; Warr, 2000a). Coates' animal costumes too are psycho-physical objects, activated by the poses and gesticulations of their wearer.

Coates' projects at Grizedale, at ACA and at Compton Verney have provided him with rural settings for his animal mergings, but they have also been rich contexts in which he could explore the relationship between nature and culture. In Grizedale, Romantic conceptions of Nature—Wordsworth's Lake District—are still everywhere. In Coates' films, *Dawn Chorus* and *Out of Season*, the sublime beauty of the forest and its birdsong, at first, seem contrasted with the ugly sentiments and gestures of the songs chanted at the birds by a football fan. But, on further consideration, we see that this is a fair analogy. The birdsong, like the football fan's chants, is aggressive, territorial and self-defining. In the middle of Grizedale Forest, an advertising billboard with Coates' photographic work *Wild Animal at its Den*, confronts the forest with a seemingly incongruous consumerist medium, appearing to be a faceoff between human culture and nature. But is the billboard in the forest an affront to nature or an acknowledgement of our commodification of nature? In the 1970s, Ana Mendieta made a film entitled *Breathing Grass* in which she lay under turf simulating breathing as part of her project to realign the body with a living nature. Mendieta's earnest intention, however, appears at odds with the inadvertently ridiculous effect of her action. In Coates' *British Indigenous Mammals* we see a microphone on moorland and hear a range of animal calls. Only toward the end of the video do we realise that the artist is lying underneath the turf, beneath the microphone, simulating the sounds. Here, rather than being a particular animal, he is being nature itself. Unlike Mendieta's work, Coates employs the comicality of his imitations as part of their effect.

At Compton Verney, Coates employs a juxtaposition between the imposing pile of the mansion house—a symbol of human culture and power, with bird song. The relay of human mimicry of bird calls from the mansion roof teeters between an attempt at interspecies communication and the ridicule latent in all mimicry. An anecdote by ornithologist Jan Lindblad describes how he was attacked by an owl that he had been imitating too much (cited in Coates, 2001). This owl certainly seemed to regard the mimicry as ridicule or affront. Coates' alignments of human and animal do not only reveal analogies of self-definitive, aggressive and territorial behaviour or debunk Romanticism. They propose an analogy between human and animal 'art'—birdsong, elaborate nests or dams, animal camouflage and displays, or the 'art' of the Bower Bird.

Like our narratives of animal-human hybrids, human mimicry of animals, has a long history in shamanic practices. Eliade and Mauss are among writers who have described how shamans, in a range of cultures, seek an intense connection to the natural world through an incantation of an animal. The animal invoked might also lend the shaman its powers—its speed, vision or power of flight (Eliade, 1964: Mauss, 1972). Such shamanic practices and beliefs evince a conception of the human as intimately connected with animals and the natural world, rather than defining itself as their opposite. Coates' art is an enquiry-into human and animal consciousness and an enquiry into the play-like methodology of art. His work presents the human immersed in a dynamic relationship with the environment, rather than defined against it.

There is currently intense interdisciplinary debate—among neuroscientists, philosophers, psychologists and others—around definitions of human consciousness and human 'being'. Artists contribute to this debate through experiential research rather than scientific experiment and analysis. Our sense of being something is, above all, defined by our anticipation of eventually not being that something and losing altogether our temporary, fluid and tentative definition against and with our environment.

11

CLAIRE COTÉ AND ANNA KELEHER: UNDER THE BLANKET OF THE LAND: RADIO DREAMING

2014. First published online in *a-n*, March, https://www.a-n.co.uk/reviews/radio-dreaming/.

[You can listen to the *Radio Dreaming* episodes online (*Dreaming Place Project*, no date; *Claire Coté*, no date) and read about the project (Keleher and Coté, 2016).]

Hold a shell up to your ear and you hear the sound of the sea, a sound that tells you maritime stories, conjures up ships, waves, tides coming in laden with seaweed, sea breezes whipping your hair into your eyes. Artists Claire Coté and Anna Keleher make artworks that do something similar but with the sound of the land instead. Their artworks and radio broadcasts invoke ancient and contemporary stories of the land: its undulations, its soils, the layers of rock beneath our feet in a subterranean world usually hidden from view. The artists use the human geography and history of landscapes to speculate about our shared future.

For *Radio Dreaming* they explored the caves and landscapes of Marble Arch Caves Global Geopark on the island of Ireland, talking with many people, making recordings. Then they toured around this same landscape and its communities with their mobile sculpture, *The Place-Dreamer Pod*, dreaming and talking with farmers, potholers, historians, scientists, geographers, and re-engaging with the many residents who inspired and generously contributed to the work. ClaireandAnna made six radio programmes broadcast on community radio stations around the world. The programmes focus on edible landscapes, dreams, local traditions and myths, geology, self-sufficiency and off-grid living.

The extraordinary Marble Arch Caves system runs beneath Cuilcagh Mountain and the border between Northern Ireland and the Republic of Ireland. The first recorded exploration of these winding caverns with their underground river and slender tangles of glistening rock filigree was undertaken by candlelight by Edouard Martel at the end of the nineteenth century. The caves however have been there for over 350 million years, their stalactites formed by millennia of rain seeping through and sculpting the porous limestone. In the landscape above this subterranean world, evidence of human presence and burial tombs is at least four thousand years old, and some of those early people must also have explored the caves long before Martel.

Above ground is a glacial landscape of limestone pavement, sandstone boulders dumped erratically by the retreating ice, peatland, ash and hazel woodland. Rock faces rise up vertically with straggling vegetation clinging to ledges and growing from unlikely crevices; freshwater pearl mussels cluster in the river; streams disappear suddenly into swallow holes. Beetles, bugs and butterflies clamber and hover around the pools and spongy hummocks of the bog with its luxuriant, brilliant green mosses. Gamine-faced golden plovers swirl in the sky overhead, their plumage flecked yellow and grey, streaked white.

The medium of radio has tremendous reach. You can listen to an online radio broadcast anywhere in the world and thousands of people do, but it also has tremendous intimacy as voices murmur seemingly directly to you, in your living room, your kitchen, your car, your ear. Anywhere on earth, you can listen to Margaret Gallagher making a cup of tea in the kitchen of her traditional three-room cottage in Boho, County Fermanagh. The radio programmes cajole us, a gentle mixture of information and imagination.

We hear human, animal, mineral, and meteorological cacophonies and whispers, sounds and stories. Wind sweeping across hills and bogs and dripping stalactites mixed with traditional music and voices singing or speaking to us. Water trickles over rock, pummels rock, branches creak rubbing against each other, language —English and Irish—is savoured, corn crakes are remembered. The drone of wind and water wash the mind, send us to sleep with a sodden lullaby. Fiddles, hard rain, tent zips, bodhran, birdsong, food sizzling in a pan, place names, weather forecasts, laughter, bee-loud glades, ukulele, sudden silence. 'The place is making an artwork for us,' Coté tells the listener as these sound textures create virtual visuals.

The distant voice brought near is important for the artists' own collaboration since Coté lives in New Mexico, United States and Keleher in Devon, United Kingdom. They are four thousand miles apart, talking with each other and sharing materials online, through a seven-hour time difference. Other distant voices emerge in their work—voices from the past stretching back to the neolithic inhabitants of this landscape. *Radio Dreaming* telescopes time and distance.

The artists are explorers into histories and geographies, into a back-to-basics future of off-grid, self-sufficient living. Food, story-telling, settlements and mobilities are central to their work. They use drawing, audio and crafted artefacts to create engagements with people as they pass through on their expeditions. They converse on the effortful but autonomous and rewarding lifestyles of people living in old stone cottages, living slowly on the road in a horse and waggon, living with the land.

ClaireandAnna's visions of the future are based on examples from the past, rather than on progressive, technological solutions to problems created by the Anthropocene and the time of climate change that we are living in now. Their work asks us to imagine sustaining life from the land and our own labour, to imagine living in a gift-giving, exchange culture. They create their artwork from extraordinary gifts of knowledge, memories, skills, and kindness they received from the people they encountered. Their radio dialogues consider ancient and contemporary methods of harvesting energy from the environment—from sun, wind, water, wood, living to the diurnal rhythms of light, dark and warmth. They are particularly interested in how human motion can generate energy: walking, running, pedal power from weaving.

They look at archaeological remains in landscapes, imagining the lives of Mesolithic people making survival tools from the environment: clay vessels, flint tools, turf fields that might contain bog bodies and bog butter. In a previous artwork on Dartmoor National Park, Devon in England, their audience struggled through rain, wind and cold, crossed a river on stepping-stones, and used a map to discover a wooden box buried in the peat, keeping homemade bread and butter cool—a peatbog larder. The participants in this project by ClaireandAnna had small containers attached to their ankles, churning cream into butter with their gait over a three-mile stretch, and then we ate our own walked butter with tea and cake. 'The primeval trek to pull histories out of the earth was a remarkable event that was multi-sensory but also opened up the imagination to the richness of place,' wrote Alan Boldon, one of the participants. In Raymond Williams' novel *People of the Black Mountains,* set in Wales, the history of the land and its former inhabitants come alive as the narrator treads the mountain paths, and ClaireandAnna's projects have a similar quality, resurrecting the past in our mind's eye.

The artists explore dreams, daydreams, and the visionary dreams of humans, animals, and of the land itself. They dream in tents, in vans and in their *Place-Dreamer Pod*, towed around the geopark. The pod is a miniature bedroom, kitchen, larder and dining table. It is a solar-powered listening and recording suite, a collaborative drawing studio, and a way to meet and talk with people who respond to its smallness and comfortable domesticity, its sense of playing at 'home'.

ClaireandAnna's work addresses ecological, economic and ethical issues with wry humour and hopefulness. They evoke the wonder of the world for us in all its minutiae. Memories of the land are a bedtime story before the blanket of the night. Dreams of the future change and reform like clouds over the blanket bog.

12

DOROTHY CROSS: UDDERS, DRILLS, AND X-RAYS

1996. First published in *Women's Art Magazine*, 70, June/July, pp. 20–21.

There are pudenda and phallic symbols—holes and probes—everywhere you look in the work of Irish artist, Dorothy Cross. Her work explores the dynamics of masculinity and femininity, but it goes well beyond a mere rejection of old stereotyped dualisms. *even,* the title of this exhibition of work made over the last two years, seems to refer to a balanced status between the two genders. Or does it imply, more aggressively, 'getting even'? Such ambivalence is characteristic of the equable humour Cross uses to soften the assertion of her blows.

Many of Cross' pieces make simple, but disconcerting, changes to everyday, found objects. She drills a hole in the heirloom family bible, she wears a cow's udder as a finger sling, a phallic cow's teat is sewn inside the gusset of a pair of women's knickers, and a series of photographs of a rugby match present the game as a metaphor for conception. Cross' metaphors are deliberately obvious, but her simple displacements and inversions are never heavy-handed. Her work is gently surrealist, turning things upside down and reversing their normal positions or relationships. *Her Stilettos* (1994), for example, is a pair of pointed woman's shoes made from hairy udders and reminiscent of Oppenheim's *Fur Breakfast.*

Her use of organic materials provokes a visceral recognition from the viewer. 'Using udders,' Cross remarks, 'generates a strange mixture of disgust, hilarity and excitement' (Cross, 1996, pp. 13–20). The corporeal, tangible, fetish qualities of skin, hair, fur and bone have a synesthetic impact. Simply looking at these materials makes us see odorous and tactile sensations. The real body seems to have crawled through the gallery of Cross' work. But on the other hand, Cross has also cleaned up after it, encasing physicality in precious metal casts, or coyly hiding it as she does with the disturbing knickers in *Trunk.* The embarrassing physicality and intimacy of these materials remains inescapable.

In *Rugby,* Cross has rephotographed newspaper photographs of rugby matches. The composition and cropping of the images place the ovum-shaped ball at centre-stage, heroine of the action. In a beautifully inverted take on the game, rugby appears as a tender soap opera of conception instead of a macho display of aggression, as the rugby players struggle for and cradle the ball. The ball is their holy grail. The muddy, bandaged players appear engaged in a valiant ordeal in its pursuit. The photographs have removed competitive aggression and turn the players' physical contact with the ball and with each other into a romantic drama.

Cross' obsessive reworking of the metaphor of the cow hides and udders in her earlier work, have appeared at times too emblematic, almost a trademark. In the recent work, serpentine metaphors replace the bovine. *The Gallows* is a theatrical installation in which a large snake hangs in the noose above an open trapdoor while other snakes swarm up the steps of the life-size wooden gallows. Are they slithering toward their own deaths or intending to assist with the hanging? Are the snakes complicit in their own execution? The piece, for me, does lack her best subtlety of touch. In *Convention,* a circle of twelve snakes are talking to each other with blown glass bubbles. In *Bandaged Snakes,* a wounded snake lies bandaged with its heart removed and preserved in a box. *The Lover Snakes* are entwined with their hearts inside silver cases. This exhibition demonstrates the range and prolixity of her work. Alongside the numerous snake pieces are more diverse works, such as *Iris, Cuttle Rings* and *Mantegna.*

At the Arnolfini, Cross' choice of layout for the exhibition was as satisfyingly obvious as her metaphors. After the busy downstairs room full of snakes, a darkened, sparse upstairs room contained only *Bible, Trunk* and *Pointing the Finger.* These three pieces are perhaps her most arrogant and defiant works—most near the knuckle—and her presentation of them incorporates an embarrassed urge to hide them. 'There are few works that I've made which I have hidden', Cross remarks (1996) about *Trunk* where a phallus-like udder is sewn onto a pair of Marks and Spencers knickers and placed inside a partially opened crate. Here, Cross is venturing into real bad girl territory. There is no mystery in Cross' work but plenty of complexity conveyed in a deceptively simple way. The exhibition catalogue quotes Roberto Calasso's *The Marriage of Cadmus and Harmony:* 'Myth, like language, gives all of itself in each of its fragments. When a myth brings into play repetition and variants, the skeleton of the system emerges for a while, the latent order, covered in seaweed' (Cross, 1996). The simplicity of Cross' metaphors works in such a way, skating on the edge of literalness but rarely falling over.

Bible is an ornate family heirloom bible with purple marker ribbons and a large, neat hole drilled through it by Cross.

> Drilling the hole was an attempt to re-invest the bible with physicality... the bible.. is full of wonderful stories... but it also harbours

some of the most destructive information. My reaction to that isn't to take a hatchet to it or burn it, but to pierce it with a very controlled void. (1996, p. 32)

The hole is positive rather than destructive, a creative, illustrative act that nevertheless puts a rather satisfying female hole through the misogynies, for instance, of Saint Paul. Writing in the exhibition catalogue, James Conway aptly comments:

At the hidden heart of the book there is a hole, and the absence is called spirit: it is the sign of something which is gone, for which symbols and substitutions multiply, numberless. It is a book because there is a hole in it... more confident than any picture: arrogant, the hole makes whole, the hollow is the real meaning. (Cross, 1996, p. 22)

In *Point the Finger* Cross photographs her finger inside a cow's udder.

By putting my finger inside the cow's teat and using it in different ways. I'm truly getting inside it, confronting that sense of disapproval (of the female interior stereotyped as dark, mysterious and unknown) and contradicting the notion that females have to be docile and harmless and obedient. (Cross, 1996)

In the three photographs, her teat-clad finger is first displayed hanging as if ready to be milked, then as if injured in a finger-sling supported by her other hand, and finally pointing upwards in a defiant gesture that is both penile and like an abusive gesture. Again the literalness of her imagery verges on going overboard but she pulls it back.

The third room at the Arnolfini presented two related works —*Close your eyes and open your mouth and see what God will give you* and *Kiss.* The first work is fifty black and white close-up photographs of children's faces with their eyes closed and their mouths open, playing the game of the title. They variously express trust, need, receptivity, anticipation, defensiveness, surrender, vulnerability, the potential of intrusion. Vision denied, the exposed mucous membranes of their mouths become conduits to the body and the self. With their eyes closed, we become acutely aware of our position as voyeurs—looking inside so many mouths, inside the children. For *Kiss,* Cross had two people kiss with their mouths full of dental plaster, forcing their tongues through the plaster. She then electroformed the resulting cast in silver. It looks like an insect or a plant.

There seems to be a new note of tenderness and pathos in recent works, such as *Lover Snakes, Rugby, Close your eyes..., Kiss* and also, notably, in *Untitled,* where an x-ray of a foetus is lodged in the x-ray of a skull. *Untitled* is a beautifully simple, complex image denoting new life lodged in a death's head, cerebral creation conflated with biological conception.

Like her pieces, the mixed connotations of Cross' exhibition titled, *even,* are a simple but effective measure of the overall temper of her work—suggesting equality, revenge, neither more nor less, emphatic comparison, balance, equability.

13
DEAR BODY: ENDURANCE AND PERFORMANCE

2008. First published in D. Kermode (ed) *Endurance*. Birmingham: Vivid, np.

Where does contemporary endurance art sit in relation to the historical work of artists such as Skip Arnold, Dennis Oppenheim, Abramović or Burden in the 1970s? Where does it sit in relation to concepts and practices of endurance in the wider culture, ranging through Ernest Shackleton's epic story of Arctic survival; religious acts of endurance by Jain monks, Himalayan yogis or Christian ascetics; entertainment spectacles and stunts by Houdini, David Blaine or Evel Knievel; feats in *The Guinness Book of Records* or Japanese gameshows? What do all these endurance acts have in common and how do they differ?

Thomas McEvilley's essay, 'Art in the Dark' (1983, pp. 62–71) remains one of the most insightful analyses of endurance art (also see Exit Art, 1996, pp. 60–70). McEvilley noted that all endurance acts—whether art or not—are 'based on an aesthetic of choosing and willing rather than conceiving and making' and 'a mode of willing which is absolutely creative in the sense that it assumes that it is reasonable to do anything at all with life'. They involve an arbitrary and rigorous style of decision-making. A very precise, very unpragmatic and demanding task is vowed for a specific length of time (such as a year or the rest of one's life). They involve an 'apparent aimlessness along with fine focus and rigour of execution'. There is a 'suspension of judgement about whether or not the act has any value in itself, and a concentration on the purity of the doing' (McEvilley, 1983, pp. 62–71). So, for instance, Tehching Hsieh's works exemplify these qualities, in his year-long vows to punch in hourly on a time clock, live outdoors in New York, be tied with a rope to fellow-artist Linda Montano, live in isolation in a barred cell (Johnston, 1984, pp. 176–179).

Blaine's works all involve an element of transparency (transparent boxes and blocks of ice) because their principle intent is to create a spectacle of heroic prowess. Just as Blaine spent 64 hours embedded in a block of ice, Chinese artist, He Yun Chang spent 24 hours embedded in a concrete block. But unlike Blaine, Chang was not visible. He became a present absence, an empathetic anxiety for the audience who knew he was in there but couldn't see him. The feats and records enacted for *The Guinness Book of Records* are about being superlative: the best, the fastest, the tallest. (In 1990, I co-curated a project in Newcastle by artist Guillaume Bijl where he set up a spoof Guinness record attempt for counting backwards in the dark (Bennett, 1990)). Unlike the Guinness feats, artist Sherman Fleming's works set the body up to fail as, for example, he tried to move in shoes bolted to bowling balls (*Rodforce*, 1989).

The 1995 survey show, *Endurance*, presented by Exit Art in New York, described it as work that tests the physical, mental, and spiritual endurance of the body,

an extreme form of presence ... an emphatic statement of existence, time, and the physical limitations of the body and will ... an
intention beyond the physical to reach the spiritual ... a way for
the artist to prove a point with themselves ... a defiance of being
your own victim ... an action between triumph and defeat.
(*Endurance*, 1995)

There is, however, an uneasy potential here for endurance to be
read as macho heroics. Lippard, for example, remarked scathingly:

In 1967 to 1971, when Bruce Nauman was 'Thighing', Vito Acconci
was masturbating, Dennis Oppenheim was sunbathing and
burning himself and Barry Le Va was slamming into walls, [body
art] seemed like another very male pursuit. (1976, p. 74)

While many of the cultural manifestations of endurance enact
superman, endurance art more often enacts everyman and demonstrates the vulnerability and incapacities of the body rather than its
prowess.

Scarry has described how the conditions of the body—its
mortality, its vulnerability to pain, disease, emotional and psychological distress, its isolation and inability to ever fully communicate
across the divide between consciousnesses—shape our generation
of artefacts that make up the world. Scarry's expansive definition of
artefacts includes both the material objects we make and the invisible ideologies that we also make, and which structure the environments we live in. She describes the body as having the status of
primary material and reference point and its use, therefore, in giving
substance to immaterial ideologies. It is the site of both ideological
control and individual resistance.

The process of the imagination ... begins ... by man conceiving of
his own body as a sign of (and substitute for) something beyond

itself, and then bringing forth other signs that can perform the work of representation in his dear body's place. (1985, p. 237)

What does endurance mean for contemporary artists and contemporary audiences? The contemporary artists showing in *Endurance* at Vivid reference their historical forebears from the 1970s, but their acts are occurring in different times, different contexts and so carry different meanings. They each do something slightly different with the genre of endurance.

When Joost Nieuwenberg chops and cooks a huge amount of onions in a tiny, cramped space he suggests endurance through the routines of daily life—eating, cooking, existing. Like Gina Pane, he addresses the small cruelties of daily life and forces awareness of anesthetised behaviour patterns. Harold Offeh's forced sustained facial expression in *Smile* reminds us of the irrepressible and indomitable human spirit, as well as the many stresses it has to rise above. Marcus Young's slow smiling and slow walking works are images of infinite patience and the aching but unfrenetic pleasure of being and interacting. Kira O'Reilly's work focuses on the fragility, mortality and vulnerability of the body and the empathy between bodies. She says, 'I use bodily utterance when words fail me'. William Hunt's absurdist feats (playing guitar upside down with his head in a bucket of paint or trying to play music and sing while maintaining his balance on a rotating circular stage) show the fallible body persisting stubbornly, despite the odds, in its efforts to create and express.

Last year I spent a day walking along beaches in Cleveland with He Yun Chang as he carried a small rock on a sixteen-week walk anti-clockwise round the edge of the British island (*Amino*, no date). He explained to me that he can do what he likes in his head and with his body and his will, despite any social and political oppression. For Chang an act of endurance is an assertion of freedom. As McEvilley noted, endurance art hopes 'to escape from one's own intentional horizon' and is 'designed to undermine the conditioned-response systems that govern ordinary life' (1983).

Artists use their bodies, not to tell us something specific about themselves, although that may be the source and starting point they work from, but to tell us something about the human condition in general. Artists use the body to ask what is it to be human and what is it to be humane.

14

WILLEM DE KOONING: NONSTOP

2016. Review of Rosalind E. Krauss, *Willem de Kooning Nonstop: Cherchez La Femme*, first published in *Times Higher Education*, 8 April.

In 1950, in a lecture on Renaissance art, the Dutch-American artist Willem de Kooning declared that 'flesh was the reason why oil painting was invented'. In his own artworks, de Kooning was fascinated with 'what paint does', its lushness, the possibilities of building it up into material substance on the canvas, evoking fleshiness. He confessed to a predilection for 'a nice, juicy, greasy surface'. What he liked about clay, when he started sculpting in later life, was that you could keep it wet.

Between 1950 and 1954, de Kooning created many large abstract expressionist oil paintings and drawings of the same subject—woman—sometimes seated, sometimes standing, sometimes two women. He worked on each painting over and over for long periods of time. Woman occurred as the subject in his work in the 1940s and recurred in the 1960s in paintings such as *The Clam Diggers*.

Although de Kooning admired Rubens, his own iterations of women in paint were not realistic fleshy nudes. Instead, with their smeared abstraction, their hideous toothy grins and exaggerated breasts, they appeared to many viewers as monstrous, ugly, even gynephobic. 'I get the paint right on the surface. Nobody else can do that,' remarked de Kooning, and indeed the woman in *Woman I*, with her 'distorted oral rictus' and transfixing stare, seems to be coming right at you, out of the painting.

In this study, Krauss sets out to account for the repetitions of compositional template in de Kooning's work. Her central question is why he could not desert woman as subject. 'I can't get away from the Woman. Wherever I look, I find her,' he said. Krauss notes that de Kooning's inability to stop working on a particular painting, or to stop obsessively painting the same subject over and over again, are at the centre of many previous critical discussions of the artist. She proceeds to outline her own 'explanatory tropes' for de Kooning's commitment to the woman-as-model template that held steady over four decades of his career. This template, she argues, formed the nexus of what he wanted to say about the status of painting as representation.

Krauss' short book is written in lucid, cogent prose, making its argument as strongly through its seventy-three illustrations as it does through the written text. She draws on the evidence of de Kooning's lecture 'The Renaissance and Order', on a fascinating series of photographs showing the changing states of *Woman I* as the artist laboriously worked and reworked the painting over two years, on her own account of the 'heated intelligence of the formal discussions' de Kooning held with fellow New York School artists, and on the well-trodden ground of contentious interpretations by the critics Greenberg and Harold Rosenberg. She discusses de Kooning's art in the context of literature that he and his contemporaries read and debated: Jean-Paul Sartre, Maurice Merleau-Ponty, Søren Kierkegaard. She engages with other critical readings of de Kooning's work ranging from Thomas Hess writing in the 1950s and 1960s to more recent studies by Mark Stevens and Annalyn Swan (2004) and by Richard Shiff (2011). Above all, however, Krauss' argument blooms from a careful looking at and pondering of the artworks themselves.

Discussing de Kooning's techniques, brushes, eradications, cutting and pasting that produced collage-like discontinuities, Krauss effectively demonstrates how he was concerned with the grammar of painting: the visual meaning of a painting apart from its overt subject matter. The pose in the *Woman* series, for instance, allowed him to explore foreshortening and perspective. He aimed to make figures and the voids around them equally active.

The 'explanatory tropes' Krauss puts forward are what she terms 'the triplex'—the combination of model, canvas and artist; the shadow (touching on her earlier work on the index); the window/mirror/windshield; the Freudian fetish, existentialism and doubt. She argues that de Kooning studied 'the triplex' of model-canvas-artist in the work of predecessors, including Vermeer, Ingres, Picasso and Matisse. She conveys de Kooning's admiration for Vermeer's ability to paint 'between the edges', Matisse's windows-rhymed-with-canvases, and Ingres' inclusions of mirrors. The point of view need not be materialised through an actual representation of the artist; instead, the artist could enter the picture as point of view, and so de Kooning saw each brushstroke in Cézanne's paintings as the artist's shifting point of view. She refers to later work, such as the indexical shadows of Lee Friedlander's photographs and the bodily imprints of Jasper Johns' *Skin* drawings. Krauss demonstrates that de Kooning was aiming to catch the totality of object and subject.

De Kooning's later paintings of abstracted highways occupied him for seven years, even longer than his compulsive fixation with *Woman*. Krauss argues that rather than a shift of topic, there is a continuity from the *Woman* paintings to the *Parkway Landscapes*.

De Kooning, a non-driver, enjoyed weekend drives in a Packard with his friend Wilfrid Zogbaum. Krauss suggests the car windshield can be equated with canvas, landscape with woman/model/subject, the view of the road with the artist's tacit point of view, and so 'the triplex' reappears.

Born in Rotterdam, de Kooning arrived in America in 1926 as a stowaway and died in 1997. He lived a life long enough to read Greenberg championing a new generation of artists and repudiating de Kooning's work as mere 'mannerism', to see (and donate the base work for) Rauschenberg's *Erased De Kooning*, and to have his dealer tell him that his late sculptural work was 'not good'. His late paintings were judged by some to be the outcome of Alzheimer's. Krauss argues that, on the contrary, there is a robust continuity of the concerns she has outlined, both in his late *Ribbon* paintings and in his sculpture.

Willem de Kooning Nonstop offers a fresh and persuasive perspective on its subject, provoking thoughtful engagement with the artist's work and with paintings by other artists who influenced him. Krauss presents her argument in an episodic, almost note-like structure. Having studied with Greenberg, the pre-eminent and often controversial critic of this generation of artists, Krauss is now the *grande dame* of revisionist theory on these artists. It was a 2011 exhibition of de Kooning's work at the Museum of Modern Art in New York that was the spur to Krauss to write this book. Many years earlier, she wrote an undergraduate thesis on de Kooning, and thus this study can be seen as the culmination of a lifetime spent pondering the paintings and the pictorial intelligence behind them.

De Kooning referred to the influence of Mesopotamian idols on his *Woman* series and saw his women as landscapes, with 'arms like lanes and a body of hills and fields'. He was transfixed by the joyousness of Matisse's paintings. His *Woman* paintings express maternity, fertility, sexuality, *joie de vivre*, life and procreation nonstop. At the same time de Kooning was painting the *Woman* series, Jean Dubuffet, in France, was coincidentally producing paintings of 'ladies' bodies', including *The Tree of Fluids*, which is displayed in Tate Modern. Georges Limbour wrote that

> the famous *Corps de Dames* seemed monstrous to those who wanted to reduce them to what they were only in part—women. The texture of these bodies shows clearly that they are not big hunks of flesh, but rather terrestrial slime, the substance of mountains and moors.

The grins and hooves of De Kooning's women evoke the copious laps of stolid, joyous mothers and grandmothers who might suddenly pick up their skirts, kick up their heels and hoof it at any unexpected moment. *Willem de Kooning Nonstop* evinces a ferocious and desperate joy in life and in the endless road—that eventually does stop.

15
FERAL CITY: PUNK ART

2007. First published in M. Sladen and A. Yedgar (eds) *Panic Attack!: Art in the Punk Years*. London: Barbican Art Gallery/Merrell, pp. 116–121.

With that backcombed orange hair, the cruel painted face and an attitude of furious and wanton destructiveness, Margaret Thatcher was a punk. The citizenry first came adrift from a belief in democratic government in the punk years. We were living in 'the city gone feral' (Solnit, 2001, p. 18). There were oil crises in 1973 and 1979, fuel shortages, three-day working weeks, power cuts, strikes, rocketing inflation and unemployment. Thatcher engaged in vandalism against the Welfare State, public services, the mining industry and its associated working-class culture. In the United States, there was the bitter aftermath of the withdrawal from Vietnam, New York went bankrupt, and Watergate and Richard Nixon's resignation exposed an untruthful government. Such political disillusion is everyday now but in the 1970s it was new. In the post-war period, people had briefly tasted and believed in the ludicrous notion that the role of democratic government was to move collectively toward equity and civil rights. As Thatcher and Ronald Reagan settled in for their long, long terms in office, we lost hope in Michel Foucault's assertion that it was 'up to individuals to become indignant and to talk, and up to government to think and to act' (Macey, 1993).

I remember the 1970s as orange, purple and brown. In 1974, I was sixteen and rebelling against femininity and the oppression of women. I read Betty Friedan and Kate Millett, left behind the needlework and cookery at my girls' school to study economics and politics at a really bad further education college. I had cropped hair and wore ties and flimsy shirts with no bra. My university lecturer fell in love with me, (partly) because I looked like his boyfriend from public school. I went to the Blitz Club, took part in student sit-ins, pogoed off sticky carpets to The Sex Pistol's *Pretty Vacant* and The Stranglers' *No More Heroes*, faghagged with male friends in London's gay clubs, pubs and swimming pools, saw William Burroughs at the Brixton Academy, wore silk ballgowns from Flip and got the back of my head shaved for my sister's wedding. In the 1980s, I worked at the ICA on exhibitions by Mapplethorpe, Jarman, Anderson and the Situationist International. I liaised with a major Sunday magazine to bring in negatives of Mapplethorpe's works, which customs had impounded, and I handled irate phone calls about *Man in Polyester Suit*, visits from the Vice Squad and a delegation of priests. I went to Anderson's *United States* at the Tottenham Court Road Dominion three times because I was three-timing. The ICA's Situationist book (Blazwick, 1989) had a sandpaper cover imitating Guy Debord's *Memoires* (1957) that had been designed to destroy other books alongside it on the shelf.

Everyone who was young in those years has to tell their own story of that time because it was about trying to really live life. It was about finding 'a more intense life... that has not really been found' (Debord, cited in Marcus, 1989, p. 433). 'In this world where we had been looking for life we found only wreckage,' wrote Michel Mourre in 1950 (cited in Marcus, 1989, p. 284). Punk expressed dissatisfaction with humdrum conventional life, with capitalism creating our desires and then selling those to us as needs: the 'degradation of being into having' (Debord, cited in Marcus, 1989, p. 140). For McCarthy, 'our culture has lost a true perception of existence ... We are fumbling in what we perceive to be reality. For the most part we do not know we are alive' (Smith, 1979, p. 50). Punk was a protest against life that wasn't living. It attacked the constructs of the media, of consumerism and capitalism with venom and passion, to snap us out of it. Punk was edgy and ugly but not cynical.

Greil Marcus outlines the historical provenance of punk in revolutions and heresies, in Dada, May 1968, Lettrist International, Situationist International (Marcus, 1989). Punk also looked back to the boycott of a sick society in destruction art (see Stiles, 1992) and the messy body aesthetic of the Viennese Actionists. In a speech after the May 1968 Revolt in Paris, President Charles de Galle declared: 'This explosion was provoked by a few groups in revolt against modern society, against consumer society, against technological society ... which do not know what they would put in its place, but which delight in negation' (Marcus, 1989, p. 32). Punk too was an incoherent shout of refusal rather than an earnest programme for social change.

The Stonewall Riots following a police raid on a gay club in New York in 1969 had led to the establishment of the Gay Liberation Front. In London, the increasing confidence of gay culture was reflected in Lindsay Kemp's outrageous performances and Andrew Logan's establishment of *Alternative Miss World*. Going out itself became a form of political action—a show of conviction and a statement of community and stance. Michael Bracewell remarked that *getting ready* to go out became an artform and sometimes people didn't even bother to go out in the end (Atlas, 2004). The getting ready was the main thing as the socialising body became a form of individual resistant expression.

Clubs, cafes and journals have been the bivouacs of resistant aesthetics since Dada (see Ades, 1978; Melzer, 1994). The self-published Dada, Surrealist, Lettrist and Situationist journals were precedents for the punk zines, including *Punk* and *Sniffin Glue* (see Perry, 2000) and the appearance of punk DIY where bands could form their own garage record labels and Leigh Bowery's band Raw Sewage could make a pop video in the Trocadero Make Your Own Booth for £15. When Bowery and Tony Gordon launched their club, Taboo, in London in 1985, they were referencing the Tabou cafe in Paris frequented by Isidore Isou and the other Lettrists in the 1950s.

The punk club haunts included Steve Strange and Rusty Egan's Bowie nights at Billy's and the Blitz Club in London, and CBGB's, the Mudd Club and Pyramid in New York. The Blitz Club was a personal catwalk for art and fashion students from Saint Martin's College. Its other regulars included the musicians who would form Spandau Ballet and Ultravox, journalist Robert Elms, Ben Kelly who later designed the Hacienda in Manchester and Boy George who was the cloakroom attendant (Rimmer, 1985). The Ramones, Blondie, Patti Smith and Talking Heads all played at CBGB's (Beeber, 2006). The Mudd Club had a rotating gallery and gender-neutral bathrooms and was frequented by David Byrne, Basquiat and Lydia Lunch. It features in songs by The Ramones, Frank Zappa and Talking Heads. The club staged theatrical theme nights, including Rock Suicide, Nuns and Victor Hugo. The explosion of the East Village art scene began with Gracie Mansion's show in her toilet in 1982 and by 1984 boasted around thirty tiny galleries in the neighbourhood. Nan Goldin worked as a waitress in Tin Pan Alley and showed her slideshow in progress of *The Ballad of Sexual Dependency* there. The Pyramid Club was part of this East Village scene created by the artists, actors and musicians who lived there. Marcus asks, 'is the cabaret where the spirit of revolution is born [?] ... it is a question of how much history, made and unmade, a cabaret can contain' (Marcus, 1987, p. 39).

The need to live life forcefully, indelibly, was expressed by the Dada Cabaret Voltaire in Zurich in the face of three million dead soldiers on the battlefield of Verdun in 1916. For the Lettrist International and Situationist International groups in Paris, it was the recent memories of the Second World War that spurred their fierce urgency. The unbearable shortness and vividness of life would be brought into sharp relief again in the early 1980s by the advent of the AIDS epidemic and its tragic mishandling by bigoted authorities.

The seventy-five prints of David Wojnarowicz's series *Arthur Rimbaud in New York* (1978–1979) show Wojnarowicz's friend Brian Butterick in various locations around the city, wearing a photo-copied melancholy Rimbaud mask with its bruised mouth and drooping eye. Drawing on his own experiences as a homeless, runaway rent-boy (see Scholder, 1999), Wojnarowicz photographs 'Rimbaud' on the shore of the Hudson River, in a diner, outside a peepshow, shooting up at the piers, in front of Coney Island, masturbating, reading a paper in a seedy room, on the subway, in Times Square. The impassive pallor of the mask jars with the living flesh of the body shooting up or masturbating. 'Rimbaud' is both immersed in New York, taking it all in, and a displaced and dispassionate alien observing it. We expect at any moment that he will break out of his impassivity and give us his observations on this city, this life, but he remains mute and uncommunicative—a mere surface. And can Butterick see through the mask at all?

Peter Hujar, Mapplethorpe and Wojnarowicz's works portray a furtive sexuality, inhabiting dilapidated urban interstices: 'in [Tom of Finland's] visions of the leather-scene and S/M sex, a habit of mind was identified which became real on the West Side piers in the early 1970s, and was photographed by Robert Mapplethorpe' (Hollinghurst, 1993, p. 11). 'The city's ruins constituted a dark playground for those... engaging in non-economic, non-productive activity, imaginative and erotic' (Solnit, 2001, p. 22). These artists' photographs, artworks and texts capture the dangerous peeling alleyways and interiors of the Hudson River Piers where gay men met for anonymous sex. Mapplethorpe stated, 'I have not set out to make distinctly homosexual photographs. I have recorded or documented a certain kind of sexuality ... these have been both perhaps my best pictures and the most difficult to make' (Nairne, 1993, p. 6). Wojnarowicz stencilled walls, made murals in the piers, painted on trashcan lids and supermarket posters and incorporated street graffiti into his collages. In these works and the street art of other artists, including Keith Haring and Basquiat, the city became both canvas and subject.

David Lamelas' *The Violent Tapes* (1975) captured the bewildering, alienated, predatory spaces of modern life. And the theme of the feral city also occurs in Jarman's bleak dystopic vision of the United Kingdom in *Jubilee* (1977). Queen Elizabeth I and John Dee travel through time to 1977, the Jubilee year of Queen Elizabeth II, and discover the end of civilisation: a punk England that is murderous, cruel, valueless, burning, grimy, graffitied and pointless. While Abba was actually winning the *Eurovision Song Contest*, Jarman's character, Amyl Nitrate (played by The Sex Pistols' singer Jordan), wins it as a mooning, suspendered, goose-stepping Britannia/Boadicea. A repugnant impresario (Malcolm McLaren?) cackles throughout the film like a hyena. There is no future and no beauty or integrity in this rebellion.

1970s body art stripped down the body at the same time as the *Alternative Miss World* was dressing and trussing it up. Abramović, Burden, Gina Pane, Acconci, Bruce Naumann and Dennis Oppenheim were among artists who were using their own bodies in performance as a field of enquiry and revitalising a bodily discourse

(Ferguson, 1998; Warr, 2000a). Body art was featured in the journals *Artitudes, Avalanche* and *Studio International.* Three important exhibitions of body art took place in 1975: *Bodyworks* in Chicago, accompanied by a significant essay by Willoughby Sharp; Francois Pluchart's *L'Art Corporel* (1975) at the Stadler Gallery in Paris; and *Magna Feminismus* in Vienna, curated by Export.

Rebellion against sexual stereotyping was reflected in persona-based work by feminist artists, including Adrian Piper, Eleanor Antin and Lyn Hershman. Hannah Wilke in *Through the Large Glass* (1976), *S.O.S. Starification* (1974–1982) and *So Help Me Hannah* (1978–1984) and Carolee Schneemann in *Naked Action Lecture* (1968) used their own stripped naked bodies to critique the treatment of the female body in art, in pornography and in the wider culture. An equally powerful but more ambiguous position was taken by Cosey Fanni Tutti in her 'magazine action' pieces created while working in the sex industry in England, which she re-presented in the controversial *Prostitution* exhibition at the ICA (1976). Abramović's *Role Exchange* also addressed the sex industry. Abramović sat in a prostitute's window in the red-light district in Amsterdam while the prostitute went to the artist's gallery opening.

Burden, McCarthy and Mike Kelley were working in Los Angeles and explicitly attacked the deadening impact of the media and Hollywood. Burden hijacked a live TV show, holding a knife to the hostess' throat. McCarthy referenced television shows and the horror and porn movie industries. Timothy Martin describes Burden, Kelley and McCarthy as reacting against the dispassionate neutrality of minimalism and conceptualism—rupturing that clean space with the living, breathing, messy body (Martin, 1994, p. 280). Kelley abjured the clean lines of minimalism for a more DIY or artisan aesthetic and drew on punk in a gleeful debunking of earnestness and pretension.

McCarthy's rituals too were irreverent. His performances equated the dining table with the altar, the dissection table, the stage, addressing social rather than autobiographical trauma. A media-generated 'reality' is violently force-fed to the gagging and effaced body. Ralph Rugoff describes McCarthy as 'molesting ... the fundamental scaffolding of civilization ... the butchered eloquence of his work speaks ... against the deadness of pre-packaged experience' (Rugoff, Stiles and Pietrantonio, 1996, pp. 35–36). McCarthy contrasts an exaggeratedly leaking body—wearing its insides on the outside—with wooden Pinocchios, bodies fitted together from Lego-like parts and pre-programmed robotic figures.

Kathryn Rosenfeld has described the merging of queer and punk sensibilities and subcultures in the 1980s. She argues that many people came out and came to queer identity politics through the radical foundation laid by punk and its direct action approach. So ACT UP's fluorescent President Reagans built on the aesthetic of The Sex Pistols. 'The central idea of identity politics—that the inscription of otherness on the body is what situates and activates one politically' could be linked to 'punk's expression of mainstream disaffection through bodily adornment',

> Punk's reliance upon the visual—its earnest insistence upon the body as a canvas for self-expression-cum-visual terrorism—made it a logical home both for the performative, visually strategic tactics of contemporary queer culture, and for art students seeking a way out of the studio and the institution and into the streets. (Rosenfeld, 1999–2000, p. 29)

Bracewell points out that bodies started to become articulate in Anthony Burgess's novel *A Clockwork Orange* (1962), in Stanley Kubrick's film of the novel in 1970 and in David Bowie's *Ziggy Stardust* (1972) (Bracewell, 1994, p. 38). In 1974, the *Transformer* exhibition in Lucerne looked at artists who employed masquerade and explored transgender in their work, including Urs Luthi, and related this to the imagery of Bowie, Brian Eno and Brian Ferry. Hujar photographed New York drag performers and Goldin intimately captured the lives of drag queens in Boston. But the most dressed up body of all was easily Bowery's.

Bowery's appearances in London clubs and the magazines, *The Face, i-D* and *Blueprint*, took dandyism to a new extreme. Appearing as a beautiful monster in his own laboriously crafted designs that were both glamorous and horribly twisted, he enacted Roger Caillois' thesis of an uncanny border between camouflage and excessive display (see Caillois, 1938 and Sarduy, 1975 in Warr, 2000a, p. 250). Bowery had a theory of embarrassment as the unexplored emotion. Bowery remarked, 'I'm interested in the human body and the way it can be changed … I had a period where my favourite fabric was flesh. I didn't wear any clothes for a while' (Atlas, 2004). Bowery's unclassifiable cultural practice is captured in Cerith Wyn-Evans film *Epiphany* and in the work of many photographers from the time. His performances at Anthony D'Offay Gallery in London in 1986 emphasised how his overly adorned body had become a mirror reflecting society and an armour deflecting penetration. In his collaborations with Michael Clark and Bodymap, there is a tension between the excessive covering of the body and the wearing of holes baring the arse and other unexpected areas of flesh.

Donning crazy masks and costumes designed by Marcel Janco at the Cabaret Voltaire in 1916, Hugo Ball had noticed how they structured his perception and behaviour. Butterick's identity is half-submerged in Wojnarowicz's Rimbaud masks. Robert Longo's *Men in the Cities* used business suits as a uniform/costume (like David Byrne), to express the alienation of his dancing/writhing figures. McCarthy's disguises—his rubber masks and his cheap female wigs and sunglasses—depersonalise him, telling us, this isn't me, it's you. Bowery danced for hours in costumes that barely allowed him to breathe and did not allow him to urinate. In the daytime, Bowery also wore wigs and costumes—of a 'normal', nerdy person—as if there was no way to really be himself in the world. The promiscuous

and delirious collage and polysemy, the uneasy composites of
Bowery's work, are also stylistic characteristics in the work of
McCarthy and Wojnarowicz. McCarthy and Bowery dress up to
perform the artist's role as clown—to speak out an extreme critical
view on society from the privileged position of court jester.

16

BRUCE GILCHRIST: SLEEPER

1996. First published in *Performance Research*, 1(2), pp. 1–19, DOI: 10.1080/13528165.1996.10871484. *Performance Research* is published by Taylor & Francis: https://www.tandfonline.com/.

[Part 3 of this article was prepared in collaboration with Bruce Gilchrist and draws extensively on his writing.]

A man is lying sleeping. It is discomforting to be looking at him in this private and vulnerable state. His eyes are covered by a visor with flashing red lights. He has electrodes attached to his arms and head. Wires and cabling stretch from his body to an array of machinery: sound equipment, some unidentifiable boxes, a red button. A gurgling, visceral sound—punctuated by static—is amplified in the space. An audience is looking at the wired-up, sleeping body. One person steps over to the red button, studies a sheet of phrases with morse code translations and taps in the long-short signals on the button. Long and short bursts of electric current are administered to the sleeper, causing his body to twitch and jerk.

> x x -- x x -- x (I'm not certain what I'm interfacing with.)
> -- -- -- (I love you.)
> x x -- x x -- (Can you respond to this question?)

PART 1: RISK AND THE ARTIST'S BODY

All art is a risk for artists in the sense that they expose their deepest personal perceptions to general view. This may make artists liable to persecution if their ideas are at odds with the dominant religious or political ideologies of their times. Artists may also be at risk—of neglect and misunderstanding—if their vision is too radical for society to assimilate. And artists risk themselves through a deliberate engagement with a disorder of the senses—Rimbaud, Van Gogh, Artaud, might be examples.

> Generally, risk remains theoretical, a kind of by-product of the masochism inherent in every creative act, and actually one had to wait for the end of the '60s and the beginning of the '70s to see the artists endanger their bodies and inflict on themselves a violent physical suffering in order to produce thought. (Pluchart, 1978, p. 39)

In 1919, Marcel Duchamp shaved his head with a tonsure in the shape of a shooting star and humorously emphasised that the artist can be his art. Piero Manzoni took this a step further by presenting the artist's biological body as art: 'In the month of May '61 I produced and tinned 90 tins of "artist's shit" (30 grammes each) naturally preserved (made in Italy)' (Manzoni, 1962). From the late 1950s, artists all over the world were incorporating themselves into their work—Hans Namuth filmed Jackson Pollock working within his drip paintings; French artist Georges Mathieu executed enormous action paintings in public; the Japanese Gutai group incorporated their bodies into *koi* (actions), including Kazuo Shiraga who painted with his feet and sculpted by wrestling mud. From 1959 onwards, Happenings, incorporating the artist and the audience, were being presented in the United States and Europe by a wide range of artists, including Kaprow, Oldenburg, Dine, Schneemann, Vostell, Knizak, Lebel, Kudo and Kasama, and artists associated with Fluxus, such as Ono, Paik and Moorman, Higgins, Beuys and Vautier, were also using their bodies in their art.

The Viennese Actionists were among the first artists to use the abuse of their own bodies to attempt to go beyond language and intensify their message. In 1962 Hermann Nitsch was tied to a wall as if crucified, and lamb's blood was poured over him. Otto Muhl and his collaborators exposed their bodies to desecration in chaotic, orgiastic tableaux, to denounce taboos and liberate the individual from the repressions of bourgeois society. Rudolf Schwarzkogler created a series of staged photographs exhibiting the body being variously mutilated, bandaged, electrocuted. He had been influenced by the work of Yves Klein and, especially, by *The Artist of Space Hurls Himself into the Void* (1960)—the fictionalised photograph by Harry Shunk showing Klein leaping from a building. To make the photograph, Klein did actually leap from the building several times into a tarpaulin held out for him below, He was slightly injured. The tarpaulin and catchers were later removed from the photograph.

Schwarzkogler's 'action aesthetics seem to reflect salvation through the slow suspension of corporeality' (Klocker, 1989, p. 49). While Nitsch, Muhl and Schwarzkogler's works were theatricalised or fictionalised presentations of the body at risk, in pain, desecrated, Gunter Brus' work gradually combined symbolic dissection with real bodily risk. *Self-painting/Self-mutilation* (1964) presented photographs of his body painted white and dissected by black stripes, juxtaposed with an axe and other implements of incision or torture. He developed an aesthetic of analysis of the body—taking his body and himself apart, in order to reconstruct both himself and the body politic.

> I dissever my left hand. Somewhere lies a foot. A suture on my wrist joint bone. I press a drawing pin into my spinal cord. I nail my large toe to my forefinger. Pubic, underarm, and head hairs lie on a white plate. I slit open my aorta with a razor blade, I slam a wiretack into my ear. I split my head lengthwise into two halves. I insert barbed wire into my urethra and by turning it slightly try to cut the nerve. (Brus, quoted in Klocker, 1989, p. 118)

Brus' *Art and Revolution* performance in 1968 involved eating his faeces, drinking his urine and masturbating while singing the Austrian national anthem. (Following this performance he had to go into exile to avoid a prison sentence.) In his final performance, *Zereissprobe* in 1970, he symbolically and actually realised a degree of self-dissection, or what Hubert Klocker has aptly described as 'psycho-archeological existentialism'. Destruction art drew on Freud and psychiatric theories of self-reconstruction through destruction —see Stiles (1992) and Berke and Barnes' (1973) *A Journey Through Madness*.

The Actionists were followed by a host of artists putting their bodies at risk. Michel Journiac created a pudding from his blood (1969). Marina Abramovic took pills for schizophrenia and depression in *Rhythm 2* (1973) and presented her passive body for six hours to an audience with an array of objects, including a loaded gun, knife, paint and feathers in *Rhythm 0* (1975). Australian artist Stelarc suspended his body with meat hooks inserted into his flesh. Dennis Oppenheim was stoned in *Rocked Circle Fear* (1971) and exposed to serious sunburn in *Reading Position for Second Degree Burn* (1971). Vito Acconci used his body as a site where he could measure different types of feeling, such as pain and fatigue and he ran the risk of exposing his secrets and fantasies to the public.

All Chris Burden's performance work involved risks 'that took art to the verge of suicide'. He was locked up for five days in a small locker in *Five Days Locker Piece* (1971), shot in the arm in *Shoot Piece* (1971), 'crucified' on a Volkswagen in *Transfixed* (1974) and lay in the middle of the highway under a tarpaulin with flares around him in *Deadman* (1972). Burden's work often turned responsibility for his body over to the public. In a few projects he also raised the question of endangering others—he fired a gun at a jumbo jet, and in a live television show he held a knife to the interviewer's throat.

Czech artist Petr Stembera grafted a rose onto his arm. Pinoncelli was thrown into the sea in a closed, ballasted bag in Naples in 1974 and in another work he attacked a bank armed with a sawn-off rifle loaded with blanks. Other artists risking their bodies included Micoch, Le Va, Parr, Fox, Paik, Weibel and Export. Art critics were groping for a new critical language to cope with this art in essays, such as Harold Rosenberg's 'The American action painters' (1952); Lucy Lippard and John Chandler's 'The dematerialization of art' (1968); Joseph Kosuth's 'Art after philosophy' (1969); Jindrich Chalupecky's 'Art and sacrifice' (1978); and Thomas McEvilley's 'Art in the dark' (1983).

Burden's projects used physical deprivation or risk as a means to access an altered state of consciousness for himself. The degree to which this could be a shared empathetic experience for his audience or a sensational voyeuristic one is problematic. As Mary Kelly has pointed out, artists who invoked 'the phenomenological body' were perhaps engaging in a form of essentialist romanticism (Kelly, 1984, pp. 30-31). There is a fine line between work such as Pane's, which successfully evokes a universal empathy, and work that is narcis-sistic and about The Artist as hero. The 'elusive factors that divide body art by women from that by men' (Lippard, 1976) have not really been addressed by feminist or any other critics. Lippard pointed out that women's body art in the 1970s seemed to be avoiding a major fact about women's bodies—birth (Lippard, 1976). Stiles comments that men's body art was mainly assertion and recuperation of identity and women's was reconstruction of the self. Archetypally, pain and bodily injury have very different connotations for men and for women. For men they are associated with initiation and manhood—for women with birth, violation, conquest, ownership. Whatever the body artists' intentions may have been, they could not necessarily escape the archetypal cultural and gender traditions they were working within and with.

Gina Pane was one of these artists who most effectively placed her body at 'the crux of empathy' in a protest against human self-destructiveness. Her performances disturbingly combined anodyne, banal, daily actions with injury and pain—swallowing rotten minced meat while watching TV news in an intentionally uncomfortable position; alternately wounding herself with a razor blade on her stomach, eyelids, face and arms and playing with a tennis ball (*Psyche*, 1974); gargling endlessly with milk until blood mixed with the spit liquid (*Sang, Lait Chaud*, 1972); climbing up a ladder of protruding razor blades with bare feet and hands (*Escalade Sanglante*, 1971).

> Gina Pane ill-treats herself in order to make one feel that violence is a daily fact, a way of denying both man and life .... During the whole action Gina Pane does not give the spectator a break. By her suffering, her risking, she disrupts his indifference and hostility, she channels his repulsion, making him aware of what they carry. Here, the body is projected as the conscience of the self. It is pure thought, an intellectual and sensitive analysis ... the body, having become a thinking and suffering matter, transforms itself into a coadjutant of thought. (Pluchart, 1978, p. 40)

SUBJECTIVITY

Body art, in common with performance art, concept art and land art, was attempting to escape the marketable art object and was part of the dematerialisation of art (see Lippard and Chandler, 1968). However, as Art and Language pointed out to Lucy Lippard, ideas were just as saleable as objects (Lippard, 1973, pp. 43–44). Documentation of the artists' bodily risks went on the market.

Also, as Brazilian artist Lygia Clark emphasised, the body artist could make himself or herself an object:

> In this apparent demystification, doesn't the myth of the artist actually grow, to the extent to which this myth is the object of the spectacle? What is the difference between [the artist who mutilates his body, and one who] cuts or destroys his canvas in order to negate it as an expressive object? This is the romantic attitude of the artist who still needs an object—even if the object is himself—in order to negate it. (1973, p. 118)

Where body art did differ from the other art trends of the time was in its complex presentation of subjectivity. 'Strictly speaking it is impossible to use the body as an object. The only case in which a body approaches the status of object is when it becomes a corpse' (Sharp, 1970, p. 16). Alan Sonfist took up this point by bequeathing his dead body to the Museum of Modern Art in his will (*Last Piece*, 1973).

The body perceives and experiences itself and what it encounters. It is narcissistic and existentialist but also universal and empathetic. Every body is implicated in the sufferings or pleasures of other bodies. It cannot be an objective observer. 'To say that one never suffers alone, is not a simple cliche. The laws of identification and of communication between images of the body make one's suffering and pain everybody's affair' (Schilder, 1950, p. 149). In the presence of another human sentience, much has to be acknowl-edged. The body forces the inescapable realisation of an essential intersubjectivity.

> The enigma is that my body simultaneously sees and is seen. That which looks at all things can also look at itself and recognise what it sees, the 'other side' of its power of looking. It sees itself, it touches itself, touching; it is visible and sensitive to itself. It is not a self through transparence, like thought, which only thinks its object by assimilating it, by transforming it into thought. It is a self through confusion, narcissism, through inherence of the one who sees in that which he sees, and through inherence of the sensing in the sensed—a self, therefore, that is caught up in things, that has a front and a back, a past and a future .... This initial paradox cannot but produce others. Visible and mobile, my body is a thing among things; it is caught in the fragment of the world, and its cohesion is that of a thing. But because it moves itself and sees, it holds things in a circle around itself. (Merleau-Ponty, 1964, pp. 162–163)

As well as undermining objectification and creating a disturbing and an, often, unacceptable access to empathy, the artists' use of their bodies was also an attack on the notion of distance and objec-tivity in assessing art, and in public behaviour. It drew on authori-sations of the autobiographical or subjective by feminist writers, such as Luce Irigaray and Helene Cixous: 'Write yourself. Your body must be heard' (Cixous, 1975, p. 165). It contained a wholesale attack on objectivity and rationality.

Kristine Stiles has tellingly compared the social and legal reac-tion to the *Destruction in Art Symposium* (DIAS) in London (featuring Nitsch, Muhl and Brus) with the *Dialectics of Liberation* conference organised by R.D. Laing and David Cooper, also in London, ten months later (and coincidentally at the same time as the trial of the DIAS organisers, Gustav Metzger and John Sharkey):

> the textual and expository exegesis of those who participated in *The Dialectics of Liberation* presented no threat, framed as it was in the vaguely sentimental idealistic terms of liberation, terminology that conformed to the authoritative, abstract, restrained, measured, and ostensibly objective code of academic discourse. By comparison, 'destruction in art' represented a direct, contentious, strident, and unsentimental discourse and its practices were raw, passionate, involved, impatient, skeptical, pessimistically critical, and sometimes dangerous and beyond control. (Stiles, 1992, pp. 85–86)

Philosophy has always used subjective experience to explore reality whilst science has purported not to. But the earliest scientists, such as Newton, were philosophers and alchemists too. Various deconstruction analyses written in the last fifty years have emphasised that there is no such thing as an objective, impartial view, but science is only slowly coming to acknowledge that all human thought, all human knowledge, bears the personal imprint and vested interest of those formulating it.

> The unprecedented achievement of the body ... in art has been to visualize the perpetually shifting but mutually identifiable relations of power and need within the exchange of subject/object relations. When the body becomes the material support, subject, and content of art, it holds the possibility of shifting the determined and fixed relations demanded by the prior objective status of art into an interplay of subjectivities established and transmitted in body gestures, systems, and relations. The private body is utilized as formal material, subject matter, and content into

which the experiences and institutions of the body politic are collapsed. (Stiles, 1992, p. 96)

Stiles describes this process as 'a reconstitution of the humanistic project, a shift from the transcendent subjectivity of holistic humanism to a polysemic humanism characterised by independent subject positions' and describes body art as a development from figuration into embodiment, a response to a desensitised society, about intersubjectivities as opposed to objectivities. Presence has to be taken a lot more seriously than representation.

The increasing absence of 'embodiment' caused by technology —global communications, including the telephone, television, satellites and the internet—all make it easier to conceive of other people as distant, and therefore irrelevant Others. Mediation through technology stifles the impact of the empathetic body—war on TV news, for instance—but the efficaciousness of the human presence should not be romanticised. While soldiers and politicians are often physically distant from the victims of their actions, torturers torture close up, using other techniques to distance their victims to non-human status.

AMNESIA

The Viennese Actionists' work involved such radical protest and over-stepping of taboos that it never was integrated, socially or artistically, in the way that a lot of later body art was: 'constant provocation of the social structures which react with rejection [is one] of the main risks run by artists since 1969' (Pluchart, 1978, p. 40). Work by artists using their own bodies, which has proved too difficult for culture to swallow, has been neutralised through marginalisation, mythologising and amnesia. For the audiences of body art, its impact is subjective and has often been so disturbing that it has had to be denied. Representation of this work as an aberration in the history of 'real' art has been vigorous. (See Lea Vergine's 'Bodylanguage' (1974); Max Kozloff's 'Pygmalion reversed' (1975); Peter Frank's 'Auto-art: Self-indulgent? And how!' (1976); Nicolas Calas' 'Bodyworks and porpoises' (1978).)

Apart from the work's being undermined through prosecution or through marginalising and forgetting it, it is also undermined by mythologising it and describing it as the output of psychosis. It has been asserted by more than one critic, for instance, that Schwarzkogler died as the result of amputating his own penis in a performance. He never amputated his penis. The myth was perpetuated by a host of commentators, including Robert Hughes in *Time Magazine* in 1972 and Henry Sayre in *The Object of Performance* in 1990. Schwarzkogler actually died after falling or jumping from a window. The bandaged penis in his photograph is that of model Heinz Cibulka, who also never had his penis amputated. Schwarzkogler's photographs were staged fictions.

In her essay 'Subject-object: Body art', Cindy Nemser commented that you can't help but recoil at the artist's pain and risk. Nemser sees the artists' bodily discomfort as being at odds with their goal of bringing the subjective and objective self together as an integrated entity. She suggests that body artists are simultaneously acting out, as well as reflecting, the alienated and schizoid condition of our society. 'Due to the unpleasant nature of the content of body art, the public may refuse to read it intelligently' (Nemser, 1971, p. 42). Many other art critics of the time, such as Lea Vergine, agreed with Nemser in diagnosing 'the psychosis of the avantgarde' (2000).

Other critics though have argued that this work cannot be reduced to an individual psychotic deviation. 'The artists are not neurotics as is often said; on the contrary, they are more sane than many modern people' (Eliade, 1963, p. 94). 'A body communicating and being communicated to, a body whose ownership has been given up, sacrificed [is a] gesture of desperate love' (Chalupecky, 1978, p. 34).

> If an artist beats himself, this does not mean that a sadistic audience is watching a masochistic artist. . . Because the exposed artist can be a substitute for the audience or even for the whole of mankind. The personal exposure to danger in an art context has a semiotic/symbolic quality in the flux of the art process, that goes beyond sadomasochism. (Weibel, 1978)

Artists working now with their bodies are working against the grain of the continuing art debate around the object inherited from formalism. The contemporary descendants of the formalist tradition are the many artists making object-based gallery work who treat consumerism ironically and take a nihilistic stance toward concepts of truth and reality. While artists working with their bodies constructively allude to the role consciousness and subjective perception play in constructing reality, rather than falling back on an essentialist notion (derived from Plato) or relying on a false notion of objective truth.

The body remains a powerful material for many contemporary artists. While in the 1960s and 1970s, artists used their bodies to test the parameters of art and society, today the artist's body is more often at the juncture of a radical interface with technology and an exploration of the nature of consciousness.

Stahl Stenslie and Kirk Wolford's *Cyber SM* (1994) is an interactive sex suit using the internet. Stelarc has moved from the suspended body to explore the body hooked up to technology. Kathleen Rogers's *PsiNet* (1995), supported by the BBC and Agema, created a parallel between broadcast technology and psychic transmission and reception. James Turrell's work experiments with brainwaves, perception and light. The Entropists are aiming to download their consciousnesses into computers. Eric Hobein's

Self Immolation Machine (1995) allows participants to be bathed in fire.

Orlan's redesign of her face using cosmetic surgery has delineated the extent of the continuing taboos around the body. 'We believe that the sky is going to fall on our head if we meddle with the body' (Orlan, 1995, p. 8). The operations are performed under local anaesthetic so that she can talk to a global audience via satellite:

> During surgery I read texts as long as possible, even while my face
> is being operated on. In the most recent operations, this produced
> an image of a cadaver under autopsy which keeps on speaking.
> (Orlan, 1995, p. 8)

In terms of risk, British artist Bruce Gilchrist's wired-up, sleeping, vulnerable body subjected to mild electrical stimulations may look alarming—but the technical risks are low. During a sudden thunderstorm at an open-air performance by Gilchrist in Fribourg, the technicians covered the sound system up first—before the audience pointed out that the wired-up sleeper might also need some protection. The risk of Gilchrist's work is more associated with the long-term effects of sleep deprivation and disruption and the common fear of confronting the mysteries of our consciousness.

Our relationship with the unconsciousness seems to have modulated from the Victorian fear of the heart of darkness into something more mixed and complex today. Freud and early psychoanalysis found penis envy, the Oedipus Complex and mass incest there and what had been diagnoses of the psychotic became popularised as the bogey men inhabitants of the universal unconscious. Antonin Artaud, who was very influential on a wide range of body artists, argued that theatre should offer to the audience 'convincing deposits of dreams in order to stir its crime inclinations and erotic obsessions, its wildness, its fancy, its utopian meaning of life and things, its cannibalism' (Artaud, 1964). Genesis P. Orridge and Otto Muhl are examples of artists attempting to wrestle with 'the dark forces of the unconscious' in modern art. Recent novelists such as William Gibson and Pat Cadigan have set about envisaging human consciousness disembodied by technology with relish, whilst others, such as Anne Rice, have pursued consciousness disembodied by the latent psychic powers of the brain and ancient, dark forces in the universe.

PART 2: VISCERA AND TECHNOLOGY

A range of positions regarding human consciousness and future technology are being pursued in scientific and cultural theory and research today. One position asserts that all life and intelligence function in ways that are analogous to, and therefore reproducible by, machines. In this theory, the machinic phylum (De Landa, 1991), the computational, the algorhythmic, is the basic principle of all life, including ourselves. Hans Moravec argues that humans are likely to be superseded by robots by 2030 and that we will download our consciousnesses into machines (Moravec, 1988). Hameroff describes brain activity as analogous to computer processes (Hameroff *et al.*, 1988). Daniel Dennett sees life and intelligence evolving through the mindless process of natural selection—'generate and test'—with data being stored and carried on by genes and DNA (Dennett, 1995). This view aligns human intelligence with a 'bottom-up' computer program, where a computer is loosely programmed so that it has the ability to learn from experience and incorporate mistakes and random elements—as the human brain does. In a 'top-down' program, a computer is programmed to perform set algorithmic procedures—and fatalist, religious views of existence correspond with this—with the programme coming from god.

According to the computational thesis of life and intelligence, all artificial intelligence researchers have to do, is design machines that mimic human physical and brain activity accurately and in fine enough detail, and they will have conscious machines.

Technology has already vastly extended our life expectancy, our physical environment, our perceptions and our memories—with glasses, telescopes, endoscopes, telephones, satellites, computers, photography, film, flight, genetic engineering, organ transplants, artificial insemination and much more. Technology as a prosthesis of intelligence seems at hand.

Already, collective thought imposed by diverse media has aimed at annihilating the originality of sensations, at dispensing with the presence in the world of people by furnishing them with a stock of information destined to program their memories. With the progress of electronics, we may envisage active prostheses of intelligence,

> For about 20 years, the neurosurgeon Delgado, one of the pioneers of the electronical phenomena of thought, has been treating and especially tranquilizing his patients with implants. Others are thinking of utilizing the 'intelligence' of the computer as internal prosthesis: 'A minuscule pastille of silicon would give a person instantaneous knowledge of a foreign language or the theory of relativity.' (Virilio, 1991, pp. 47–48)

Artificial intelligence and robotics research have already taken the machine a long way—endowing it with combinations of artificial perception, speech, mobility, decision-making abilities. Although one part of the human brain alone has eighty thousand synaptic endings, compared with the computer's equivalent at the moment of three or four, some theorists envisage the gap between human and machine as one that will soon be closed by new technological developments.

There are obvious reasons why scientists are not experimenting directly on the mystery itself—the brain. While we graft ears onto mice and test everything on animals, it would not be ethical to experiment physically on live human brains. Studies of dead human brains and animals' brains have been taken as far as they will go. Studies of injured or abnormal brains have provided the most illuminating clues so far. But madness and 'abnormality' are taboo, and we prefer to anaesthetise and remove them from view rather than look at them head on. In addition, studies using live, and perhaps not sane, subjects must rely heavily on their subjective reporting, which is problematic for a science which still has not fully come to terms with subjectivity.

Artists are not so queasy about experimenting on themselves as live subjects or about the validity of subjective experience. Both in his writing and in his performance work, Australian body artist Stelarc is pushing at the edge of the hybrid human-machine. He contends that the body is obsolete, no longer able to cope with its physical environment, overloaded by undigested information and intimidated by its own technology.

> It is time to question whether a bipedal, breathing body with binocular vision and a 1,400 cc brain is an adequate biological form. The body is neither a very efficient nor a very durable structure .... Skin was once the boundary of the self. As interface it was once the site of the collapse of the personal and the political. Skin no longer signifies closure. (Stelarc, 1997)

He envisages a synthetic skin designed to absorb oxygen and other nutrients, which would do away with the need for internal organs so that the body could be hollowed out to allow for technological implants. There would be no birth and no death—merely repairs. Consciousness would somehow manage to stay put and alive during the process of grafting this cyberbody onto the physical body (rather like 'Robocop' or 'the Borg'). This solution would do away with the tricky problem of how to transfer or plug a human consciousness into a machine or how to create consciousness in a machine from scratch.

After his *Suspensions* of the 1970s, Stelarc's more recent work has included the development of a third robotic arm, a virtual arm programme and performances with an industrial robot. His *Stomach Sculpture* was a moving object inserted by endoscope. (He submitted it to the site-specific section of the *Sydney Biennale* unsuccessfully.) Stelarc's most recent work, *Remote Body*, employs a touch screen, the internet and his body hooked up to muscle stimulators, and gives anyone, anywhere in the world, the ability to jerk the artist's body around. However, for me, Stelarc's work remains unavoidably visceral and human in its impact. Compare his *Stomach Sculpture* with Mona Hatoum's much less nauseating exploration of her body cavities by endoscope, for instance. The image I take away from his performances is of the fragility and ingenuity of the human body dwarfed and pinned down by the surrounding technology and still eliciting empathy and awe.

While Stelarc's reasoning is profoundly stimulating, it seems to me that rather than revealing that we are frightened by our own technology, the theories that reduce us to machinery show instead a fear of the unknown elements of our consciousness. The only reason we need fear technology is because science, whilst emphasising ethics on a small scale, has such a bad track record for being adequately empowered to take responsibility on a large scale for its discoveries. There is good reason to fear what applications might be developed from any discoveries about consciousness, and a substantial history of passing the buck of responsibility to a fictional, inaccessible, omnipotent, collective force: 'Man', 'Society', 'Fate'.

Another position in the debate on consciousness and technology is taken up by mathematician Roger Penrose, in his books *The Emperor's New Mind* and *Shadows of the Mind*. He contends that there is a 'noncomputational' ingredient to consciousness, which will be comprehended only by a new type of physics, which will take subjective perception in the construction of reality into account.

While machines may be programmed to learn like humans from mistakes, while they can have random elements built into them, they still seem a long way short of a vast range of *qualia*—of subjective human experiences: intuition, happiness, pain, love, aesthetic sensibility, will, understanding, nostalgia, planning, dreams. The human mind's fallibility and inaccuracy may be as vital a part of intelligence and thinking as logic and reasoning. Human brain function seems to vary drastically from individual to individual. Some people, for instance, would solve a mathematical problem by using geometrical thinking (perhaps located on the right side of the brain), and others would address the same problem by using analytical thinking (perhaps located on the left side of the brain). Will computers ever lose their train of thought or forget what they were going to say? Will they ever respond intellectually to physical stimuli such as soaking in a bath or walking? Will they ever need to sleep?

PART 3: SLEEPER

For the last year, artist Bruce Gilchrist has been experimenting with sleep and dreams and presenting live performances using his own and collaborators' sleeping bodies. He is employing radical methods of human-technology interface to communicate with the sleeping body. He was recently awarded the ICA/Toshiba Art and Innovation Award to develop his project.

> We can't escape the pervading new message from the quantum experiments, which suggests that consciousness plays an active and indivisible role in what we know of as the physical universe. Western science has until now been at considerable pains to be as objective as possible, shielding all experiments from any subjec-

tive corruption by the observer. It is now proposed, by an increasing number of scientists, that consciousness, rather than being a phenomenon to exclude from proper experiments, might actually turn out to be the only phenomenon that exists. Reality proves to be more a nothing-ness than a something-ness, and about as substantial as a passing cloud. (Gilchrist, 1995, p. 1)

Gilchrist's background research for his project included visits to the Clinical Psychology Sleep-Research Laboratory at the University of Texas at Austin (see Price and Cohen, 1988 and La Berge and Gackenbach, 1988) and to British researcher, Keith Hearne.

During the seventies, both Stephen La Berge at Stanford University and Keith Hearne at Liverpool and Hull Universities, were conducting successful communication experiments in the sleep labs. They had both managed to develop methods of inducing lucidity in dreams and, through the use of the electroencephalogram (EEG), were sending messages from rapid eye movement (REM) dreaming sleep to their colleagues in the waking world. It is now accepted among the scientific community that lucid dreamers are able to consciously alter the content of dreams. The lucid dreaming machine developed by La Berge is being marketed by Synetic and Hearne's version, using a thermal, nasal probe measuring temperature and respiration, will go on the market soon.

Before the successful lucid dream experiments in the sleep labs, the activation/synthesis theory of dreaming sleep was prevalent. This theory suggested that dream content was a result of the brain being so hell-bent on assigning meaning and significance to the images thrown up by the random firing of its nerve cells that it found itself, even when there was none, making unfamiliar or bizarre images fit as best they could. In other words, it interpreted these apparently random bombardments as dreams. In the light of the work of La Berge and Hearne, this theory has been revised to acknowledge psychological significance.

What is remarkable about the activation/synthesis theory is that it sees the brain as a dynamic, self-sustaining organ, which generates its own information. The mind-brain appears to deal with the external world by having ideas about that external world. It then automatically sets about imposing those ideas, which it sees as its own truths, upon that external world. So it could be said that the internally manufactured dreamworld is then presented to the consciousness as the external universe.

The whole process of dreaming starts in the brain-stem, which appears to send triggering messages to both the hippocampus and the neo-cortex. This initiates the generation of theta waves (4–8 hz), which appear to be a necessary ingredient in the processing of memory. There is substantial evidence that theta rhythm encodes memories during REM sleep.

One way of modelling the brain, and finding increasing support, is as a dynamic, multi-dimensional holograph. This is believed to constitute the miraculous complexity of our minds and to create our ideas of the world around us. The holographic model of the mind-brain suggests that reality is really a frequency domain, and our brain an encoder (or is it decoder?) that converts these frequencies into what we see as the phenomenal world. 'Countless layers of ideas, images, feelings, have fallen successively on your brain as softly as light. It seems that each buries the preceding, but none has really perished' (Baudelaire, cited in Gilchrist, 1995, pp. 1–2).

Among the precursors of Gilchrist's work on the sleeping body is Susan Hiller's *Dream Mapping* (1974). In her project, a group of people slept for several nights in a field of mushroom 'fairy' circles in Hampshire. They recorded their dreams and mapped the positions of their sleeping bodies in the field.

Gilchrist first experimented with his sleeping body in *The Last Sweat of Youth*, curated by Rob La Frenais at London's Air Gallery in 1987. In summer 1994, he presented *A Way of Asking for Reasons* in the *Earth Wire* project in Loftus, East Cleveland, organised by Rob

La Frenais and myself, in collaboration with Village Arts (see Warr, 1994; La Frenais, 1994). Four performers, including Gilchrist, first inverted their sleep patterns with the aid of neurosynchronisers (brain machines) loaned by the UK distributor Lifetools. During their waking hours, they undertook conditioned learning sessions to recognise language encoded within electrical stimuli. With their neurosynchronisers tuned to the theta frequency, a transcutaneous electrical stimulation unit (TENS) gave them mild electric shocks in morse code. Drawing on his own recurring dream landscapes, Gilchrist chose a shale heap as the site for the public presentation of the work. The shale heap represented subterranean material brought to the surface and it commanded a spectacular view of the landscape, which the sleepers attempted to incorporate into their dreams. Once the performers were sleeping on the shale heap, the audience could send messages to the sleeping bodies by administering the electric shock morse code. As well as the expected outcomes, the four performers also found themselves suffering from a number of unpredicted effects from sleep deprivation and inversion. 'If we really live a poetic image ... we will aggravate the boundary between inside and outside' (Bachelard, 1969).

In his next performance presented in Trinity Buoy Wharf in London in 1994, Gilchrist experimented with a galvanic skin response unit (GSR), which allowed the electrical skin responses of his sleeping body to be amplified into the space. Gilchrist's TENS and GSR were both engineered by inventor Tony Bassett.

At the Zap Club in Brighton, UK in early 1995, he used a photic device designed by the Lucidity Institute in California, which, by using an infra-red sensor, told the audience when REM sleep (dreaming) was occurring, and therefore when they could attempt to communicate with Gilchrist's sleeping body using the learned morse code phrases administered by electric shocks.

Gilchrist presented the work again at *The Incident*—a symposium on non-explicable phenomena organised by Rob La Frenais in

Fribourg, Switzerland in July 1995 (see Warr, 2008, included in this book). Gilchrist used the GSR, TENS and morse code to reach toward a tactile dialogue between his sleeping body and the waking audience—his body responding audibly by amplified electrical skin sounds to the electric shocks sent by the audience.

> After the *Earth Wire* project, I became increasingly interested in the way that external stimuli appear to be incorporated into dream content. Sometimes these stimuli (initially electrical) were incorporated symbolically, at other times more directly. Later I obtained a device from La Berge's Lucidity Institute, which detects REM sleep using an infra-red sensor, and then delivers photic stimulation. I have learned from experience that the electrical and photic signals can be incorporated in very different ways: the signal from a TENS unit can be incorporated into dream content as an earthquake, as fluid bursting through skin or as a collapsing building; photic signals may appear less dramatically as sunlight glancing off a reflective surface or being photographed by a flash-camera. (Gilchrist, 1995, p. 3)

In *The Discarnate*, presented in Glasgow, United Kingdom in February 1996, Gilchrist worked with an auric healer and a warlock from the Glasgow Theosophical Society (see Gilchrist, 1996). In addition to Gilchrist's sleeping and dreaming body, his two collaborators also presented themselves in out-of-body states. The audience could see a digital EEG visual display of their brainwaves and experience the skin responses of the performers through the GSR connected to a feedback jacket and pair of shoes. Gilchrist was again reaching for a tactile language between sleeping or out-of-body bodies and the waking audience who experienced vibrations through the soles of their feet and at body points based on Chi and acupuncture.

Gilchrist's project at the ICA in London later in 1996 used a feedback chair for the audience. Moulded to the body, the chair allows audience members to experience through their skin the electrical output of the sleeper. The output was driven by the sleeper's brain-waves. The left side of the chair correlated to the left side of the brain and vice versa.

Gilchrist worked with computer programmer Jonathan Bradley on the creation of a computer database and synthetic neural network. This enabled the sleeper's internal dream experience to be externalised into the audience's environment, which was inhabited by amplified sounds and projected images so that the audience could experience the palpable sleeping mind-brain.

The relational multi-media database consists of brainwave patterns recorded using a digital EEG and computer, specifically during periods of REM sleep, which constitute the physiological component of the database. Simultaneously, using the programmable Lucidity Institute device, the sleeper is woken up after predetermined amounts of REM (including photic and/or elec-trical stimuli) to make a report of the subjective experience: the heterophenomenological component. Using the Code Warrior program, Bradley programmed the neural network to make increas-ingly informed guesses as to what the physiological data 'mean' in terms of the dreamer's report. This then controlled the triggering of audio-visual recordings from the database in live performance, drawing, for instance, on the entopic imagery recounted by clair-voyants.

'Sleepers are in separate worlds, the awake, in the same' (Hera-clitus, cited in Gilchrist, 1995). Sleep relieves the body of fatigue. We grow in our sleep. Sleep provides us with regular breaks in the continuity of our consciousness. Is this because a ceaseless consciousness would be unbearable? Both creativity and madness have been associated with an unusually high degree of continuity of consciousness and associated sleep deprivation. Sleep provides a regular shutdown of our sensory perceptive systems, which appears to be necessary to the unconscious processing of data—our extraordinary memory, editing, cataloguing and retrieval system. Certainly, the brain seems to get overloaded if it cannot close down its sensors and reorganise its data. People subjected to sleep deprivation suffer from problems with verbalisation, perspective and irritation.

Over the last centuries, our conscious data-processing system—rationality—has had the emphasis. Brain research into the cerebrum controlling conscious actions is quite advanced but the cerebellum, controlling the unconscious, is equally complex and relatively unexplained. Unconsciousness is perhaps the right place to be looking for explanations about consciousness. However, if we discard old dualistic notions of the mind/body, rationality/irrationality splits, we have to face up to the implications of consciousness being integral to the mortal, short-lived body.

17

ELPIDA HADZI-VASILEVA: RAW PRESENCE

2009. First published in E. Hadzi-Vasileva (ed) *Motectum*. Gloucester: University of Gloucester, pp. 15–18.

Elpida Hadzi-Vasileva produces artworks that are carefully balanced between the beautiful and the brutal. There is a disjunction between the materials she uses: a cow's stomach, pigs' caul fat, one ton of butter, duck heads, salmon skins—and the exquisite sculptures and installations that she creates. 'Matter out of place', Mary Douglas writes in her great study of pollution taboos, is dirt, and yet she explains, dirt has a powerful creative charge (1966, p. 35). The materials Hadzi-Vasileva uses have a raw, uncanny presence to them because we know (and can sometimes smell as well as see) that this matter was formerly part of a living organism: an animal, bird or fish. Her work is full of paradoxes, between animate and inanimate, transcendent and abject. She recomposes decomposition into gorgeous forms.

Trees, animals, birds, food, clothing and architecture are recurring motifs in Hadzi-Vasileva's work, as she sets up a visual and material dialogue between the structures of the natural world and the structures of human culture. Her work is responsive to specific sites and engages with local industries, communities and environments: the fishing industries in Berwick and Brighton, for example, or Indian restaurants in London's Brick Lane.

The culmination of her year-long residency in Gloucester Cathedral is *Motectum*, a work which has three parts linked by the overarching theme of birds. She has created a sound installation mixing human and bird song in the cloisters and re-landscaped the cloisters garden. A crinoline dress was made by stitching together translucent yellow chicken skins. She made forty portrait busts of the feathered heads of dead ducks, pheasants and chickens.

When you step over the threshold into Gloucester Cathedral, time seems to slow and stop—partly because of the weight of history here, but also because of the sheer volume of still air. The columns, buttresses and vaults of the cathedral rise up around the visitor like a great stone forest. The earliest parts of the cathedral were built in 1089, alongside the Benedictine monastery that had been on the site since 678. The cathedral has witnessed the crowning of Henry III, the burial of Edward II and the burning of Bishop Hooper. The monastery was dissolved under Henry VIII and the cathedral narrowly escaped demolition under Oliver Cromwell. Its stained-glass windows include the earliest image of golf (1350) and a fabulous beaked two-legged grotesque. An angel orchestra play their instruments in the ceiling above the choir. Inside the cathedral are forty carvings of Green Men, and outside, gargoyles funnel rainwater away from the walls.

It is easy to imagine monks in the twelfth century pacing the quadrangle of the cloisters underneath the intricate stone latticework of their fan-vaulted ceilings, or to see them seated at the stone carols contemplating the enclosed garden through a colonnade of arched windows. The monks were mostly silent, so the cathedral was the sounding space where voices could burst out.

Hadzi-Vasileva's work repopulates the garden with trees, shrubs and birds and reinhabits the cloisters with the soaring sound of Thomas Tallis' *Spem in Alium*. Tallis' sixteenth-century composition is a forty-voice motet. Hadzi-Vasileva has combined the human voices with recorded birdsong and live birdsong relayed from microphones in the garden and in nearby Highnam Woods. The sound installation along the four sides of the cloisters represents birds commonly found in four areas of Gloucestershire: the Forest of Dean, the Severn Estuary, the Cotswold Hills and Cotswold Water Park. The sound moves randomly between forty speakers placed in the cloisters, harnessing the extraordinary acoustics of the space. The ambitious scale of Hadzi-Vasileva's work matches the vastness of the cathedral itself.

Hadzi-Vasileva's chicken-skins dress creates a frisson of disgust. Dead skins, usually sloughed off, are here put back on, and worn against living skin. We sense, or imagine, a faint whiff of decay. 'A voluntary embrace of the symbols of death is a kind of prophylactic against the effects of death' (Douglas, 1966, p. 177). Jean-Paul Sartre discussed stickiness as the queasy boundary between the self and other matter. Hadzi-Vasileva's materials occupy this distasteful zone of inbetweenness.

The laborious cleaning and preparation of organic materials in this artwork are reminiscent of the medieval textile processes of tanning, fulling, lacemaking and needlework. The chicken-skins dress, housed within the carapace of the cathedral itself, recalls Bachelard's discussion of a building as a nest or garment in his book *The Poetics of Space* (1969, pp. 90–104). What is underneath and inside a material world of membranes and skins are recurring obsessions in Hadzi-Vasileva's work. She takes dead waste materials and transforms them into new artefacts that show us the latent beauty of this discarded matter.

Hadzi-Vasileva's portrait busts made from feathered duck, pheasant and chicken heads are in a dialogue with the heads of stone angels and saints in the cathedral, which have been worn down by erosion or damaged by Cromwell's soldiers. The cathedral's angels and gargoyles are already hybrid bodies: composites of human and bird or animal. Hadzi-Vasileva's work highlights this uncanny hybridity.

When the cathedral was built in the Middle Ages, people did not have our contemporary euphemisms and squeamishness about food. They reared, killed and butchered their own animals, and would have trapped and eaten the songbirds too. Partridges, storks, cranes and larks were among the many species of birds that were eaten. Peacocks and swans were often skinned and cooked and then presented with their original plumage put back in place.

Sing a song of sixpence a pocket full of rye
four and twenty blackbirds baked in a pie.

When the pie was opened,
the birds began to sing.
Wasn't that a dainty dish
to set before a king?

A sixteenth-century Italian cookbook includes a recipe for pies with live birds inside, which flew out when the pies were cut open. These illusion foods were known as *entremets* or subtleties.

Hadzi-Vasileva's work skirts, but will not be pinned down to, any straightforward thematic reading. She evokes political topics, such as animal welfare and ecological issues, but she is not judgemental and does not explicitly engage a subject. She makes us aware of the discord between our attitudes toward the garden songbirds and our attitudes toward domesticated birds. While we protect and preserve the songbirds, the chickens, ducks and pheasants are being exploited for food and sport. The difficulty she had in getting well-feathered heads for the project is evidence of the often-appalling conditions in which many domesticated birds are kept. The abject birds are revalued in her work.

Her concern with craft and husbandry suggests pre-digital and pre-industrial eras, and ecologists' current advocacy of the need for the reacquisition of old skills and lifestyles in a time of climate change. Her work questions the human control and structuring of the natural world. Hadzi-Vasileva's work, however, is materials-led rather than concept-led. She allows the materials to unfold into their own potentiality rather than imposing an idea on the forms that the work takes.

The bird is a symbol of the soul. Like the angels, the birds are of the sphere of transcendence. 'A thing of the field that loves the air between', wrote the Gloucestershire poet and musician Ivor Gurney (Kavanagh, 1982, p. 206). Angels and birds are messengers from the divine to the human. Alongside the raw presence of offal in Hadzi-Vasileva's work, birds, angels and song transcend. 'That which is rejected is ploughed back for a renewal of life' (Douglas, 1966, p. 167).

18

IMAGE AS ICON: RECOGNISING THE ENIGMA

2003. First published in A. George (ed) *Art, Lies and Videotape: Exposing Performance*. Liverpool: Tate, pp. 30–37.

Four contradictory discourses pull in different directions in performance photography: the discourses of the document, the icon, the simulacrum and the live act, and in all four 'truth' is the issue.

Performance photograph as document would have the image perform the role of materialist evidence and proof—showing us exactly what happened so we can 'know' it. Performance photography as icon presents us with a manifestation of the unknowable and an encounter with that manifestation in a state of belief. Performance photograph as simulacrum explores fakery, the performative and representation. The fourth discourse emerges from the conflicting demands placed on performance by theatrical and fine art traditions. The theatrical tradition envisages the live act as primary, cathartic, witnessed and ontological, and any document of it has only a subsidiary status. In the history of fine art, however, representation and simulation have always had an integral role. Add to all that the ambivalent status of the body itself as representation and in representation, as both material thing and signifier of immaterial consciousness, and the image of the artist variously as everyman, performed self, and celebrity, and you have a rich, contradictory brew in performance photography.

No art object has a single fixed meaning. Each is influenced by the differing contexts in which it is displayed and received. At least, with the traditional art object, there is a fixed referent, subject only to physical deterioration. Performance on the other hand has no fixed referential basis. It continues to exist only through an accumulation of documentation and discourse. The photographic documentation of performance continues a question posed by Duchamp: where is the art? Is it in the art object or is it in the relationship between a provocation by an artist (painting, photograph, live gesture, document) and an individual viewer? Duchamp argued that there are 'two poles of the creation of art: the artist on the one hand, and on the other the spectator who later becomes the posterity'. The gap between the artist's intentions and his or her realisation is where the spectator gets to co-create the work of art (Duchamp, 1957, p. 138).

Each performance work may have at least three layers of audience: the immediate audience, the audience that experiences the work through its distributed and fragmentary documentation, and the audiences of posterity, doing the same, but adding more layers to the discourses, texts and interpretations of the work. We might add, then, photographers, editors and writers to Duchamp's inclusion of artist and spectators as co-creators of an artwork.

Pane's *Je* (1972) can only be constructed as a whole work through its documentation published in *Art & Artists* magazine (Stephano, 1973, pp. 20–27). Pane stood on an outside first-floor window ledge, clinging to the window frame and looking at a family inside the apartment. During the live event, the audience in the street below could only see Pane up there. In the later publication, we see three views—the audience's from the street; the artist's through the window; and the photographer's, of the artist outside the window.

The photograph as document usually assumes authenticity and authority, yet it is neither objective, necessarily factual nor a complete record. The creativity, selectivity and filter of the photographers and subsequent editors frequently remain invisible. The photograph has a compromised status as evidence and proof. There is plenty that the photograph leaves out (sound, time, space, often the audience). The photograph frames, composes and constructs. Lengthy, complex performances with audience participation are reduced to just one image. The 'good' image from a performance is likely to be the most composed image, one that immediately conveys a clear reading: 'giving a different reading as a symbolic portrait rather than as part of a messy and active performance' (Grant, 2002, p. 44). Some sixties and seventies performance photography cultivated a deliberately raw aesthetic, resembling crime reportage. Peter Moore, who produced many of the memorable images of Fluxus and other sixties New York performances, describes himself as taking a 'truth-telling' stance, aiming to 'make the best images he could of exactly what was occurring' (Zelevansky, 1981–1982, p. 39). There can be, however, no objective, stable, 'truth' in performance photography. The photograph always thwarts the idea that it can show the complete or 'real' performance to us: 'desire for traditional narrativist closure will always be short-circuited by the limited information available' (O'Dell, 1998, p. 13).

Discussing Namuth's photographs of Jackson Pollock, Fred Orton and Griselda Pollock ask: How far does the photographer document what happened and how far does he or she create the 'documented' phenomenon? Photographs, they argue, produce meanings that are 'contingent on the spectator's interests' (Orton and Pollock, 1996, pp. 65–76). Namuth's photographs of Pollock painting cannot be interpreted simply as historical documents. They are Namuth and Pollock staging Pollock and those images are open to a range of interpretations coloured by the expectations and needs of later commentators, such as Harold Rosenberg in 'The American action painters' (1952) (reprinted in Warr, 2000a, pp. 193–195).

In a 'theatrical' reading of performance, an 'actual', live interaction between performer and audience is given priority over the record. The photographer must use available light and silenced, unobtrusive cameras. An aesthetic and theoretical influence from dance, music and theatre are certainly part of the interdisciplinary impetus in sixties performance. In the fine art tradition, far from having a subsidiary or merely documentary status, photography and performance have been an integrated practice, as in Duchamp's performative photographs, including *Tonsure* (1919) and *Rrose* (c. 1920s). A substantial number of sixties and seventies 'performances' are, in fact, hybrid performance photographs, which were not performed for live audiences but for the camera. Art magazines, such as *Avalanche, Artitudes, Art & Artists* and *Studio International*, provided a vital arena for such performance photography.

Catherine Grant points out, in her discussion of Abramović's *Rhythm 0* (1974), that in looking at the photographic document we are identifying and empathising with the passive, suffering artist's body and are simultaneously put in the positions of sadistic actor and complicit voyeur (Grant, 2002). A similar complexity and perplexity occurs in looking at photographs of Burden's *Trans-fixed* (1974). We are forced into a position of imagining the actions and state of mind of the 'friend' who hammered the nails into Burden's hands or tied his hands behind his back before he crawled over glass in *Through the Night Softly* (1974). The photograph has a distance and a detachment at the same time as it allows an empathetic, imaginative entry.

What might be the difference between watching the eye-slitting in Bunuel's film *Un Chien Andalou* (1930) and actually seeing it done? Or of looking at a photograph of Pane climbing a razor-sharp ladder with bare hands and feet in *Escalade* (1971) and actually being in the space with her when she did it? We might still have a gut reaction to a photograph, but we can't intervene. We don't have to respond publicly. In live performances, people called out, 'Don't do it' to Pane, as she raised a razor to her face, rescued Abramović when she passed out, and called a halt to some of Burden's performances. That responsibility for others' actions, what O'Dell sees as a complicity and a contract between viewer and performer, is absent for the viewer of a document. As a live audience we are more likely to respond with a corporeal response, a reading below and before language, whereas we are already in interpretation mode in looking at a document. We can also believe that what we are looking at might be fictional.

Traditionally, an icon was a sacred image of a sacred person. The icon is a distillation of an unknowable, incomprehensible mystery to a visible, tangible manifestation. It is both a reduction of that mystery and capable, through belief, of fully expanding into an encounter with that mystery. The icon makes the intangible and invisible accessible in portable form and, therefore, creates a market for the priceless and the immaterial. We now use the terms 'icon' and 'iconic' in an expanded, secular sense to mean representations of people who seem to gather into themselves a complex cultural significance (Marilyn Monroe, Princess Diana)—bodying forth all our desires and needs as a power-fetish. The essential ingredients of an icon are that it must be universally familiar ('iconic') and that it must be enigmatic—the paradox of the known and forever unknowable. The icon is concerned with belief rather than dispassionate evaluation and evidence. Fakery and scepticism are concomitant with belief. We raise up our contemporary, secular icons and then delight in tearing them down in a continual flux between belief and scepticism.

From the whole field of artists active in any period, a canon emerges of particular artists endorsed through repeated use by curators, editors and critics, exhaustively 'received'. 'Millions of artists create, a few thousand are discussed or accepted by the spectator, and many less again are consecrated by posterity' (Duchamp, 1957, p. 138). An artist's whole oeuvre may be reduced to one or two works that we take to be 'iconic'. With the disappearance of the original source in performance, the performance photograph itself takes on the role of icon, whereas for the painting or sculpture there is always an authentic source and then representations. Burden's *Trans-fixed*, in its title and documentation, conjures the discourse of the icon: 'the spectator experiences the phenomenon of transmutation; through the change from inert matter into a work of art, an actual transubstantiation has taken place' (Duchamp, 1957, pp. 139–140).

The photograph as icon is compromised and contradictory because it is both indexical (like the Turin Shroud) and documentary, so that it purports to show us something real and actual, which, in turn, compromises its status as a manifestation of an unknowable to be believed. However, the very incompleteness and paucity of photographic documentation enhances its iconic capacity, encouraging the development of legend by giving us enough but nothing too definite.

The photographic document also has an uneasy status between art document and artist's publicity stunt. In the images of Pollock and Beuys, the artist is the icon as much as the artwork. Burden's *Chris Burden Promo* (1976) was a television advert shown on channels in New York and Los Angeles. It had a stereotypical brainwashing visual with names of famous artists (Leonardo da Vinci, Michelangelo) appearing and being enunciated, culminating with Burden and the final credit stating, 'paid for by Chris Burden, artist'.

Burden's comments in interviews suggest a nonchalant attitude to documentation (see Butterfield, 1975, pp. 68–72; Horovitz, 1976, pp. 24–31; Sharp and Bear, 1973, pp. 52–61). This apparent nonchalance is belied by the ways in which he sought to control and amplify the legend of his actions, through his self-publications, *Chris Burden 1971–1973* (1974) and *Chris Burden 1974–1977* (1978), his film compilation *Chris Burden: Documentation of Selected Works 1971–1974*, and his use of television media. Beuys' photographic documentation rarely has a self-contained legible quality. He worked with collaborative documenters, such as Caroline Tisdall, to provide an exegesis for both performances and performance documents (Tisdall, 1976, pp. 36–40). In Burden's documentation, on the other hand, there is deliberate obfuscation through the cryptic nature of his texts and the explanatory gap between the text and the image, which allows the viewer to co-create an 'excess of meaning'.

Many of Burden's performances and performance photographs work with invisibility. In *Five Day Locker Piece* (1971) and *White Light/White Heat* (1975), he is an invisible presence—inside a locker in the former and out of sight on a high ledge in the latter. In *TV Hijack* (1972) Burden destroyed the tape of the live broadcast as part of the action. In these performances his 'brute presence posited some large and serious conundrum that elided articulation ... the dumb body ... was a source of frustration' (Ward, 1999, p. 15), with neither curators nor audience quite sure whether to interact with Burden as human being or as sculpture.

His works emphasise the point beyond which the experiences and consciousness of another person cannot be mediated at all—either live or in photographic record. It can only be empathised with and imagined. Burden's work points out the seen and the unseen in the photographic record and our perpetual hope and failure to find truth and revelation there. Cameras now enter the body, image the brain's activity, show us the body dissected and reconstructed, but still we cannot see what we want to see. The more we interrogate the embodied consciousness with technology the more aware we become of its impenetrability.

19

THE INCIDENT

2008. First published in *Mute*, 1(3), October.

The Incident symposium in Fribourg, Switzerland in June brought together diverse artists and researchers dealing with non-explicable phenomena. Jacques Vallée discussed UFOs, Budd Hopkins presented his evidence of alien abductions, Rod Dickinson talked about crop circles, Ulrike Rosenbach described her work on angels, drugs guru Terence McKenna enthused about DMT and tried to persuade all the symposium delegates to take it, Jeremy Narby described the paintings of an Amazonian shaman that feature both DNA diagrams and UFOs, Keiko Sei and Kathleen Rogers discussed psychic phenomena and Swiss artist H.R. Giger showed his work, which informed the aesthetic of the *Aliens* movies. Between them all, whether you subscribed to belief or scepticism on any particular issue, you had to observe that our accepted notions of reality were being severely questioned from all angles.

Overall, *The Incident* asked what contribution artists might make to the debates around non-explicable phenomena and raised the notion, as symposium organiser La Frenais commented, that 'artists might be better equipped to deal positively with the ambiguous subjectivity that such extensions of perceptivity bring'.

Turrell's keynote address characterised phenomena researchers and artists as pioneers—akin to the criminals, deviants and delinquents who sailed to the New Worlds in previous centuries—venturing into the unknown that would become the future. As Turrell commented, the brain has capacities for which we have not yet invented a vocabulary. Whatever interpretation you put upon them (military conspiracy … benign or evil intentioned aliens … god), there seems to be an overwhelming mass of evidence of physical phenomena that are neither adequately measured nor explained by the current sciences. Consciousness, perception and phenomena are now the research subjects of reputable academic institutions around the world, including the universities of Austin in Texas, California, Duke in North Carolina, Edinburgh and Tucson in Arizona. La Frenais' contention was that 'at the point at which science breaks down, at which results are anomalous or evidence appears to point at non-provable conclusions, artists can take over where rationality stops'.

20

THE INFORME BODY

2000. First published in *Body, Space and Technology*, 1(1), July.

[Most of this article was first presented as a paper at the *Liminality and Performance* conference, Brunel University, Twickenham, UK, April 2000. Additional material on consciousness and the artist's body was presented in a paper at the *Toward a Science of Consciousness Conference*, University of Arizona, Tucson, US, April 2000. An earlier version of some of these ideas appeared in my book review, 'The Informe Body' in *Performance Research*, 3(2), 1998, pp. 118–121.]

Victor Turner's notion of liminality is a state of 'betwixt and between, a fructile chaos, a storehouse of possibilities' (1982). Other writers have also described some kind of position outside binary thinking, a state disruptive of unity and closure.

Bataille invented the term *informe*—referred to in the title of this article—in his 'Critical dictionary' published in the French journal *Documents* (1929). The 'Critical dictionary' was a paradoxical project

—a disordered pile of non-definitions of non-words. *Informe*, according to Bataille, has no definition but is performative, like an obscene word. It performs the operation of creating taxonomic disorder and a perpetual maintenance of potentials.

In *Purity and Danger*, anthropologist Mary Douglas discussed pollution taboos concerning the unassimilable waste that is outside the constitution of things that are defined (1966). And the Brazilian artist Helio Oiticica argued that art has no autonomous object state, but is instead a searching process, a constructive nucleus, an enactment (1969).

While Turner's *limen* is the threshold and a striving after new forms and structures, Bataille's *informe* is an inchoateness through which meaning briefly emerges, and Mary Douglas describes pollution and dirt as a 'fearful generative site'.

Of course there are many differences between the ideas sketchily outlined above, but the focus of this article is a perception of a shared notion in liminality, *informe*, pollution and process art of an oscillating flux that does not halt. This is an idea that is also present in contemporary scientific developments in chaos theory and quantum physics. This article discusses this oscillating flux in relation to a range of visual artists using their own bodies in their artworks—in performance, painting, sculpture, photography, film and video.

Visual artists using their own bodies as the site for art wreak havoc with categorisation from several angles. The artist's body is an art object that will not stay put and fixed in its role. It is contingent and gets up and walks back into the artist's life. As art object the artist's body is always ephemeral.

Alan Sonfist has bequeathed his body to the Museum of Modern Art after death; Orlan is planning to leave her mummified body to a museum; and Bob Flanagan left instructions for art projects after his death, including a video link into his grave that would allow access to the sight of his decomposing body. But until delivery of a corpse is taken, the artist's body will always walk off, leaving only its imprint or trace in gelatine, paint, microchips or its relic in cast objects, its indexical mark or stain, or simply its memory burnt on the retina and the cortex (see Ferguson, 1998 and Warr, 2000a).

Artists leave their trace behind—in the body prints that Yves Klein made in *Anthropometries*, in Francesca Woodman's enigmatic photographs of herself as an almost insubstantial body in flight through a world of materiality, or in Mendieta's imprints of her silhouette in mud, grass and ash.

The artist's body does not allow its audience the luxury of an academic, objective stance. It commands a bodily as well as an imaginative empathy from its viewers. It employs the shared ontology of the body. Antonin Artaud had argued that 'metaphysics must be made to enter the mind through the body' (1974, p. 76). The audiences for artists' body work are compelled to look with their own bodies, as well as their eyes, to feel on their pulses as well as rationalise and interpret.

Artists' body work emphasises how the body is at once subjective and an interface with the objective world, how it is a conscious thing and how it is a mess and flux of viscera on its way to death.

Jayne Parker held a dress of knitted entrails up against her naked body in her film *K* (1989).

> I bring my intestines up out of my mouth and let it fall in a pile at my feet. I take the end and proceed to knit, using my arms in the place of knitting needles, until I have knitted the whole length.... I make an external order out of an internal tangle. (Parker, quoted in Export and Justenssen, 1996)

In her performance *Warm Milk* (1972), Gine Pane drew a razor blade across her cheek and forearm. These artists ask us to remember the guts and bone beneath the skin. This is a consciousness vividly evoked in Keith Douglas' poem, *The Prisoner*, written in 1940:

> *Today, Cheng, I touched your face*
> *with two fingers, as a gesture of love,*
> *for I can never prove enough*
> *by sight or sense your strange grace ...*
>
> *but alas, Cheng, I cannot tell why,*
> *today I touched a mask stretched on the stone-*
> *hard face of death. There was the urge*
> *to escape the bright flesh and emerge*
> *of the ambitious cruel bone.*
>
> *(Graham, 1979, p. 67)*

The body has one foot in the camp of material, defined, boundaried matter and one foot in the camp of the amorphous and dedifferentiated. While the body—like all matter—looks and feels real and solid enough, it is in fact only its patterns that are stable, not the material itself. And within this flux of matter, consciousness is shifting at a vertiginous velocity across eighty thousand synaptic endings in one half of the brain alone.

A lot of theory discusses 'the body' as if it could be considered in isolation—but the artist's body is self-evidently self-reflexive. Because the artist's body is a sentient presence, consciousness must be part of the package presented and received. As Willoughby Sharp pointed out, a corpse is an object, but a live body must be both subject and object (1970, p. 16; reprinted in Warr, 2000a, pp. 231–233).

Adrian Piper's performance series, *Catalysis* (1970–1971) included her walking around New York wearing a t-shirt reading 'WET PAINT'. 'Making artificial and non-functional alterations in my own bodily presence of the same kind as those I formerly made on non-art materials.... I exist simultaneously as the artist and the work' (1976, p. 167). In body art, the artist's body is an ephemeral, contingent art process that is both absent and present.

From the 1920s on, performative and multi-disciplinary approaches in the work of the Dadaists and Surrealists began to incorporate time, space and the body into art (see Melzer, 1994). The action artists of the forties, fifties and sixties continued this impetus, in Jackson Pollock's drip paintings, Georges Mathieu's action paintings and Kazuo Shiraga's paintings made with his feet and his sculptures made by diving into a mound of mud and wrestling it. In the work of the happenings artists, including Allan Kaprow, Jim Dine, Claes Oldenberg and Wolf Vostell, a real space or the unboundaried real world replaced the framed canvas. The happenings artists added bodies, junk, the audience, time, fragments of words and music to their palettes. Rather than an autonomous object, art could be events in time co-created by audience, material world and artists.

Brazilian artists Oiticica and Clark explored the tangency of bodies and objects. They perceived form—whether in the material world around them or in their own bodies—as neither autonomous nor stable. Bodies and objects engage in a dynamic loop of mutability and reciprocity in their work. Their objects adumbrate bodily functions—breathing and pulsating. These objects only come into existence through their animation by the spectators' or artists' bodies. At a recent exhibition at the Whitechapel Art Gallery, *Inside the Visible*, Clark's objects lay around like deflated balloons waiting for someone to insert a bodily part into them (see de Zegher, 1996). With works such as Oiticica's *Parangoles* series (capes designed for particular wearers, many of them inhabitants of Rio de Janeiro's impoverished *favela* district) and Clark's *Bichos* (*Animals*) series, rubber geometric shapes that perch in trees, these artists cajole a geometric art language into speaking of the pulsing body.

The liminal, the *informe*, the abject and the taboo undo the work of rationalisation. According to French Fluxus artist Ben Vautier, art is dirty work, but somebody has to do it. And 'messy' body artists, such as Carolee Schneemann, the Viennese Actionists and Paul McCarthy certainly bear him out. Janine Antoni washed and painted a gallery floor with her hair in the performance, *Loving Care* (1992). Cheryl Donegan made prints of shamrocks with her green paint-smeared buttocks in the video *Kiss My Royal Irish Arse* (1993).

Rugoff has described McCarthy's work as depicting 'a body whose borders were collapsing, whose insides seemed to be gushing out as though its thin bag of skin had ruptured' (Rugoff, 1996). In his performances, McCarthy's body is obliterated by a messy deluge of images, constructs and spectacles as well as a lot of tomato ketchup, bandages and hot dogs.

Gilles Deleuze's analysis of Bacon's paintings emphasises their depiction of the human body as 'meat' (1981, pp. 197–198). In an, often unsavoury, vision, many visual artists present to us their visceral and leaking bodies. Duchamp's *Sinning Landscape* (1946) was made with semen on black velvet. Piero Manzoni's *Artist's Shit* (1961) is ninety 30-gram tins of the artist's own excrement. Carolee Schneemann's 1964 performances of *Meat Joy* were orgies of flesh, fish and meat. Shigeko Kubota's *Vagina Painting* (1965) was a performance in which she crouched over a large sheet of paper on the floor and painted with a red-daubed paintbrush attached to her knickers.

In the Viennese Actionist group of artists, Otto Muhl made chaotic, orgiastic tableaux, painting with dirt and food stuffs; Herman Nitsch's *Aktions* were bloody catharsis drawing on a blend of Dionysian, Catholic and depth psychology influences and Gunter Brus took himself apart, dissecting the individual body and psyche and the body politic in acts that critic, Hubert Klocker has described as 'psycho-archaeological existentialism' (Klocker, 1989). Andreas Serrano has made sumptuous photographs of bodily fluids—*Piss*

Christ (1987) and *Untitled XIII (Ejaculate in Trajectory)* (1989). Kiki Smith creates life-size sculptures of human bodies full of pathos, with their blood, muscle, body fluids exposed on the surface. Matthew Barney's wounded, seeping, birthing, excreting objects are made from wax, lubricants and petroleum jelly. Antoni uses lard, lipstick and chocolate to reference the body. Sherman's photographs explore the non-boundary between inner and outer, form and *informe*, human and thing. Marc Quinn's self-portrait is a refrigerated cast head made with eight pints of his own blood—*Self* (1991). (For rewarding and more detailed discussion of 'unpleasant' body art, see Jones, 1994, pp. 546–584; Kaufmann, 1998; O'Dell, 1998; Pluchart, 1978, pp. 80–82 and pp. 39–40; Richard, 1986, pp. 64–73; Stiles, 1992, pp. 74–102).

Chilean artists Diamela Eltit and Raul Zurita made performances in the eighties using their own bodies, protesting against inhumanity in an oppressive regime. Critic Nelly Richard comments on their work,

> The threshold of pain enables the mutilated subject to enter areas of collective identification, sharing in one's own flesh the same signs of social disadvantage as the other unfortunates. Voluntary pain simply legitimates one's incorporation into the community of those who have been harmed in some way—as if the self-inflicted marks of chastisement in the artist's body and the marks of suffering in the national body, as if pain and its subject could unite in the same scar. (1986, p. 66, p. 68)

Critic Cindy Nemser commented that 'due to the unpleasant nature of the content of body art, the public may refuse to read it intelligently' (1971, p. 42, and see, Warr, 2000a, pp. 233–235). But whether we like it or not, visual artists working with bodily fluids, decay, death and visceral flux are endemic. They present the body as a consuming, excreting, conceiving, transforming conduit. This view of the body is still largely taboo in Western culture. Filmmaker David Cronenberg has described the basis of horror as the fact that we cannot comprehend how we can die (cited in Kaufmann, 1998). At the same time, medical, scientific and technological advances relating to the body's health, reproductive function and death, seem to make the body's functions increasingly conceptual and euphemised.

In Western culture, death and the body as flux is a taboo vision. Most critiques of this type of body art cannot get past the Western cultural obsession with the central, terminal, cumulative self—the individual ego—to see beyond to a use of the self as universal. Talking about Dada dance, Hugo Ball commented that 'Dance ... is very close to the art of tattooing and to all primitive representative efforts that aim at personification' (1996). With his use of the word 'personification', Ball seems to be getting at a notion of the individual body inscribed, carrying the weight of collective ideas, rather than the individual engaged in self-expression.

In complete contrast to the visceral artists, however, many other artists have used their own bodies to try to lift invisible aspects of consciousness into the visible world. These aspects have included the operation of hopes, desires and aspirations, being, the liminal spaces of sleep, dream, meditation, hallucination, intuition, vision and somatic or non-symbolic thinking. So in their performance, *Nightsea Crossing* (1981–1986), Abramović and Ulay sat opposite each other across a table for a total of ninety days, not moving, not speaking and fasting. The complete performance was undertaken over several chunks of time in different cities around the world. Their longest continuous presentation lasted sixteen days. The artists presented themselves as embodied consciousnesses, in the process of being. For Abramović, the job of the artist is to reveal the mystery of existence and to act as a transmitter of energy. 'The deeper you go into yourself, the more universal you come out on the other side' (Abramović, quoted in Pijnappel, 1995).

In Fox's performance *Levitation* (1970), he lay on a pile of soil in a San Francisco gallery for six hours trying to levitate (see Fox, 1982 and Sharp, 1971). In 1972 Burden spent twenty-two days in bed in a gallery in Los Angeles, not speaking or interacting with gallery visitors or staff. 'They had to deal with me simultaneously as an object and a person.... My days were full, rich and purposeful' (1975). Susan Hiller's *Draw Together* (1972) was an experiment in telepathy and *Dream Mapping* (1974) was an experiment in group dreaming. Hiller describes art ideas as existing below a verbal recognition level where artists grab on to them (see Einzig, 1996, pp. 170–181 and 121–131). Turrell's work experiments with perceptual psychology, light and states of being. He has remarked that art is about bringing images back from the dream world to here. Shelley Sacks' *Thought Bank* (1994) was based on the idea that water remembers and that thought can be imprinted on water. In live performances, Gilchrist has attempted to externalise images and sounds from the interior of his sleeping body (*Divided by Resistance*, 1996) (see Keidon, 1996 and Warr, 1996a, 'Sleeper', included in this book). Working with a BBC Outside Broadcast Unit, a group of mediums, a thermal camera and sound equipment, Kathleen Rogers' *PsiNet* (1994) set up a parallel between psychic transmission and reception and technological transmission and reception (see La Frenais, 1994).

The body itself is liminal—between material thing and immaterial consciousness, a shifting interface between subjectivity and the world, a seemingly solid reality that is nevertheless a flux of viscera, time, consciousness and space. Anthropological studies have been a fertile source for visual artists interested in exploring an alternative semantics of the body.

> Speech has been over-emphasised as the privileged means of human communication, and the body neglected. It is time to rectify this neglect and to become aware of the body as the physical channel of meaning. (Douglas, 1978, p. 298)

21

IN THE DARK ABOUT ART

1998. First published in E. Stankevicius (ed) *Twilight/Sutemos*. Vilnius: Centre for Contemporary Art, pp. viii–xv. [Lithuanian and English.]

In twilight, the normal, everyday objects in the field of vision are bathed in a lurid, navy-blue, light that seems artificial, eerie, transformative. The light of twilight seems to come from nowhere in nature, not from the sun nor from the moon and stars. Perhaps it is stored in the rocks. It is like the light inside dreams and memories generated by the body, by consciousness.

Twilight is a hybrid time, a hybrid space. It is a shimmering membrane between light and dark, day and night, consciousness and unconsciousness, clarity and obscurity, real and surreal, life and death. Twilight is the soft near-visible edge of intangibles. It is almost alive and breathing down the back of your neck. A hybrid of inanimate and animate.

Are we in twilight or at twilight? The artists in *Sutemos/Twilight*, Lithuania's first international exhibition of media art, constructively employ this ambiguity of time and light, of process and space, this lack of concreteness either way, in the exhibition's theme.

Perception is altered and transformed by twilight. The world is turned inside out. When vision is obscured, our other senses are heightened. You must hear and feel your way in the dark. (Something I experienced strongly on my first visit to Vilnius in 1993 when there were no streetlights at night.) The body, rather than the optical senses alone, becomes a heightened sensory perceptor. With this twilight vision we can almost see the edges of consciousness. Twilight is anxious and full of phantasms we cannot quite see.

In *The X Files*, Mulder and Scully stumble in a darkness that is both style and content. We want them to turn on the light when they venture into those scary places or at least carry a more powerful flashlight than the standard FBI issue. But without this ubiquitous semi-darkness there would be no story, no mystery.

Dusk (*sutemos*) is the undertime, the point that materialises the compulsive continuity of time. There is no escape from the continual recurrence of day and night, nor from birth and death. The many short video loops in the *Sutemos/Twilight* exhibition enact this relentless continuity. Arturas Raila's bikers ride into the Contemporary Art Centre over and over. Kathleen Rogers' old woman trudges on the spot on the same path through the forest endlessly. The picture in Jutempus' video installation of recycling garbage treads round and round its spiral space. Jane and Louise Wilson's surreal ball continues to leap out of the lake and push over the figure in the foreground. These video loops are not arrested. Nor are they linear temporal sequences. Here, compulsion is an expression of continuity rather than neurosis, a topic that Hal Foster discusses in *Compulsive Beauty*, his study of compulsion and anxiety in the work of the Surrealists (1993).

The *Sutemos/Twilight* exhibition presents media artworks that flourish and function in the dark, or rather, in the semi-dark, like twilight itself, as the many video and slide installations and projections flicker against each other's light and rupture the dark of the Contemporary Art Centre's large main gallery.

Peggy Phelan claims for performance art the privilege of being the art closest to consciousness, because of its transience and awareness of its own imminent absence (1993). But media art has at least the same claims to make. These images flicker against the walls of the space traversed by the silhouettes of exhibition visitors like dreams flickering against the black canvas of closed eyelids in REM. Silhouettes promenade through Ann Lislegaard's projections of melting offices, Algimantas Maceinos' footage of the uprising in Georgia, Joachim Koester's images of Christiania in twilight. Barbara Visser gives us a film in which we hear the familiar Schwarzenegger soundtrack of *True Lies* but see only a blurred image vaguely discerning the action of helicopters, planes and rushing people. We watch a near-invisible film. Marshall McLuhan described electric media as appealing to feelings rather than to thoughts (McLuhan and Zingrone, 1997) and some of these artists are exploring the positive aspects of that notion.

The American light artist Turrell makes work that is concerned with vision that is not purely visual. His works may address spiritual or mystical vision, but they also present us with the sight of the body. He describes how we have latent optical rods in the backs of our hands, our foreheads and the backs of our heads. His hairdryer installation in Germany bathed the backs of visitors' heads in three different coloured lights. In his *Gasworks* (1993) installation at Dean Clough in Halifax, United Kingdom, the visitor's view was the same with their eyes closed or open—a kaleidoscope of light effects corresponding to brainwave patterns.

In *Sutemos/Twilight* we have visions with closed eyes. We have Algis Garbatlauskas' film of a blind sculptor modelling Garbatlauskas' head. Watching the blind man's hands feeling the model's face, his forehead in close proximity to the emerging clay bust, we can almost see his hands and forehead looking, seeing. The optical mediation is bypassed as hands transmit direct to brain and brain transmits directly back to hands. The eyeball vision of Garbatlauskas the model, and we, the viewers, seems quite bland in contrast to the vision that we can see going on in the blind artist's working process.

In Gilchrist's work *The Discarnate*, we witness again a vision that has nothing to do with sight. A healer sits in deep meditation with electrodes connecting him to an array of biofeedback technology. A Macintosh computer gives us the healer's drastically altered brain-waves as visible shifting patterns on the screen and converted into audible tones. His brainwaves drive small motors in a jacket and shoes massaging a member of the viewing public.

Garbatlauskas and Gilchrist allow us awry glimpses into the inward visions of others, the blind artist, the healer. We are voyeurs, just as our alter-egos, our shadows, promenade through the large-scale wall projections in the exhibition, like those dreams where we appear to be interlopers in an architecture, a space, a narrative that seems none of our making.

To return to compulsion, Bataille asserts that life shatters the continuity of death and desire (1970). Many artists today approach this subject of the amorphous flowing continuity of death and formless matter, of compulsion, of the recycling of consciousness and creativity. Twilight, we remember, approaches the convergence of animate and inanimate, organic and inorganic. Is it then a time when we dimly perceive our connection to this timeless, formless, inorganic flow (Batallle's *l'informe*). Many of the works in this exhibition are attempting to give us these edges of consciousness, subjectivity, emotion, compulsion.

In his essay, 'Art in the dark' (1983), McEvilley discussed seventies performance work as art activity that 'flowed into the darkness beyond its traditional boundaries and explored areas that were previously as unmapped and mysterious as the other side of the moon' (1983). He described how artists, such as Nitsch, Brus,

Schneemann, Beuys, Stelarc and the U.S. West Coast performance artists—Burden, Edelson, Jones, McCarthy, Montana, Oppenheim —were engaging in an appropriation of ritual activities from ancient and primitive sources with the 'desire to reconstitute primitive sensibility within Modern civilization'. These artists drew on a shamanic repertoire of female imitation, animal mimicry, performance of taboo acts and self-injury. McEvilley drew a parallel between the performance artists and 'the preparation of his or her own body as a magico-sculptural object' in the shaman's performance. 'Such activities have necessarily involved artists in areas where usually the psychologist or anthropologist presides'. McEvilley sees these artists taking on a quasi-religious role as shamanic healers, their individual acts being therapeutic for society. He argues that since religion was burdened with the weight of institutionalised beliefs, art could be the zone where culturally bound things could be liberated into direct experience. 'The art context is a neutral and open context, which has no proper and essential contents of its own'.

In the early eighties, McEvilley perceived a tendency for contemporary art to contract again around the commodifiable aesthetic object. Now, in the late nineties, artists are exploring this twilight terrain again. Again, they are using themselves, their own bodies and consciousnesses, now often meshed and in conjunction with flickering, pulsating electronic technologies, that are more accessible, informal, less self-consciously 'artistic' than traditional art mediums.

Gilchrist attempts to use technology to communicate with the body in a state of REM dream sleep or trance. The body 'speaks' back to witnesses through galvanic skin responses and its projected EEG brain waves. Jane and Louise Wilson's disturbing video installations are latent with unspoken narratives. They are luridly filmic, drawing on the horror, gothic and sci-fi genres and exploring abnormal states of consciousness dreams, trauma, madness, drug and hypnosis-induced states. Kathleen Rogers' work examines parallels between the knowledge systems of ancient civilisations and patterned codes in nature, between psychic and technological transmission and reception. Her new work in *Twilight* explores what Deleuze and Guattari have described as the 'resonance and redundancy' of the codes of place and identity' (1987)—drawing on Lithuania's long history as a contested space, inscribed with violent identity conflicts.

Some of these projects in *Twilight* bypass conscious language and tentatively probe in darkness for an alternative language of body images, gestures and actions. This is art that flourishes in the dark, in a state of doubt, ambiguity and hybridisation. It is art in the dark about mortality, consciousness and art itself. It is art plunging into that darkness.

Jutempus' video installation *Recycling* presents the recorded sound and image of walking through the massive rubbish dump on the outskirts of Vilnius where many people make a living scavenging. The oval image in the installation stomps audibly round the spiral space as the artists trod through the tip themselves, making the work, looking for art materials to scavenge.

In contrast to British artist Gilchrist's use of customised, medical 'high' technology, some of the Lithuanian artists come up with interesting mechanical engineering solutions to what they want to materialise in their works. Jutempus' self-generated revolving video projector, for instance, or Audrius Novickas' pneumatic installation of 'breathing' black and white animals. Vytautas Zaltauskas' kinetic sculpture is delightfully simple. Three computer screens are revolving on metal arms and the image of the moon appears in turn on each, leaving the other two screens black.

The artists in *Twilight* have responded to the complex suggestions of the exhibition theme in a variety of ways. Responding to the notion of light, Saulius Mazilys' large colour image of a sunny childhood moment stands out in the rain, bathed in that mysterious golden light of memory, and French artist Rose-marie Martin's installation of fluorescent painted strings leaves ghostly afterimages on the retina.

Other artists respond more to the 'undertime' aspect of the exhibition theme. In Raila's work, one video monitor shows Kestutis Kuizinas, the director of the Contemporary Art Centre, repeating over and over, 'It is a great and difficult task for an artist to dub a motorcycle', while a loop of the Crazy Rockers riding their bikes through the entrance of the Contemporary Art Centre is projected alongside the monitor. This work by Raila, like his earlier piece in the *Mundane Language* exhibition, dislocates norms, combines fine art practice with popular culture, hip-hop rappers and skateboarders. His art edges into awkward collaborations with alien areas of culture.

Magnus Wallin's excellent computer animation depicts disabled, paraplegic figures desperately trying to escape from some holocaust in a cityscape. Aida Ceponyte and Valdas Ozarinskas project a film of an elderly woman in a hospital bed. Giedrius Kumetaitis, Mindaugas Ratavitius and Simonas Tarvydas project their 'caught in Lithuania' series, and the projections of Lars Wellejus and Mindaugas Navakas inhabit the Centre, cropping up all over the building. Gintaras Makarevitius presents the outmoded hairstyles and facial styles of an old police identikit. Egle Rakauskaite's saint on the box of a screen, in the box of a monitor, in the box of a carved wooden shrine ponders on his condition. If, as McEvilley argues, art is a neutral zone with 'no proper and essential contents of its own' then can we propose art or the artist, as a void into which content can rush.

Rationalist notions of creativity conceive of the artist as a born genius, creating out of some 'given' subjective quality that comes from god or nature. Barthes, Foucault and other writers propose the hybrid creator of artist and audience, or artist and culture. Duchamp offers creativity as a combination of artist, audience, chance and posterity (1957, pp. 138–40). But can we perhaps propose the artist as channeller or electrical conductor for eons of collective recycling unconscious. The artist, then, would draw on emotion and subjectivity as intelligent access routes to that source material. I am not using the word subjectivity here within the confines of the discourses of identity politics or subject/object debates. Rather I am using subjectivity as the equivalent of 'consciousness' within a metaphysical context of cosmos and geological time.

> The aerial view reveals the vitality of the earth and the passing and reemerging of cultures. Geology reinforces that view with the movement of continental plates, with subduction and volcanic reemergence.... I wanted an area of exposed geology where you could feel geologic time. (Turrell, 1993, p. 26, p. 58)

When artists walk into their studio or lay down to sleep in their bed to create, they bring with them all their perceptions, experiences, memories, rationalisations, knowledge. They also bring their body twitching with electrical and chemical reactions, crawling with an invisible quantum life and motivation of genes, cells, DNA and enzymes, which are linked back in an unbroken chain to our ancestors and forward to our imminent progeny. The body and consciousness are leaking membranes between the world, time and the self.

When we communicate with ourselves within the space of our bodies, with no motivation to articulate and exteriorise that communing, we do not think in language as rationalism or structuralism would argue. We use the chemical, electrical, emotional, if you like physical, language of the body. I am not talking here about the primal drives hypothesised in psychoanalytic theory from Freud to Kristeva. I am speculating and gesturing rather toward the emerging science of consciousness that discusses the chemistry of emotion, the genetic quantum life inhabiting our bodies. We understand the language of our bodies perfectly well. We only resort to language, take language inside ourselves when we are trying to find a way to translate that chemical, electrical body language into form that will be comprehended on the outside, by someone else, by posterity. The last few decades of critical and psychoanalytic theory focused on language, on decoding, on deconstructing ideology, have finally run into an inevitable dead-end. Evaldas Jansas' work in *Twilight* gives us a comic counterpoint between human consciousness and potato consciousness. The simple potato shoots are twisting, deforming, growing toward the tiny light source in stark contrast to the complexity and confusion of the talking heads of his friends on film, expressing their life wishes for themselves and for him.

Kathleen Rogers argues for 'the existence of sacred places in the landscape that can organise memories, feelings and imagination'. Reaching around those edges of consciousness in twilight, perhaps we can begin to perceive the temporary coagulation of matter into form that we share with animals, plants, rocks, that sedimentation of memory and matter that our DNA has in common with geology. In a range of phylogenetic theses, from Freud and Jung to Bataille or Deleuze and Guattari, we can begin to speculate on how life shatters the continuity of death and desire.

22

JOAN JONAS: WHAT A PERFORMANCE IS

2004. First published in S. Foster (ed) *Joan Jonas*. Southampton: John Hansard Gallery, pp. 17–24.

'I rarely perform for my students, though I think I should, and probably will, since they don't exactly know what a performance is.'

—Joan Jonas (Smith and Niesluchowski, 2003, p. 131).

REDUCTION

One of the things that strikes you about Joan Jonas' performances is a tactic of reductive signification enabling her to engage with the big stuff: war, society, history, culture, time, media, life, death. So a couple of thin, wobbly planks of wood waved around in the air signify a river, as they might in a children's play, but they also signify flux in a very expanded sense. The flux, instability, non-fixity that is life, history and society that won't be pinned down and stay still. (The descriptive examples of elements of Jonas' performances throughout this essay, unless otherwise stated, come from *Lines in the Sand*, first presented at *Documenta 11*, Kassel in 2002, re-performed at The Kitchen, New York and at Tate Modern, London in 2004.) A scrappy bit of gauze tied around Jonas' forehead and eyes signifies the obfuscation of vision (vision in an expanded sense).

Nothing is literal or singular in meaning in Jonas' work. Each image, symbol, action is multi-layered. It will signify something in the contemporary context—U.S. military policy in relation to Iraq, for instance—but it will also gesture at historical, mythological, poetic, metaphysical meanings. Marina Warner writes that Jonas finds 'her inspiration in ... embedded, primary, and structural symbolic order, visiting its manifestations polymorphously, even promiscuously' (Warner, 2003, p. 91). A sandpit in which performers and Jonas draw and erase lines and circles and build up and break down small pyramids, signifies the deserts of Troy, Egypt, Iraq and the shifting sands of time, the mind, mortality. A pile of breeze blocks placed by performers signifies the walls of Troy, a fragment of a pyramid, a screen on which history is projected, a physical and psychological barrier to climb across.

The whole complex thematic resonance of Jonas' *Lines in the Sand* performance is contained and packed into its title, which evokes the impermeability of human life and individual identity and the confrontational stance of identity—a line drawn to mark and defend territory. And the lines also indicate the role of art in asking what is this activity of drawing or writing lines all about?

INTERMEDIA

Another striking feature of Jonas' work is her use of mixed media. It is impossible to apply any straightforward categorisation to her work. Her performances employ time, rhythm, pace, text, costume, video, sound, drawing. Their concern with space and volume is sculptural and their use of composition and colour is painterly. Her performers interact with projected images and sound. She mixes live performance with technological mediation. The projection screens and monitors in her performances are props, sculptures, part of the action and the set. 'My sets were always installations anyway' (Hynes, 2003, p. 13). Equipment and props are littered across Jonas' performance space—slide projectors and wiring are unconcealed. There is no effort to create a smooth illusion, a suspension of disbelief, we are made aware throughout her performances that this is a made image.

Jonas' work is that very rare thing—the intermedia art that Dick Higgins advocated in the sixties.

> For the last ten years or so, artists have changed their media ... to the point where the media have broken down in their traditional forms and have become merely puristic points of reference. (Higgins, 1966, reprinted in Armstrong and Rothfuss, 1993, p. 172)

Higgins argues that the 'intermedial approach' is to emphasis the 'dialectic between the media'. Higgins, along with many other artists and critics, envisioned the breakdown of traditional artform categories and the mixing and mingling of dance, visual art, music, theatre. To some extent this did happen—but, from the perspective of the early twenty-first century, we can see that the categories did not fully break down—they remain with us. Instead, artists' experimentation in the sixties and seventies expanded the categories and blurred their boundaries. What is the difference between visual performance and theatrical performance? Is there one now?

Sixties visual artists made performances drawing on and collaborating with contemporary performing artists and vice versa—dancers, actors and musicians drew on and collaborated with visual artists. Some of the most famous examples being *Pelican* (1963), a collaboration between Rauschenberg, Carolyn Brown and Alex Hay; the collaborative happening at Black Mountain College by John

Cage, Rauschenberg, Merce Cunningham and others; the collaborations of Nam June Paik and musician Charlotte Moorman; many Fluxus performances; visual dance work, such as Trisha Brown's *Roof Piece* (1973); and the performances of the New York Happenings scene by Allan Kaprow, Jim Dine, Robert Whitman, Claus Oldenburg, Carolee Schneemann and others. When Jonas made her first performance in 1968, she was part of this New York scene—on the one hand, living with and collaborating with sculptor, Richard Serra, and, on the other hand, attending workshops with dancer Trisha Brown and drawing on the work of other dancers, including Lucinda Childs, Yvonne Rainer, Simone Forti and Deborah Hay. She sees her work as 'in between dance and sculpture' (Simon, 1995, p. 75).

Dorine Mignot describes Jonas' performances as consisting of 'movements, speaking and singing (which are not to be understood within the traditional disciplines of dance, theatre or opera)' (Jonas, 1994, p. 9). The toolkit of techniques, strategies, histories, and discourses that a visual artist approaches performance with, differ from the toolkit carried by an artist coming out of a training and background in theatre, dance or music. In the eighties, Jonas worked as a performer with the Wooster Group—venturing into 'acting'. But her own work remains determinedly improvisational, raw, instinctive, amateurish even. Simon equates Jonas' performance with the moment when an actor is in her dressing gown, 'the transfigured moment between the theatrical and the ordinary' (1995, p. 73). Rudi Fuchs describes it as 'a manner of working that is forever experimental' (Jonas, 1994, p. 5).

> Body, space and time provide the circumstances of the performances Jonas has developed since 1968. In doing so, she distinguishes performance categorically from the acting out of a role in which the acting follows someone else's literary model with only limited room for autonomous play. (Schmidt, 2001, p. 12)

The type of venue in which a performance is presented and, therefore, the flexibility of how it can interact with its audience, has little bearing anymore on what type of performance it is. Both visual performance and theatrical performance have been located in galleries, theatres and beyond. Contemporary visual-art-based performance comes out of a tradition of making static images and working with techniques, materials and framings to accomplish that. Contemporary theatrical performance comes out of a tradition of enacting animated and illustrated narratives, using bodily techniques and illusion and effects to accomplish that. I would argue, for instance, that a distinction could be made between Oleg Kulik as visual performance and Forced Entertainment as theatrical performance, or between Abramović as visual performance and Annie Sprinkle or Karen Finley as theatrical performance. Influences from other cultures and especially from ritual have had a profound influence on both types of performance. Over the course of the last century, the two types of performance have been in constructive dialogue with each other. Visual performance and theatrical performance, nevertheless, continue to be fundamentally different. Jonas' work, however, unusually, occupies a middle ground between them.

A lot of visual performance has a close relationship with documentation—the performance is conceived of as a construction of an image or images and the documentation will capture some of those, allowing a secondary audience, beyond the one that witnessed the original event, to enter imaginatively into the image and the act (see George, 2003). In Abramović's *Biography*, for instance, when the artist cuts a Star of David on her stomach, in the time-based performance, the audience live through the act of creating the image with the artist, empathising with her experience bodily. The secondary audience, encountering this work through the documentary image, will have a different experience. They are not complicit witnesses to the live act. But they will, nevertheless, seek to empathetically and imaginatively enter into Abramović's act as imaged in the documentary photograph. Jonas' work is not like that. Documentation has a hard time dealing with her work, because there is no clear image points as there are in the work of, for example, Burden, Pane or Abramović. In part, those clear image points are constructed by the process and reception of documentation—the repetitive dissemination of the iconic image extracted from the performance, but they are also part of the artist's structuring. It would be impossible to pick out any moment, any image in a Jonas performance to stand for the rest. On Jonas, Crimp writes,

> Performances can never exist in the integrity of their scripts and descriptions, just as the notion of art that we can take away from these works is that it can now exist only in the process of its enactment, not in its integrity as an object. (1983, p. 10)

REFLECTION

In Jonas' early *Mirror Piece* performances, mirrors were used to foreground 'the audiences' understanding that *it* is what is being seen' (Wagner, 2000, p. 69). In *Mirror Pieces*, mirrors are walked around the space by performers capturing and reflecting back the audience like photographs. 'The audience is at risk, severed from its windowed mirrorings, from its framed certainties to be thrust adrift to the tumultuous throes of subjectivity and narrativity' (Jonas, 1994, p. 17). The mirror brings about an enforced presence/presentness for the audience. The 'mirrors function to edit what aspects of the performance can be seen' (Crimp, 1983, p. 20). They bring into question the authority, completeness, veracity and stability of the visible.

23
PAUL KLEE: THE VISIBLE AND THE LEGIBLE

2015. Review of Annie Bourneuf, *Paul Klee: The Visible and the Legible* first published in *Times Higher Education*, 3 September.

'Three days in Weimar and one can never look at a square again for the rest of one's life,' Paul Westheim wrote of a 1923 exhibition that included grid paintings by Paul Klee. Annie Bourneuf's study shows Klee critically engaging with ideas around him, questioning and probing his peers' theories and practices. Although she discusses Klee's explorations of children's drawings, fantastic art and synesthesia, her primary focus is the graphic elements of his work.

She ties her argument to close discussion of Klee's paintings from the late 1910s to early 1920s. These works incorporate myriad systems for making marks on a surface, including cartography, typography, diagrams, alphabets, handwriting and notation, as Klee explored picture writing, hieroglyphs, runes, pictograms and Chinese characters. He was concerned with the relationship between seeing and reading, asserting that writing and drawing had a common origin. One of his paintings is titled *Concentrated*

Novel; others attempt visual representations of Chinese poems, and still others he described as 'watercoloured writing'.

Bourneuf also examines the theoretical sources that Klee was influenced by and reacted against, in particular Gotthold Ephraim Lessing's influential text *Laocoon*, which claimed poetry as temporal and painting as spatial. Clement Greenberg said that Picasso 'sees the picture as a wall, while Klee sees it as a page'. Bourneuf shows that 'grazing' the painting, as Klee called it—scripting the viewer's gaze and laying down paths for the viewer's eye—is modelled on reading. Her discussion of New Typography and modernised reading theory at Bauhaus is illuminating. There was a sense in the 1920s, as now, that 'the archaic stillness of the book' had had its day.

Art theory then, as always, was tied up with the politics around it, and Bourneuf discusses Klee's work in the context of the First World War, the failed socialist Bavarian Republic of 1919, and a general rejection of moribund culture expressed so forcefully, for example, by the Futurists. The form and modest scale of Klee's pictures address the viewer as private individual at a time when this was seen as capitalist luxury and the very opposite of a collective address that artists should be searching for. Making private art or literature for the individual was a political statement in an age when, as Bourneuf observes, 'the typographical avant-garde sought to make printed matter that would refuse a contemplative mode of reading as withdrawal'.

Bourneuf's cogent and scholarly discussion illuminates Klee's critical engagement with the ideas and practices of other artists, including Kandinsky, van Doesburg and Moholy-Nagy. She sometimes labours her points, but the points themselves are nevertheless strong and insightful. She shows Klee working counter to the Bauhaus ideals of a new union between picture and architecture and the reimagining of the artist as engineer, and indeed there was resistance to his appointment as a master at the Bauhaus in 1921.

This book offers a salutary lesson for artists who mistakenly imagine painting to be simply about technique and making and who have constructed an illusory division between practice and theory. Bourneuf effectively demonstrates how Klee's artwork is itself a critique of theories and practices, and she conjures up for the reader the muscularity of artists' thinking about art in that period.

24

LONDON FIELDWORKS:
TUNING IN

2002. First published in B. Gilchrist and J. Joelson (eds) *Syzygy/Polaria*. London: Black Dog, pp. 6–11.

Gilchrist and Joelson's *Syzygy* and *Polaria* projects are poetic investigations into human consciousness and physiology in relation to the external phenomena of weather and light. These projects provoke a number of questions. Are the artists suggesting that these phenomena are metaphors for the processes of the human embodied consciousness, or are they arguing that there is actually a link and continuity between these two things? What, anyway, is consciousness? And how do these 'poetic' propositions relate either to science or to art?

SYZYGY: WEATHER AND MIND

Syzygy took place on the remote and uninhabited Scottish island of Sanda in summer 1999. The tiny island is a high green rock in an expanse of sea, at the edge of the Atlantic. A team of artists, writers, musicians, computer programmers and kite flyers spent several days on the island, surrounded by sky and sea, living in the weather. They took with them a range of computer, communication, atmospheric diagnostic and biofeedback technologies and kites. Between them, they attempted to corner their notoriously elusive quarries, consciousness and weather, with a range of different techniques. Kaffe Matthews, literally collaborated with meteorological events to play music. Rather than recording and manipulating environmental sound, she used software that allowed the weather to generate its own music. The kites, flown up to 1,000 feet by international stunt team AirKraft, carried sensors that measured light, temperature, wind speed and orientation. The kite flyers wore electroencephalogram (EEG) monitors recording their brain activity. On first consideration, that taut, nylon line holding a kite seems like a very fine conduit to carry the proposition of a link between mind and weather. The thin lines of the kites were more than simply an image of a connection between consciousness and the environment—they were a responsive conjunction between the two. Both atmospheric and EEG monitoring equipment materialised these immaterial processes.

Simultaneous weather and mind data were metaphorically correlated, by their transmission and manifestation in a 'smart' sculpture 700 miles away at the ICA in London. This sculpture was a glass bowl suspended on a steel spine, encrusted with light-emitting diodes and housed in an electro-luminescent glass tank. The glass bowl looked like a large cranium, being a little larger than head size. It contained an electro-rheological fluid that responded to the transmitted brainwave data by pulsing and freezing. The electrical current was transmuting the fluid's viscosity. Sometimes the changes in the sculpture were dramatic and at others they were lethargic, reflecting the human and environmental conditions on Sanda. The interaction between the mind and the weather data affected the viewers' relationship to the sculpture. At times, the visibility of its inner workings was obscured when light data rendered the glass opaque. Occasionally, the fluid appeared as shadows, frozen in time against the glass, illuminated by the internal light. There was often no way of knowing whether it was the weather or the mind data that were causing the mutations within the sculpture or whether it had become a cauldron in which a new combined brew was in action.

Among the four writers on the island, Walwin based her activities on the tidal timetable and historical characters who had had connections to the island. She imagined herself into the island's human history and wrote with the waves. Tony White became the embodiment of a fictional character—half Jack Bruce, the Cream bass player who had previously lived on the island, and half a cloaked sorcerer from science fiction. White engaged in what he describes as 'cartomancy', mapping invisible forces on the island, becoming part of the land and the weather. Mark Waddell wrote as the voice of an anthropomorphised Weather, talking egomaniacally about itself and commenting on its rare human visitors. Steve Beard used a list of British islands to create a computerised method of sampling *The Tempest*. He dubbed his invention the *Sanda Island Spirit Generator*. The poetry of Shakespeare's lunatic play set on a transformative place that is right on the edge, survived this fragmentation remarkably well—appearing like globs of a torn script slapped in our faces by the wind.

In its engagement with awesome natural phenomena, *Syzygy* was a legacy of the monumental works of the American land artists —Nancy Holt's *Sun Tunnels*, Smithson's *Spiral Jetty*, De Maria's *Lightning Field*, Charles Ross' *Star Axis* or Turrell's *Roden Crater*. But *Syzygy*'s approach to the forces of nature was much more ephemeral. Gilchrist and Joelson propose that the body is a mobile laboratory, a set of instruments in itself. They use the body in the environment, rather than the intellect, as a means of knowing. Our sensory and cognitive systems have always related to and interpreted our immersive environment. Contemporary scientific technology is just a way of materialising and imaging this relationship.

POLARIA: LIGHT AND BODY

For their latest project, *Polaria*, Gilchrist and Joelson travelled to north-east Greenland in August 2001 to conduct fieldwork on Arctic light and human physiology. They travelled to their research location, Hold with Hope, a remote corner of the world's largest national park. Gilchrist and Joelson were assisted in Greenland by a Danish guide who had previously worked with the Sirius Sledge Patrol. The light in this region is a special kind of light that disorientates temporal and spatial expectations. The idea of the sun rising in the east and setting in the west simply does not apply here. The summer midnight sun seems to suspend time. Photographers, Anthony Oliver and Jo Outram, were part of the fieldwork team. They documented the fieldwork and the changing Arctic light by photographing the landscape it defined. While Joelson measured and 'collected' the light, Gilchrist measured and collected physiological responses to the light.

Returning from their research trip, Gilchrist and Joelson worked on producing an art installation that recalls body states and light conditions experienced in Greenland. They used the fieldwork data to create a relational database that enabled these experiences to re-emerge in a virtual light chamber placed in the context of art gallery spaces. A visitor sitting in the chamber triggers responses through direct connection to the database, via a physiological interface. The chamber makes explicit the nature of the body as technology in itself. The body is both the source of the data and their receptor, both recorder and transducer of phenomena. We are used to the visual sense being dominant in our interaction with the environment, but the whole body is an environmental sensor. Airflow and temperature contribute to the sensory information we collect about the space we are in, as well as the more obvious senses of sound, smell and touch. There is evidence that those with sensory impairments compensate with heightened other sensory abilities, such as blind sight. Ved Mehta, the blind writer, talks about 'sound shadows'—a kind of facial vision that responds to acoustic shadows and changes in air pressure as a way of navigating the environment (1987). Gilchrist and Joelson's work makes us think about sensory experiences in new ways, to appreciate how 'The curved reality of sense perception operates in and out of the straight abstractions of the mind' (Smithson, 1979, p. 113). Gilchrist and Joelson's interactive installation gets us to stare into the light, into the void. Like Turrell's work there is no subject in this art, no image, no representation. The viewer's own perception is the subject. As Turrell says about his work: 'you are looking at your looking' (1993, p. 26).

This interest in light and the body arises from the conjunction of concerns in Gilchrist and Joelson's previous work. In his earlier work, Gilchrist employed biofeedback technologies to measure and materialise brain and physiological activity in his own sleeping body. Joelson has a background as a lighting designer and installation artist. Part of her childhood was spent living in the United Arab Emirates, in the intense light at the edge of the desert. She has worked with the medium of light for ten years, often borrowing from nature and synthesising natural phenomena in artificial environments. Between them, the two artists are seeking ways to define the relationship between human observation and sensation. Gilchrist and Joelson's work clarifies an enquiry into the unknown that is the common, fundamental motivation of art, science and exploration.

METAPHOR OR CONTINUITY?

Is Gilchrist and Joelson's combination of mind and weather in *Syzygy* simply poetic license or do they intend us to consider it as a literal relationship? Is it a metaphor for consciousness or are they asserting that there actually is a continuity between human consciousness and physiology and the natural environment? Some theorists have tried to apply new ideas about materiality and causality observed in natural phenomena to the processes of human consciousness, quantum mechanics, chaos and emergence, for instances. Neurophysiologist William Calvin, remarking that ignorance is scary, claims that 'we badly need a metaphor... that successfully bridges the gap between our perceived mental life and the neural mechanisms responsible for it' (1998, p. 197). But he is sceptical about the various metaphors that have been applied:

> [I]s the invocation of QM [quantum mechanics] in the consciousness context just another mistaken instance of suggesting that one area in which mysterious effects are thought to lurk—chaos, self-organising automata, fractals, economics, the weather—might be related to another, equally mysterious one? (1998, p. 46)

Christopher Tyler, on the other hand, has recently argued that 'In respect to its transcendent quality, consciousness seems more akin to cooperative processes such as fire, lightning, waves, tornadoes or nuclear reactions' (2000, p. 30). He is using the word transcendent here to mean that 'a background level of activity intensifies into a self-organising state that transcends the original activity state'. He goes on to argue that 'The strength of process metaphors, such as the tornado, is that they reveal the difficulty of the philosophical analysis of consciousness based on non-transcendent concepts of things in the world' (2000, p. 30). Tyler argues that consciousness is emergent, it is a dynamic process with evanescent qualities rather than the stable properties of material objects.

The idea that there is a dynamic relationship between our neurophysiology and that stuff out there, that human consciousness is embedded in and somehow linked to a wider distribution of consciousness, is an idea that has been voiced by an impressive range of thinkers, including Alfred North Whitehead, Carl Jung and William James, as well as more recent commentators, such as psychologist, Max Velmans, and artist, Bill Viola (1995). But before we can consider the validity of this idea of continuity between human consciousness and environment we need to define what we mean when we talk about consciousness.

WHAT IS CONSCIOUSNESS?

'The ultimate passion of the Western mind over two thousand five hundred years has been to understand the ground of its own being.' (Velmans, 2000, p. 3)

Our subjective experience confirms the existence of consciousness (our own at least) and intuitively we know it is central to human life, but science is currently unable to explain what it is, how it works and what its functions are. In the tangle of muddled terms and theories that surrounds the word 'consciousness', other words, such as mind, soul, knowledge, self, are all often used interchange-ably with it. Debates are raging over consciousness in neuroscience, cognitive science, psychology, philosophy and other disciplines. Gilchrist and Joelson contribute to this debate from within the discipline of art. One common definition of consciousness is to make a distinction between being conscious or wakeful, and uncon-scious. But this leaves out a whole range of experiences. We have visual and auditory experiences in dreams for instance. Another definition is that consciousness is what we are conscious of (Velmans, 2000, pp. 3–8). This, then, includes thoughts, feelings, images, dreams, body sensations and sensory experiences.

However, this second definition excludes preconscious and unconscious brain and body activities. It excludes autonomic bodily functions—heartbeat, blood flow, vasomotor activity, pupil dilation —the neural, biochemical and bioelectrical activities carried out by our bodies of which we are unaware and to which we have no conscious access. Our bodies are twitching with electrical and chemical reactions, crawling with invisible quantum life, animated by the motivations of genes, cells, DNA, hormones and enzymes. This definition of consciousness excludes all our pre-conscious activity, such as dreamless sleep, knowing without knowing, experience that is 'below language'. Much of our experience exists at a non-linguistic and non-symbolic level, it is not consciously voiced but it hovers on the edge of what is consciously known. This may be experience retained in the body, in emotion, in the soma. Information processing and long-term memory are unconscious brain activities.

There is clinical evidence that we have the ability to make discriminations below the threshold of conscious awareness. Pre-conscious semantic processing is required for many skills that we think of as conscious, such as reading, thinking and speech, but consciousness—defined as being conscious of something—arrives too late to influence input analysis in reading, overt speech and covert thought (Libet, 1999, pp. 47–58). Pre-conscious activity may influence actions, enter into the creation of our expectations, affect our judgements and create emotional reactions to events—what we mean when we talk about gut reactions, instinct and intuition. Isn't all that part of what we think of as consciousness? Most Western thought is premised on versions of dualism, idealism or materialism. Dualism splits the universe into two fundamentally different substances—mental and physical. In this definition, consciousness is an entity, a wholly different substance from the physical. It remains essentially mysterious and unknowable. The so-called 'hard problem' in the science and philosophy of consciousness is that if consciousness is fundamentally different from physical energies and events, what is the relationship between the two? How can the behaviour of neurons be affected by desires? How can the electrochemistry of the brain relate to subjective experiences? Gilchrist and Joelson attempt to bring about a collision between scientific and subjective measurements of consciousness phenomena.

Definitions of consciousness remain contested but theorists in all disciplines now agree that only a serious study of contributions from 'first person methodologies'—art for instance—will move the debate on. The brain can be studied objectively using imaging techniques: EEG, positron emission tomography (PET) scans or magnetic resonance imaging (MRI). While the brain is the aspect of our bodies that seems most closely involved with consciousness, 'no discovery that reduces consciousness to the brain has yet been made' (Velmans, 2000, p. 13). The only evidence about what conscious experiences are like comes from first person, subjective, sources. Attempts to make a scientific study of this first-person phenomena in the past have included the introspective methods of Wundt, Kulpe and Titchener, and the study of responses and stimuli in behaviourism. The drawback of both methods, however, has been their reliance on linguistic reporting. The phenomenology of experience cannot always be unambiguously and exhaustively described in words. Even though science uses protocols and methodologies generally established and agreed to be 'objective', the scientific observer is still a subjective observer. There is no real basis for assuming that it is possible to designate one human being a subjective subject and another an objective observer. The interpretation of observations and results are always subjective.

So is there no sure knowledge? Phenomena experienced subjectively and individually may be verified through intersubjective agreement about what has happened. There are shared consensus realities created by communities of knowers. Velmans has pointed out that science itself is a form of communal knowledge with transcultural procedures. Art is an inter-subjective process. Recognition plays an important role in art. In successful art, viewers recognise that they are being presented with something—whether it is a painting or an ephemeral action—that they can relate to, that expresses something essential about them.

What unifies the consciousness of a particular being? What constitutes being? The dictionary defines 'being' as existence and essence—so it is clear that it is distinct from the other terms discussed—mind, soul, knowledge, self—but it seems similar to the contemporary meaning of the word consciousness. The term 'self' is problematised in cultural theory by issues of identity construction and the social projection of persona. Nevertheless, there remains an overwhelming subjective sense of a continuous and coherent being. This I is experienced as being identical through time, forming a coherent whole, a base from which perspective, as well as perception, is gained. Drawing on his sleep research, neurophysiologist Stuart Dimond discusses consciousness as 'the running span of subjective experience' (cited in Velmans, 2000, p. 241). The word 'being' implies existence and, therefore, raises the issue of non-existence. It implies the self existing within a span of time, it implies mortality. The sloppy wiring of the brain creates smears rather than connections. Much of consciousness is unconscious, unlanguaged, unplaced. Only a small amount of our thinking is pragmatic—devoted to surviving in our environment. The majority of it is concerned with metaphysics—how to understand life, mitigate death—and what George Steiner describes as 'The drive to be interested in something. For its own enigmatic sake. Because it is there' (1978, p. 213).

SCIENCE AND ART

So what could artists possibly contribute to these debates around consciousness? Science is the metaphysics of the late twentieth and twenty-first centuries, whereas the function of art in Western society is far from clear. In the past, artistic methods of enquiry have been seen as directly opposed to scientific methodologies. William Blake, for instance, criticised Isaac Newton's reduction of a rainbow to optical theory, seeing deduction as sterile in contrast to instinctive response. Art is a different form of approach to knowledge than science. While science devises methods to test a hypothesis, proving or disproving it, art speculates based on intuition. Artists make things up and move toward knowledge through fictions rather than facts. Art makes us feel knowledge—it addresses being rather than thinking. Gilchrist and Joelson's title *Syzygy* refers to the astronomical phenomenon of planets aligning. It suggests not only an alignment between weather and consciousness, but also between science and art. Despite an appropriation of scientific language, tools and methodologies in Gilchrist and Joelson's projects, there is as much shamanism as science going on in their work. *Syzygy* and *Polaria* are instruments of the heart rather than instruments of reason. What they present us with is 'not scientific evidence but poetic debris' (La Frenais, 1994, p. 5).

The small number of scientific papers published on art and consciousness have mainly dealt with the neurology of looking at art (see Goguen, 1999). They also only address traditional, representational art and make no attempt to engage with the last hundred years of non-representational art—Dada, Surrealism, abstract art, conceptual art, body art, and so on. Many artists have contributed to a speculative exploration of consciousness through these non-traditional forms. Artists have used the body itself as a technology to explore consciousness and creativity. This tradition stretches back at least to the Romantic artists and writers experimenting with laudanum and opiates, visions and dreams. This interest continued in the experiments of the Surrealists who tried to 'tune in' to the ether, like the mediums and Theosophists they were interested in. Just as Theosophists Annie Besant and Charles Leadbetter had drawn invisible 'Thought Forms', the Surrealists experimented with automatism and other 'irrational' techniques, such as Max Ernst's *frottage* or Oscar Dominguez's *decalcomania*, to try to materialise the immaterial. But the rational/irrational divide is a cultural construct and they found that rationalised interpretation always crept back in somehow.

In the 1970s and 1980s, Hiller revisited the Surrealists' experiments, making work concerned with telepathy, dream, automatic writing and reverie in *Draw Together* (1972), *Dream Mapping* (1974), *Sisters of Menon* (1983) and *Belshazzar's Feast* (1983–1984). Writing about her dream work, Hiller commented that

> This is not an attempt, in any sense, to make an equivalent to a scientific experiment. This is an experiential... this is a structure that invites possibilities of intensified subjective experience. It's not oriented towards 'results'. (Einzig, 1996, p. 180)

The premise of *Dream Mapping* was that the group of seven people dreaming together in a field in Hampshire would demonstrate a shared subjectivity. Hiller's work asked whether ideas are individual or whether they have a collective origin. She was interested in exploring 'knowledge that's embodied, not split off and relegated to the mind separately. One needs to re-feel everything as an artist'. In Abramović and Ulay's *Nightsea Crossing*, 1981–1986, the artists sat in art galleries fasting, unmoving and silent for stretches of up to sixteen days at a time. They presented themselves as embodied consciousnesses in the process of being. For the final four days of this marathon work, they were joined by a Tibetan lama and an Aborigine Pintubi tribesman, indicating how they had drawn on the meditative and spiritual traditions of those cultures for the work.

Gilchrist's earlier work concerned with sleep and dreaming investigated the objectification of phenomena associated with cognitive processes within a poetic application of technology. In works using his own sleeping body, he employed brain imaging and galvanic skin response measurement to try to externalise what was going on inside his unconscious mind (see Keidon, 1996; Walwin, 1997; Warr, 1996a). He attempted to observe how external signals became symbolically incorporated into his dream content. 'Detached from our critical faculties we are passive witnesses to the extraordinary inventions of the under-mind'. He used physiological and neurological impulses as material for the expression and examination of disembodied states. Using the empathetic imaginative link across bodies, he devised an experience for his viewers' bodies. Burden made the private experience of sleeping a public activity in his work *Bed Piece* (1972). Gilchrist took this a step further, using technology to demonstrate what was happening inside as well as outside, trying to make his viewers feel his sleeping body and EEG on their own pulses. Visitors to his work *Divided by Resistance* (made in collaboration with Jonny Bradley) at the ICA in 1996 could feel vibrations through sitting in a tensile chair and wearing a special jacket and shoes. These vibrations were translations of Gilchrist's sleeping EEG so that the viewers were literally wearing his dream brainwaves.

TUNING INTO THE OCEANIC

All of Gilchrist and Joelson's work challenges the model of the artist as a unique self-expressor and offers something other than the affirmation and extension of the individual. Gilchrist says that his role falls 'somewhere between invigilator and collector, emphasising the process and transformation over the act of making'. Gilchrist and Joelson examine the immaterial through material. They 'tune in' on the manifestation of the non-manifest in order to make it accessible. Is Gilchrist and Joelson's proposition of this link between human consciousness and external phenomena merely a contemporary Romanticism, revisiting the sublime?

Freud's friend Romain Rolland described the experience of a

dissolution of individual self in the cosmos or oneness with the universe, as the 'oceanic' feeling, 'a sensation of "eternity", a feeling as of something limitless, unbounded'. Freud could not discover this 'oceanic' feeling in himself. He viewed it as a 'consolation' despite Rolland's assertion that 'it brings with it no assurance of personal immortality' (Freud, 1930, pp. 64–65). But other thinkers, notably William James and Jung, have acknowledged this immersive and reciprocally creative relationship between individual consciousness and the universe.

Bachelard describes the human as 'the being that lies half open', envisaging a fine membrane between inside and outside: 'Through their "immensity" these two kinds of space—the space of intimacy and the world space—blend' (Bachelard, 1964, p. 203). Gilchrist and Joelson's proposition does revisit the sublime and the Romantic, but there is more than a projection of internal emotions onto the external world going on. They manifest the embodied conscious-ness in the immersive environment, through a combination of instrumentation and subjectivity.

25

LONDON FIELDWORKS: MEASURING BEAUTY IN THE UPPER ICE-WORLD

2005. First published in B. Gilchrist and J. Joelson (eds) *Little Earth*. London: London Fieldworks, pp. 11–19.

MEASUREMENT AND EXPERIENCE

Gilchrist and Joelson's art project, *Little Earth*, began with two rime-encrusted atmospheric observatories on mountains in Scotland and northern Norway. The artists researched the lives and work of Victorian scientists, C.T.R. Wilson—who worked at the Ben Nevis Observatory at the turn of the last century investigating electricity in storm clouds, and Kristian Birkeland—who was investigating the aurora borealis at Haldde Observatory. Gilchrist and Joelson engaged with the scientists' experiences by being at the observatories themselves, encountering the weather conditions there and working with the nearby communities in Fort William and Alta. The *Little Earth* project examines the interaction of embodied consciousness with the natural environment. This is a recurring issue in Gilchrist and Joelson's work—in, for instances, *Syzygy* (1998/1999),

KnoWhere (2000/2001) and *Polaria* (2001/2002). *Syzygy* interrogated the relationship between consciousness and weather; *KnoWhere* was a collaborative work with blind and partially sighted artists exploring sensory modalities in interaction with the natural environment and *Polaria* was concerned with embodied consciousness and natural light phenomena (Gilchrist and Joelson, 2001; *London Fieldworks*, no date; Warr, 2001c, 2002a, included in this book).

The conditions worked under by Wilson, Birkeland and other meteorologists at the mountain observatories were extreme. In the winter, they had to dig their way out of the buildings through piles of snow or heat up instrumentation and hands paralysed by the freezing temperatures. The imminence of an electric storm could be presaged by the experience of having your hair stand on end. There were lightning strikes and battering winds. For long periods, the mountaintops and the meteorologists were inside heavily saturated clouds that reduced visibility to a few inches of wet, white, near-tangible fog. Haldde Mountain, above the Arctic Circle, was subject to twenty-four-hour darkness in the winter and twenty-four-hour daylight in the summer. During the summer, the meteorologists could experience clear days with endless views of landscape and sea, and balmy temperature inversions when it was hotter at the top of the mountain than at the foot (see Ashcroft, 2001; Roy, 2004).

The atmospheric phenomena the meteorologists witnessed from the mountains were also extreme. The aurora borealis appeared as spectacular curtains or streamers of green or coloured lights reaching down from the high altitudes of the night sky. They saw glories, haloes, coronas and Saint Elmo's fire—an electrical discharge that can be seen during thunderstorms around high projecting objects. The Brocken Spectre, observed by Wilson on Ben Nevis in 1894, is otherwise known as a 'glory', a phenomenon where the observers see their own magnified shadow thrown onto a cloud-bank and encircled by rainbow-like bands. Brocken is the highest peak in the Harz Mountains in northern Germany. It is reputed to be the scene of witches' Walpurgis-night revels. The relative position of sun, observer, mist and the size of the raindrops and the reflections and refractions of the sun's rays within the cloud droplets cause the Brocken Spectre phenomenon.

There were good scientific reasons for undertaking observations on mountaintops. Before the invention of radio it was the only way to investigate the vertical structure of the lower part of the atmosphere and to study the ionosphere—the electrically charged conducting layer in the upper atmosphere—with its electromagnetic forces. Birkeland's research at Haldde linked geomagnetic activity with the aurora. Wilson's observations from Ben Nevis led him to a major contribution to atomic physics and a Nobel Prize.

But there appears to have been some resistance to the mountain observatories from the Victorian scientific establishment. The Ben Nevis Observatory was built and mostly maintained through public subscription and was repeatedly unsuccessful in achieving any serious financial support from the government or the Royal Meteorological Society. After twenty-one years of operation, it was allowed to fall into disuse, with funding going instead to the Low-Level Observatory in Fort William. Despite the hardships involved in collecting the Ben Nevis weather data, which were sent daily down a heavily armoured telegraph cable, it appears that the mountain-top observatory was barely used in weather forecasting.

Perhaps part of the resistance to the mountain observatories was an uneasy awareness of their contingency with a Romantic engagement with nature. There was intensive activity and interest in the nineteenth century in both mountaineering and polar exploration. The numerous polar expeditions included attempts to find the Northwest Passage, to reach the North Pole, and to explore Greenland and the Bering Straits. The first International Polar Year occurred in 1882, with fifteen polar stations being established. The intrepid nineteenth-century polar explorers included Ross, Peary, Shackleton, Amundsen and Scott. The glamour of these adventures was only heightened by the fact that the hostile environments took the lives of many mountaineers and polar explorers, including Franklin (1845), De Long (1881), Scott (1912), and their crews. The northern mountains the meteorologists chose to perch on were steeped in associations with the sublime, the mystical, the heroic.

Sublime landscapes are familiar territory in Gilchrist and Joelson's work. Among their previous projects, *Syzygy* involved fieldwork on the uninhabited Scottish island of Sanda, the *KnoWhere* project took them to Lundy Island in the Bristol Channel, and for *Polaria* they conducted research in remote north-east Greenland. One of their central concerns is an interrogation of the contemporary in relation to Romanticism.

A fascination with awe-inspiring landscapes and natural phenomena—waterfalls, canyons, mountains, storms—developed in the eighteenth century and was addressed by many writers, including Burke, Kant, Goethe and Ruskin. Emerson, Thoreau and Muir also all wrote rapturous essays on mountains. ('The upper ice-world' is a quotation from Ruskin in *Peaks, Passes and Glaciers* (Alpine Club, 1862). Also, see Macfarlane, 2003.)

Throughout the nineteenth century, this fascination is imaged in the work of many painters—ranging from the lurid emerald polar seas and threatening icebergs of Church, the stormy wrath of God in John Martin's work, the maelstrom of weather and sea in Turner's paintings, to Constable's cloud studies. Church's painting, *The Icebergs* (1861), is based on studies he made off the coast of Newfoundland, Canada during a voyage in 1859. Church was rigorous in his attempts to accurately represent what he saw in nature. The ice in the foreground looks wet and glistening because it has risen from under the water, the changing level of the sea has left horizontal stains on the main iceberg and the brilliant blue veins in the iceberg are caused by water frozen in the cracks of a glacier.

Many of Friedrich's paintings, including *The Wreck of the Hope* (1823) (also known as *The Polar Sea*) and *Wanderer Above a Sea of Fog* (1818), emphasise that there was a direct relationship between these artists' work, the activities of gentlemen (and occasionally gentlewomen) explorers and scientists and the dilemma widely felt in European and American nineteenth-century society in relation to religion and science. Discoveries arising from astronomy and geographic exploration, as well as an increasing emphasis on the individual in the fifteenth and sixteenth centuries had already challenged the Christian church. The impacts of the theories of Darwin and other scientists in the nineteenth century further undermined religious belief. Friedrich's work, in particular, images a world where divinity is either transferred to nature or absent altogether and yet nature is redolent with awe nonetheless (see Gamwell, 2002).

There was a chasm between the handwritten records of hourly observations of temperature, wind speed and direction, and rainfall kept for twenty-one years at the Ben Nevis Observatory, for instance, and the stunning beauty of the phenomena the meteorologists were witnessing there. There is a gap in articulation between measurement and experience.

Taxonomy, dissection, reduction and disassemblement have been key scientific strategies, along with the dualist construct of an objective subject examining an object. Mark Dion's recent artworks critique the exercise of power, dominion and closure in a taxonomical methodology. Much of Duchamp's work critiques the reductive idea of knowing through measuring and quantifying. The mathematician and physicist Henri Poincare who had expressed a fundamental doubt as to the possibility of objective scientific knowledge influenced Duchamp's ideas. Poincare argued that laws believed to govern matter and its behaviour were created solely by the minds that 'understood' them and that science could not reach the things themselves—only the relations between them.

Duchamp's *3 Standard Stoppages* (1913–1914) involved inventing a new unit of measurement based on chance by dropping three-metre-long lengths of thread and then creating wooden 'rulers' based on their chance position. He explained: 'the unit of length, one meter, was changed from a straight line to a curved line without actually losing its identity [as] the meter, and yet casting a pata-physical doubt on the concept of a straight edge as being the shortest route from one point to another.' He then used these wooden templates in mapping the diagrammatic painting *Network of Stoppages* (1914) and for positioning the 'Bachelors' or 'Nine Malic Moulds' in *The Bride Stripped Bare by her Bachelors, Even* (also known as *The Large Glass*) (1915–1923). Duchamp's *3 Standard Stoppages* was made at a time of widespread scepticism concerning the objectivity of scientific knowledge. In *Science and Hypothesis* (1902), for example, the philosopher of science and mathematician Henri Poincaré asked whether or not it would be 'unreasonable to inquire whether the metric system is true or false?'. The concept for *3 Standard Stoppages* may also be linked to Alfred Jarry's pataphysics, or 'science of imaginary solutions', explicitly designed to 'examine the laws governing exceptions, and ... explain the universe parallel to this one'.

Traditionally it has been assumed that it is efficacious for the scientist to observe and record data with no reference to the human measurer. Hiller argues that 'objectivity is a fantasy that our culture has heavily invested in'. Thomas Kuhn's theory of paradigms (1962) suggests that experiments can produce meanings that are 'contingent on the experimenter's interests'. Subjectivity shapes science, just as it shapes art. Belief, and the limits of belief dictated by the current paradigm, must influence 'knowledge'.

The myth that science works with empirical truths and that art is the unique expression of a born genius is a strong myth. Neil deGrasse Tyson, for instance, in an essay entitled 'Science as the Artist's Muse', suggests that

> The most important scientific discoveries ... those that came from the minds of undeniably great scientists, would all have been discovered eventually by one or more other scientists... In art, however, Cezanne didn't have to rush-paint his Mont Saint-Victoire out of fear that somebody else was going to create the identical landscape. (Gamwell, 2002, p. 6)

Both art and science are the result of individuals or teams of individuals working with the material that is in the collective milieu. Cezanne's innovations were as likely to be, if not replicated, at least approached by other artists, in the same way as a scientist's theories might be.

Despite the overstatement of the notion of construction in some postmodernist theory, the immanence of reality is central to both art and science. Scientific interpretation has been embedded in methodology and worked toward achieving a stability of knowledge while art has always had a capacity to allow fluid interpretations. The understanding in the humanities is that meaning cannot be definitively deciphered, that interpretation is an unending play with infinitely varied meanings, that art is contingent on its context—the contexts of its framing, the context of its making and of its reception (see Ede, 2000 and Wilson, 2002).

Dissection and taxonomy have taken us a long way in the technological and scientific developments of the last two centuries. However, the issues that science is probing now—such as quantum theory or human consciousness—are not yielding at all well to this methodology. There is now a recognition in the scientific community of the value and indeed need for first-person methodologies and an engagement with subjectivity, which was hitherto unthink-able, a new understanding of the fluid, dynamic, creative process of interaction going on between subject and object (see Gilchrist and Warr, 2000; *Toward a Science of Consciousness*, no date).

Gilchrist and Joelson's work is an on-going enquiry into the ways that the data of natural phenomena is interpreted and made manifest in both science and art. In *Syzygy* they worked with Impe-rial College and Cranfield University to develop a smart materials sculpture that was responsive to physiological and weather data being transmitted to it. In *Polaria* an interactive light installation responded to the physiological state of the visitor. In *Little Earth*, they take a different approach—a theatrical engagement with the scientists' experiences—using strategies of re-enactment and stag-ing. In particular, they focus on Wilson and Birkeland's invention of idiosyncratic instrumentation, and mirror this in their work with the invention of their own instrument—the *Little Earth* installation.

INSTRUMENTS OF ART AND SCIENCE

Stan Cowley and Marjory Roy locate Wilson and Birkeland's work at the turning point in a shift from naked-eye observation and specu-lation, based in a natural philosophy framework, to a science increasingly dependent on instrumentation and technological simulation (Cowley, 2005 pp. 64–93; Roy, 2005, pp. 50–57). These developments show an increasing distance between the scientist and the raw materials or phenomena under examination. Both Wilson and Birkeland invented instruments. Wilson's cloud chamber visualised the tracks of ionising particles and Birkeland's terrella machine demonstrated the aurora and its relationship to solar activity.

Instrumentation and simulation reduce the vast scale of natural phenomena to a human scale where it can be seen, played with (like a doll's house), manipulated and harnessed. The cloud chamber and terrella are, in effect, models of the atmosphere—the atmosphere in a bottle, a storm in a teacup.

The four-screen video installation of *Little Earth* is also an instrument for understanding and manipulation. The work is a fictional recreation of the activities of the two scientists at the observatories. The artists describe this as an audiovisual poem. Incorporating a script by James Flint and sound score by Dugal McKinnon, the video work is projected onto the four sides of a cube suspended from an architectural rigging. The projection structure was designed by architect, Ed Holloway. He was inspired by radar dishes and antenna arrays that the artists had photographed at scientific installations on the island of Svalbard. Drawing on these and other images of the Cluster satellites, the installation requires the audience to orbit the work.

Little Earth, however, is not simply the art installation shown at Wapping, Fort William and elsewhere. Gilchrist and Joelson's work characteristically employs a process of interrogating their subject through several modes of artistic 'output'. In *Little Earth*, this process has included a series of residencies at the Headlands Centre for The Arts, San Francisco; ACA in Northumberland and at Dartington Gallery in Devon; Joelson's Arts Council/Arts & Humanities Research Board Art/Science Fellowship working with Professor Stan Cowley and the Radio and Space Plasma Physics Group at University of Leicester; an official twinning ceremony for the Haldde and Ben Nevis Observatories held at Fort William in October 2004; and a publication in which the artists collaborated with a number of writers (Gilchrist and Joelson, 2005).

During the Headlands Centre for the Arts residency, the artists made a series of visualisation experiments to represent the methods and ideas of Wilson and Birkeland. They were inspired by the vagaries of the San Francisco microclimate, from the fogs rolling through the Headlands and the Bay Area to temperature inversions at the top of nearby Mount Tamalpais. They were given access to contemporary space weather science for the first time at University of California Berkeley Space Sciences Lab and were introduced to the phenomenon of sprites. Part of the artists' enquiry included discussions with a Stanford researcher who is an authority on the recently imaged sprite phenomena, which are upper atmospheric, electrical discharges occurring above storm clouds. She created a linkage with Wilson, relating how he predicted the existence of sprites in the 1920s. They were photographed for the first time in 1989. (A sprite event has been linked with the 2003 Columbia shuttle disaster: a photograph taken by a San Francisco astronomer appeared to show a purplish bolt of lightning striking the shuttle during re-entry.)

At ACA, Gilchrist and Joelson conducted a series of interviews with particle and quantum physicists about how contemporary scientific knowledge is disseminated to the lay public. They became interested in the possibility of fictions being created through the interpretations of the lay imagination. At Dartington, they experimented with ferro liquids and magnetic materials in a lab-like construction of glass vessels and clamps and invented 'proto-instruments for the sub-conscious'. At each residency location, they were at pains to engage audiences in their developing ideas.

Their work is collaborative in a wide-ranging and interdisciplinary way—involving, for examples, members of the mountain communities of Haldde and Ben Nevis, a composer, script writer, architect and writers for *Little Earth* and a team, including stunt kite flyers, computer programmers, materials scientists, writers and musicians for *Syzygy*. Their work is also participatory, and it is unusual for artists' practice to span both the gallery world of the art cognoscenti and a range of localised communities. The twinning of the observatories was initiated by Gilchrist and Joelson. They designed the official twinning document with its swathe of aurora across the sky between the mountain-top observatories. They brought together a range of people from the two remote communities to make it happen, including the John Muir Trust, who own the summit of Ben Nevis; the Fort William Justice of the Peace; the Highland Council; Fort William and Alta Museums; bagpipe players and a Sami musician. Gilchrist and Joelson's working process has enabled the reconnection of aspects of history and identity for these two remote communities and has been a catalyst for a new dialogue. The director of the John Muir Trust told the community of Alta, for instance, 'Our mountain is now your mountain'.

A lot of current 'sci-art'—where artists collaborate with scientists and work with the concerns and materials of science—is still mired in the idea that art can be an illustrative, accessible, user-friendly mediation for science or that science offers art an alluring range of kit and language to be appropriated. There is still a mutual lack of understanding of functions and methodologies in many science-art projects and above all a misunderstanding of the role of art. Gilchrist and Joelson's work bypasses the binary fallacy of sci-art. Rather than attending to agendas proposed by the artificial construct that is the 'science-art' domain, the artists instead see it as 'part of their creative freedom to measure using their own scale and methods, inspired perhaps by the rigours and questioning of science but unsatiated by its self-imposed limitations'.

Cultural authority currently resides with science and not with contemporary art. A puritanical or sceptical streak in traditional science tends to evince a fear of the frivolous and pointless, a fear of the credulous and superstitious. Gilchrist and Joelson's work approaches a complex knot of belief, desire, creativity and knowledge. It reminds us of the play, the intuition, whims and idiosyncrasies in both art and science. By walking in the scientists' shoes, and through a process of theatrical fictional re-enactment, they have been able to image the intuitive leaps of the scientists and the ways in which they were inspired by the beauty of natural phenomena, and then to relate that to the contemporary world. While they engage aspects of the mimetic and simulation, their work also emphasises the direct engagement of being and becoming. They explore both direct and mediated experience in their work. They enact the role of the generative human imagination in making and unmaking the world and examine how ideas leak out into the manifest world.

26

LONDON FIELDWORKS:
REMOTE PERFORMANCES BLOG

2019. First published as a daily blog online 4–9 August by Live Art Development Agency at https://www.thisisliveart.co.uk/2014/08/05/remote-performances-day-1-what-is-remoteness/.

[*Remote Performances* was a collaboration between artists London Fieldworks, Resonance 104.4fm, (the world's first art radio station), and the Live Art Development Agency. Twenty specially commissioned artist performances and programmes created with local residents were broadcast live from *Outlandia* in Glen Nevis, Lochaber, Scotland. *Outlandia* was created by artists London Field-works (Gilchrist and Joelson). *Remote Performances* was broadcast daily for a week in August 2014 (see Gilchrist, Joelson and Warr, 2015; *Remote Performances* (a), no date; *Remote Performances* (b), no date).]

DAY 1 – WHAT IS REMOTENESS?

MONDAY 4 AUGUST, LOCH AILORT, SCOTTISH HIGHLANDS

What is remoteness and where is it? Twenty artists converge on Fort William to engage with mountains, forest, loch. Resonance 104.4fm radio decamps from London to a temporary studio in *Outlandia*, an artists' treehouse in Glen Nevis. A *cèilidh* band cram into the tiny tardis space. It is a struggle to broadcast in the face of grim weather and difficult topography—Ben Nevis mountain opposite, large trees in the way. A satellite moves overhead hoping for an ecstatic jolt of connection with the antenna, a thwarted technological mating.

Travelling fifteen hours to get here, driving in pitch-blackness, rust and green roadside foliage lit by headlights, teeming with deer. Arriving at the artists' shared house, four people in the kitchen sit, hooked up to laptops, headphones, screens showing sound graphics. Is anywhere really remote?

The sea is a few feet from the house. This morning a yellow lobster trawler circles the bay, waves colliding with rock ramparts. Fingers of wet volcanic rock test the waters. The view shifts minute by minute with weather and tide. Low roiling clouds look at the sea and at the land as if in a mirror. The ground is wildly hummocky. Air smells of soil, seaweed and pinecones. A stone seat lodges like a cushion in the crooks of a tree's many elbows. Water drops silver in matted grass, trickle to part long reeds, slip down banks, barge past rocks in the stream, thunder over small falls, linger in peaty rock pools.

Chinnery builds a human nest, Kirsteen Davidson Kelly plays piano in the woods. Mark Vernon, Gilchrist and Joelson's broadcast *The Sound of Lochaber*: milking cows, shearing sheep, reducing duck fat, a cockerel's crow, the animal auction bell.

Even here, the sound of roads is relentless as wind. Sixty-one million people in ninety-three thousand square miles of land in Britain, thirty million cars, two hundred and ten thousand miles of road, but five thousand islands, five hundred mountains, three hundred rivers (Macfarlane, 2008, pp. 9–11).

Sarah Kenchington clambers across a litter of huge rocks on the beach. Washing machine hoses, a trumpet, inner tubes, a foot pump, marigold gloves wave loose like tentacles from her backpack. Everything is connected together with balloons, improvised washers and sticky tape and then fixed to a long pipe washed up in the wrack line. The sea adds its own spit and low bass note to this wind instrument in the surf. Dusk falls over the bay. Rocks are black hump silhouettes like whales against pale blue and pink streaks of sky. A pine marten comes to eat a jam sandwich on the deck.

Remoteness is fluid. It is spatial and temporal, psychological and geographic. In remoteness, removed from daily routines and networks, the self and the world become strange new locales for exploration and reportage.

DAY 2 – SOUNDINGS

TUESDAY 5 AUGUST, FORT WILLIAM, GLEN NEVIS, LOCH AILORT

This morning mackerel are boiling in the waters of the bay and Lee Patterson spots otter spraint on the rocks. Bram Thomas Arnold borrows a desk and chair from New Start Highland charity shop, lugs it up to the top of Cow Hill and performs *Swearing an Oath to a Scottish Glen* against the distant backdrop of Loch Linnhe. Later in the day, Bram reads an introduction to particle physics to a river. Lee, Benedict Drew and Lisa O'Brien are foraging for sound up the glen. The tiny space of the *Outlandia* treehouse reverberates with Gaelic music: Ingrid Henderson's *clàrsach* and The Cèilidh Trailers.

Geoff Sample has been recording nature sound in the Highlands for twenty-five years. Glen Nevis, he says, is the most extreme glen with the highest amplitude of relief in Britain, an unbroken drop from 4,400 feet to sea level, and a unique acoustic space. Fewer insects and amphibians here mean that dominant sounds are wind, running water, birds and mammals.

Working with seven other writers—Nuno Sacramento, Alison Lloyd, Gillian Ness, Lorna Finlayson, Anne Claydon-Wallace, Gay Anderson and Carol Brock—I explore maps at the Lochaber Archive Centre. Words on maps are rearranged into our own texts. We imagine our way into the maps. Lorna Simpson's enigmatic flash stories prompt us to use maps as visual aids to write our own. Map Reading OS Explorer 392 Ben Nevis and Fort William: forest, stone, hill, ford, cairn, ridge, waterfall, steppingstones, gully, shelter.

In the afternoon, we start at the Glen Nevis Visitor Centre, take some lines for a walk, write about portable objects we pick up on our walk. I pick up a brown stone with four flattened sides from the stream. As it dries, it reveals itself as skin-coloured, freckled like a lover's arm. Ed Baxter joins us, recording some of the writings and discussions. Arriving at the Wishing Stone, Ed hops around it three times. It used to revolve to tell the future, but now it's given up moving itself and we have to do the revolving.

This evening, Gilchrist and Lee are out on the bay in a canoe at dusk with hydrophones recording shrimp cracking underwater. As twilight falls, Peter Lanceley plays a haunting guitar accompaniment to White's performance of his story *Stormbringer*. Words roll and rollick like pebbles in the surf.

I am learning the moon for the new novel I am writing. Tonight the moon is waxing gibbous. Moon jellyfish dangle tentacles in the sliding, dark waters.

DAY 3 – OFF THE GRID RADIO

WEDNESDAY 6 AUGUST, GLEN NEVIS AND LOCH AILORT

Trying to make live radio broadcasts from an off-grid studio up a steep track is of course, perverse. Malfunction, as Johny Brown observed at breakfast, is part of it—and that malfunction might be both technological and human. The *Remote Performances* project, with Resonance 104.4fm broadcasting from *Outlandia*, a hut up a tree in Glen Nevis, has been a challenge, but beyond that, the artists and other contributors are on a rollercoaster of making, editing and broadcasting, with not much time to draw breath between. The complexity of the logistics is fierce: generators, satellites, transport, harsh walks uphill in rain and midge, with heavy and fragile equipment, and above all juggling time, but this difficulty is proving to be wildly constructive.

Today's broadcast ranged across Mozart, Morse Code, Johnny Rotten and Fleetwood Mac's *Albatross*; and included Kenchington's whale-wave-wind-like music, played on DIY instruments in the sea, producing melodic wheezings, groanings, snorings and huffings; Lisa O'Brien's sound artworks inspired by weather and landscape in the Highlands; White's new story *High-Lands*, written here over the last few days from a desk looking out over islands, sunsets and cormorants.

Sheep farmer Ian McColl made the journey up the precipitous peat track to *Outlandia* for a discussion with Nevis Radio presenter, Isobel Campbell, who also runs the Lochaber Rural Education Centre. Ian had with him a very finely carved wood and horn shepherd's crook, the black and ivory handle worn glossy and marbled from the slide of a hand over the years. He and Isobel discussed changes and challenges in farming in Lochaber.

Tam Dean Burn interviewed historian Alex Du Toit from the Lochaber Archive Centre. They talked about the Clearings, the Jacobite Risings and the nineteenth-century Kirk's attempt to curtail whisky consumption at funerals to a maximum of six glasses. Alex described how the Harry Potter Quidditch scenes were filmed at the viaduct in the glen. Researchers at the archives include the Local History Society and Scottish Diaspora visitors from Canada, Australia and New Zealand, who are looking for information on their ancestors.

Continuing his series of absurd and effortful interactions with 'nature', Bram Thomas Arnold threw rocks at trees today, but nature appeared as impassive to this as to his oaths and particle physics lecture yesterday. Geoff Sample experimented with a lyrical performance drawing on experiences of working in the landscape, recording stags and eagles.

So at the end of four hours of broadcasting, when Johny Brown gently told the listeners: 'We have to leave our nest in the trees here now and the mist is coming down over Ben Nevis opposite', there was a sense of reluctant withdrawal from an eclectic, evocative soundscape ... until tomorrow.

DAY 4 – AND THEN ...

THURSDAY 7 AUGUST, LOCH AILORT AND GLEN NEVIS

The kitchen is littered with booms, mics, amps, cabling, laptops, and guitars. A pod of dolphins in the bay witnessed from the kitchen window. Emerald vegetation clothes craggy mountains and loch banks, looking like a snug snooker cloth draped over them from the sky.

Chinnery, dressed in feathers and whistles, making birdcalls, is a cross between a camouflaged hunter and a shaman. Baxter is whistling up sheepdogs and Burn is yodelling Shakespeare across the glen.

Broadcasting today in the *Outlandia* hut: Alex Gillespie and Willie Anderson tell yarns of their experiences as veterans of the Nevis Mountain Rescue Team; White and Lanceley perform *Stormbringer*, a story set on Sanda Island; Finlayson and I present *Taking Four Sentences for a Walk*, an account of the writers' workshop; and Ruth Barker's electric performance is a retelling of ancient myths.

'Nature! my arse!' declares Nuno Sacramento in the writers' workshop, responding to roads, fences, trails, and other signs of control and exploitation in the managed landscape. There is a hubris in the presumption of ownership of this place or any other natural environment. Inhabitants are only slightly less temporary, less frivolous, than tourists in the scale of things.

Late at night on the road a stag confronts us in the headlights—like a dream.

DAY 5 – CLIMBING A MOUNTAIN IN BLUE SUEDE SHOES*

FRIDAY 8 AUGUST, GLEN NEVIS

Performance—A display of exaggerated behaviour or process involving a great deal of unnecessary time, effort and fuss.

Artists and guests are performing on Resonance 104.4fm at *Outlandia*, and the weather is performing too with rain slewing in. Many visitors from the local community and some of the contributing artists are encountering *Outlandia* for the first time: a little hut in the forest that has become a big performance space this week—cramming in several bands, a harp, a host of live guests, and broadcasting to an international audience.

The Sound of Lochaber today, from Vernon and London Field-works, was reminiscences during a journey on the Jacobite steam train from Maillaig to Fort William. Tam Dean Burn was in conversation with Emma Nicholson from Atlas Arts on Skye and with John Hutchison, chairman of the John Muir Trust and the Isle of Eigg Heritage Trust. Emma described the current Atlas Arts' project, *Are You LOCATIONALIZED* by Joanne Tatham and Tom O'Sullivan, and she talked about coming to the *Outlandia* opening event four years ago, when the cloud was beneath the level of the treehouse. John Hutchison discussed the John Muir Trust's guardianship of the top of Ben Nevis and other wild lands quoting, 'You cannot own the land, the land owns you'. The Ben Nevis footpath, he said, is used by two hundred thousand people a year.

Laura Davies and Liam MacLean from Fort William presented a music performance and talked about life as young musicians in the Highlands with Baxter. Bram Thomas Arnold read Scottish poetry to a rock in his *Actions for and Against Nature*. Alec Finlay and Ken Cockburn performed *The Road North*, a panegyric to the landscape, revelling in the beauty of the natural environment. Johny Brown and James Stephen Finn presented *The North is Another Land*, with lyrics ranging through lost love to Scottish Independence. Michael Pedersen and Ziggy Campbell's broadcast was a visceral mix of poetry, song and found sounds, including pigs and a crackling fire. Lee Patterson's new soundwork, made on the shores of Loch Ailort and in Glen Nevis, mixed 'natural' sounds with human and especially technological noises: the drama of thunder and rain mixed with the noises of a failed satellite connection and the conversation of the anxious, coping radio crew: 'don't worry'—'what's that, Sarah? —'What have we got now?'—'Nothing'. Cutting in amidst waterfall, water drips and the pulses of underwater life were thrummed piano strings, a tapped microphone.

Another exaggerated and necessary day up the steep peat track and across the bog board walk to the *Outlandia* treehouse radio station.

* Michael Pedersen

DAY 6 – WILD RADIO

SATURDAY 9 AUGUST, GLEN NEVIS

The final day of broadcasting from *Outlandia* included a discussion with John Ireland from the Forestry Commission, more music from local musician Ingrid Henderson, and a series of new artworks responding to the Glen Nevis environment. Johny Brown's radio drama, *Into Outlandia*, performed by Tam Dean Burn, took an old folk tale of four hunters and four vixens and updated it, evoking the urban, outsider dream of the Other Remote Place. Benedict Drew's *The Brave Tapes* and the broadcasts by Goodiepal and Baxter took different approaches to forms of communication—whistling, yodelling, shouting across spaces, fragmented texts concerned with nature and technologies—fragmented experiences and histories. Geoff Sample's recordings of bird and animal calls suggested a parallel with the human voices tickling or assaulting our ears via the medium of radio.

Outlandia, Goodiepal remarked, is an urban dream: a romantic, magical treehouse, architect-designed, hanging in the trees with a view of mountains, visually expressing a hankering for return to childhood, escape from social convention and rules, immersion in Another Green Place. It is a microcosmic expression of a world and a life we would like to make and have that is so very different from the world we have made and move in. *Remote Performances* was broadcasting live to London via an almost silent hydrogen-fuel-cell generator and tooway satellite, engaging with the off-grid.

What is the result of mixing sessions with local musicians and interviews with local people giving a slice of local life, with works made by artists coming from around Scotland and further afield? This mix reflects back to Lochaber inhabitants their own experiences and contexts and expresses outsider longings for a far and different place. It captures hereness in Glen Nevis from many angles.

Before the inventions and widespread use of TV and the internet, radio was the dominant mode of mass communication. Now broadcasting offers a space for performance and reflection that is archaic and yet also a future form, a potentiality, a 'free space' (another Goodiepal concept) for self-definition unencumbered by the conventions and assumptions of previous generations.

Radio whispers its voices and sounds intimately into your ear, seeming to speak only to you. Radio satisfies the old need to hear stories reflecting human experiences.

27
PIET MONDRIAN: THE AFTERLIFE

2014. Review of Nancy J. Troy, *The Afterlife of Piet Mondrian*, first published in *Times Higher Education*, 7 April.

'The living fight over the bones,' Robert Motherwell remarked after Piet Mondrian's funeral in 1944 in New York. Seventy years after the Dutch artist's death, sale prices for his artworks have rocketed to $40 million (£24 million) from a maximum of $800 during his lifetime, and his style continues to find echoes in design, fashion and architecture. American art historian Nancy Troy takes the reader on an eye-opening tour across the battleground of the artist's posthumous reception. Mondrian's works did not simply appear or speak for themselves but were instead disseminated through the filter of the many vested interests of his heirs, friends, collectors, dealers, curators, scholars and artists. Troy candidly acknowledges her own place in the ranks of those implicated in these processes, which Duchamp referred to as 'the posterity'.

Troy vividly evokes the uneasy pact between impecunious artists with utopian and egalitarian ideas and corporate interests manipulating the artists' work for their own agendas. She tracks Mondrian's afterlife through court cases, auctions, exhibitions and 'the promotional juggernaut' of the 1994 Year of Mondrian in the Netherlands with its Mondriania of mugs and tea towels, taking us behind the scenes to witness a series of unholy alliances and unsavoury spats. The tale she tells veers between the sorry and the comic, full of misguided conservations, dubious attributions and items thrown out by cleaners or lost by auctioneers.

Mondrian was not a prolific artist and as the monetary value of his works climbed there was a temptation to find ways to 'expand' his oeuvre, or as one commentator put it, to make something from 'the dregs of the estate'. This urge was entangled with a desire to revere everything the artist had touched, like a saint's relics. Sustaining a polite tone throughout, yet nevertheless damning with the devil of the details she uncovers, Troy writes:

> Copies of one of his most important works (*Victory Boogie Woogie*) have stood in for the original; historical documents have been marshaled to support the authenticity of reconstructions (the 'Wall Works'); and what began as the artist's furniture was later presented as sculpture. (2014)

Throughout *The Afterlife of Piet Mondrian*, we catch glimpses of neglected aspects of his work: the gulf between the painted surfaces of his originals and the graphic power of their glossy reproductions; the significance to him of watching Europe devastated a second time by world war, his homeland and adopted country of France occupied by Nazis, and the deaths of fellow artists and intellectuals. Troy's focus, however, remains firmly on dissemination rather than on a reading of the artworks.

Mondrian's work provoked controversy over the value, monetary and otherwise, of modern art, and he continues to be perceived as an abstract artist whose works are difficult to understand in the context of a persisting preference for figurative art. Yet his work pervaded popular culture, from L'Oréal cosmetics packaging to jigsaw puzzles to Yves Saint Laurent dresses.

This is an important, meticulously researched contribution to the story of how modern art was embedded in and exploited by corporate wealth and how it influenced every aspect of visual culture. Troy asks whether becoming a brand laid waste to the depth of meaning Mondrian invested in his art. Despite their posthumous adventures, perhaps Mondrian's paintings are not unduly threatened by the discourses they provoke, or perhaps those discourses themselves, as Duchamp suggested, constitute the art.

28

HAYLEY NEWMAN AND EMILY SPEED: THE PRACTICE OF SPACE

2013. First published online http://www.castlefieldgallery.co.uk/event/hayley-newman-emily-speed/. Manchester: Castlefield Gallery.

'To live is to pass from one space to another, while doing your very best not to bump yourself.'

—Georges Perec, *Species of Spaces*

WHAT WE MOVE ABOUT IN THE MIDST OF

Hayley Newman and Emily Speed's artworks consider the body in space and depict a bodily understanding of spaces. They address the social production of space and the social construction of needs. They are making work about dwelling in the body, in houses, in cities, on the planet, in the universe.

In her work *Inhabitant* (2009), Speed moves around Linz wearing an accretion of cardboard boxes and model houses. In this performance, she becomes one of her own drawings of hybrid body-buildings in which buildings are worn like armour or a shell, with just two bare legs protruding. She wears ephemeral architecture that conceals and protects her, but also blinds her, making her dependent on passers-by to keep her moving safely.

In her novella, *Common* (2013), Newman presents a fictionalised account of one day as self-appointed artist-in-residence in the City of London. She moves through the spaces of the city, charting riots and the crash of global markets and currencies. Newman engages in a critical inhabiting of the city.

Space is not fixed, but always being made, always unfinished and open. It is not a given but is socially constructed. Henri Lefebvre describes space and the political organisation of space as expressive of social relationships but also reflecting back on them (1991). Edward Soja writes that social relations are both space-forming and space-contingent (1989). We are always inhabiting some kind of space—bed, shed, house, garden, office, car, train, street. Spaces hide us, defend us, express us and constrain us. They are shelters, refuges, retreats, snugs, perches and nooks. In spaces we generate, store, recuperate, regenerate, are intimate, private or public. Spaces are our territories, our castles, our nests. They make us comfortable or agoraphobic or claustrophobic. The spaces we make reflect our psychological needs, our physical needs, our social, economic and political beliefs and structures. We wear space, formed from the inside, like a carapace, and Doreen Massey writes that space presents us with a continuous series of encounters between bundles of trajectories (2005; also see Rendell, 2006; Scarry, 1985).

A GARMENT-HOUSE AND THE FUNCTION OF INHABITING

Speed's *Human Castle* (2012) was shown in a park as a live performance during the Edinburgh Festival, and also exists as a moving image work. Ten acro-balancers, directed by Speed, gradually converge, the women wearing strange shapes strapped to their backs that look like geometrical wings. At first, in pairs, they try balancing on each other knees, hands, shoulders, and then eventually they form a circle with the women on the men's shoulders, unfolding their 'wings', which are revealed to be drapes resembling castle walls topped by felt crenellations. The performers sustain the shape, or the collective costume, of the ephemeral castle briefly, before the women carefully regain the ground and the castle collapses. At the Beaux Arts Ball in New York in 1931, the architects of the Chrysler Building and other skyscrapers wore cardboard versions of their own structures.

In her work, Speed variously wears buildings, furniture and boats, which evoke defensive shells for the frail human body that can be glimpsed merely with bare legs and feet. Bourgeois' *Femme Maison* drawing depicts a naked woman whose head and torso are concealed by a house. Speed also cites literary influences on her work, such as Italo Calvino, Kobo Abe and Mark Z. Daniewleski. Her architecture costumes are usually constructed using the consumer detritus of packaging, which, in a harsh irony, is often used by the homeless as flimsy shelter.

Speed's hybrid body-buildings express a paradox (or two). On the one hand, they are concerned with the construction of the self. Playing house, playing with dolls' houses, building childhood base-camps are all ways in which we use habitats to explore and project our own sense of identity. These spaces also express the desire to conceal who we are or to conceal ourselves altogether, to be invisible and invulnerable behind a mask or costume. On the other hand, the hybridisation of body with building expresses a sense of fragility and mortality. A huff and a puff could blow the house down that is bodged from cardboard.

Spaces habitually inhabited make an impression on the body and our bodies and their actions imprint themselves on our environments. The novelist Thomas Hardy noted how one side of a stone floor in a church doorway was worn down by countless feet. Space can become a habit, a well-worn garment, and our bodies become habituated to moving in well-known spaces. Bachelard writes that he longs to know the psychological history of each of our muscles (1964).

In her new work, *Build Up* (2013), Speed works with acrobats in the Toastrack building in Manchester, creating a series of construction exercises, where the body engages in a cyclical repetition of movement that becomes a rhythm of building and collapsing. In some of the still images produced, dancers' limbs clad a stairwell, describing space with the body. Speed's work relates to Oskar Schlemmer's examination of the body in space in paintings such as *Group of 14 in an Imaginary Architecture* (1930) and *Bauhaus Staircase* (1932), and his recently renovated murals of figures and dancing bodies in the stairwell of the Bauhaus Workshop Building in Weimar. In *Slat Dance* (1920s) or *The Triadic Ballet* (1922), Schlemmer padded and riveted geometric shapes and inflexible materials onto the body, shaping it, modifying it and constraining it, articulating space with costumed bodies rather than delineating characters (Gropius, 1961). Speed's work depicts the body moving about in the midst of space, defining, and being defined.

SERIOUS BUFFOONERY

Many of Newman's works also use costumes and masks. In *Volcano Lady* (2004–2006), she made studio photographs and a performance wearing a costume that resembled an erupting volcano: first ashy and smokey, and then, when she does a headstand, revealing flaming lava-red bloomers beneath.

The work references Toyen's Surrealist painting *Relâche* (1943), which depicts a female body upside down, her feet merging with the wall and her head covered by her inverted clothing. But while there is a dreamlike irrationality to Toyen's image, Newman's

Volcano Lady comically enacts an uncompromising image of natural force—erupting volcano and female sexuality.

In *Domestique* (2012–2013), Newman created 'portraits' with seventy worn-out dishcloths. In a performance with one of these cloths covering her face, she references the nameless, faceless people labouring in sweatshops where the cloths are made. The dishcloths are abject and almost without value. *Façadism* (2013) is a selection of short stories about faces and references the facades of buildings, which, like the dishcloths, can often have an uncanny resemblance to faces. The stories examine the honest, masked, and false faces people present to the world and to other people. Not all faces can be read like an open book.

In *Histoire Economique* (2013), Newman performs a series of bank rubbings, treating banks as part of a bygone heritage like a castle, a stately mansion or a knight's grave, the pun of bank rubbings suggesting robbery, erasure and brass rubbings. In several works (*Connotations, Common, Daily Hayley*), Newman uses faction—playing imaginatively, fictitiously with real space and times subjected to fiction to question the validity of the information that is disseminated, that we receive. Newman's imagination and focus is civic and social, driven by and through political philosophy, making manifest the invisible ideological architectures we create and live in (hierarchies, capitalism, dogmas).

Her work employs a Dadaist absurdity to address serous issues in our ecologies and economies. At Cabaret Voltaire in 1916, one of the founders of Dada, Hugo Ball, had to be carried on and off stage in a shiny blue cylinder costume with lobster hands since he couldn't move. Like many ritual costumes, Ball's outfit as a 'Magical Bishop' was both ridiculous and serious. Newman's use of costumes and masks also has this aspect of both satire and uncanny. She manifests the invisible, turning it into an entity with her costumes and actions (*Spoon Lady, Suicide Cat*) so that it can be looked at with pinned-open eyes, its injustices lanced with ridicule. Clowns and jesters wore costumes and facial masks or makeup to look ludicrous and comical but also to give them some protection from the backlash against the hard truths they spoke, the things it is just not polite to actually say.

Singing in the collective, The Gluts, and co-founding Capitalists Anonymous, the humour in Newman's work has an uncomfortable, iconoclastic edge. We don't want to look at a spot on the end of a nose; it's a bit awkward to observe *Volcano Lady*'s red drawers; we'd rather not have to think about sweatshops or really changing our lives because of climate change.

IN THE WOODSHED

Newman's *Woodshed* was a temporary structure built in Beaconsfield Gallery in London, referencing the slang definition of 'woodshedding' as a slightly removed place for practising (usually music), but, in this case, a range of creative skills and making. While there are points of connection between Newman and Speed's work: employing performance, sculpture, photography and text to explore the body's relationship with space, the emphasis of their individual approaches to this topic and the materials they draw on differ. Speed's emphasis is on the psychology of space in relation to the body. Newman concentrates more on a political satire of social space in relation to the body. They effectively and differently embrace the spatial turn in critical and creative practice, manifesting the rich potential of space as a tool for making, thinking and being.

29
ON THE TIP OF MY TONGUE

2013. First published in *Journal of Writing in Creative Practice*, 6:1, pp. 107–125.

'I hate writing' is a commonly heard refrain from artists and art students and voiced again at a Writing Pad workshop at Arnolfini last March. In 1959, Situationists Guy Debord and Ager Jorn published a book with sandpaper covers aiming to erode all other books placed alongside it on a bookshelf (Debord and Jorn, 1959). One of the arguments of Modernism was that visual art was concerned with the 'unsayable' and entirely separate from literature. Richard Serra declared that 'art is not a descriptive discipline ... linguistic mapping or reconstructing, or interpretation or explanation is a linguistic debasement' (cited in Weiss, 2004, p. 212). 'I don't like the incorporation of the nameable in sculpture,' wrote Carl Andre (cited in Weiss, 2004, p. 212). In 1992, I worked as a curator with Czech artist, Cerny and set up a TV interview for him. When the TV crew turned on the cameras and the microphones, he just said: 'I make art. I don't talk about it', so I was forced to gabble about his work instead of him. There is a notion that art conveys ideas and feelings that are best expressed visually so therefore why overlay it with text. Nevertheless, many artists have extensively used language, as part of artworks, in titles for artworks, in manifestos, in critical and self-reflective texts. In 1968, Smithson used the phrase, 'language in the vicinity of art' in the title of one of his artworks.

At the same time as professing to hate writing, the artists at the Writing Pad event at Arnolfini took to writing with relish. They relished sited writing that enabled them to write in different places —on the wall, on the floor, on the ceiling. They relished a materials and tools approach to writing: choosing ink, diverse pens, pencils and means of making a mark, post-its, big sheets of paper, other surfaces. The appeal of materials and forms for artists, in conjunction with writing, was also evident in an Art Writing workshop at Modern Art Oxford, which I led with Jerome Fletcher in 2011, where the participants made boxes to write in and on.

The conviction for artists that they can't write has its counterpart in writers who are certain they can't draw—me for one. Yet surely writing and drawing have a kinship in marking and expressing? Is it writing itself that artists really hate, or is it the ways in which it is taught? Is it the straitjacket of academic writing that they are really reacting against?

Dyslexia is very high among Fine Art students. I teach 'theory' to Fine Art undergraduates and postgraduates at Oxford Brookes University. Among my own students, around 20% are dyslexic and this takes various forms. Many dyslexics are extremely good at writing but have to come at both reading and writing in their own adapted and different ways. Dyslexia, however, is not the whole story of the writing phobia among Fine Art students. Many students who are not dyslexic also profess an allergy for writing—at least at the beginning of their studies. I try to win them round by showing them how text—reading it and writing it—can inform and inspire their art practice, by getting them to look at other artists' writings, such as texts by Duchamp, Turrell, Smithson, Carl Andre, Bill Viola, Bacon. We study various modes of artists' writings—from the essay, interview and artist's talk to the letter, blog, website, artist's book. One of my students constructed a series of postcard exchanges with Charles Baudelaire. Another constructed an exchange of letters between someone with her first name and someone with her middle name. Another wrote to a cupboard in her kitchen that was significant in her childhood. We look at how some artists use text as their material, such as Fiona Banner, Alec Finlay, Matthew Buckingham. We look at art journals and magazines, including *Cabinet* and *The Happy Hypocrite* and at publishers, such as *Black Dog, Book Works, Revolver* and *Visual Editions*.

I wrote that I teach 'theory' above in inverted commas, because this is something of a misnomer for what I actually teach. There is some theory in there, but we don't limit our explorations to art theory, promiscuously hunting too (as the artist does for their practice research) through philosophy, literature, geography, history, ecology, political philosophy and science texts. I am not interested in trying, in a few short modules, to get Fine Art students to attempt to become partial art historians or art theorists. Instead, I aim to help them find ways to draw inspiration for their own practice from text, to enable them to enhance their research skills and their means of articulating their concerns.

My 'theory' lectures include asking the students to produce and present their own manifestos and in the third year I run an Art Writing module, where they produce written work relating to their own practice. We draw on the Oxford Brookes Special Collection of Artists' Books for inspiration and many of the students produce hand-made books or use Lulu or Blurb or produce websites and blogs, as well as interviewing themselves or each other or preparing a gallery talk on their work. One student had herself photographed reading the Dada manifesto while sitting on a toilet. A few have written film scripts and made moving image works about their own work. Last year, an Oxford Brookes student, Tiffany Horan, was one of the winners of the *an* 'Degrees Unedited Blog Award'. Others produce creative writing that runs parallel to their practice, drawing on inspirations such as Don DeLillo and John Berger. I encourage them to see writing as part of the palette and material they can draw on, alongside the other elements of their art practice, rather than something difficult and in opposition to making art.

The Writing Pad event at Arnolfini, Bristol invited manifestos and papers, so I worked with my students to produce a 'Manifesto Wall'. I stuck sheets of blank paper on a wall with the invitation to comment, draw or otherwise manifest attitudes to text in relation to art practice. For the first day, there were only a few contributions to the wall, and I thought that it wasn't going to take, but then, gradually, it became a rolling stone gathering moss. More and more contributions began to appear. The students also contributed via email, Facebook and Twitter. Several students kept coming back, having had new ideas they wanted to get up there. When there was a significant amount on the wall, they then began to 'edit' it—moving things around, cutting things out, grouping, highlighting. After four days, there was next to no blank paper visible. We took it off the wall, rolled it up and took it to the Writing Pad event in Bristol.

One of the students wrote on the Manifesto Wall: 'art can speak for itself', and of course it can, but we do not need to perpetuate a resentful division between art and writing that stems from earlier traditions in which writing meant singular, authoritative art judgement and interpretation. We do not have to perpetuate the fallacious idea that art is a creative practice and writing is not. *Ekphrasis*, the interplay between the visual and the linguistic, is an ancient art.

Now that critics no longer have to function as authoritative interpreters, deliverers of a singular meaning, we can cease warfare with the logocentric and look instead for the contingencies between language and art. We can acknowledge the subjectivity in writing, that writing is always situated and incorporates the subjective act of witnessing.

Artists and writers were always functioning in tandem in the avant-garde art groups of the early twentieth century and used the space of the journal or magazine as an art space. Jeffrey Weiss has noted that 1960–1975 was a period when art was

> attended by massive quantities of artists' words', including lists, inventories, tables and lexicons. Many artists in this period were significant critical writers, including Donald Judd, Smithson, Mel Bochner and Robert Morris ... writing about the paradigm shift was a way of processing it on the run ... artists became their own best witnesses. (2004, p. 214)

In June 2012, Writing Pad organised another workshop, this time in London, called *Translating: Pairing Practice*, examining the relationship between writers and artists. Since this is central to my own practice, I ran one of the workshops in collaboration with artist, Bruce Gilchrist. Gilchrist and I have repeatedly worked together as writer and artist over the last two decades (see, for examples, Warr, 1996a, 2001c, 2002a, 2005, 2010). Our workshop was an exercise enabling participants to actively explore what happens in the exchange between writers and artists. Working in pairs, they described to each other one of their artworks currently in progress. Then they undertook a performative action some-where in or around the building that related to what they had just heard. Then they wrote on newsprint on the wall or floor a short text on their partner's work in progress. Then they read each other's texts and discussed what was unexpected about what had been written. Then they selected one of the texts (not from their own pair) and drew something in response to it. We ended with a discussion on what had emerged from listening and translating a description of an artwork into a text and from translating a text into a drawing.

Writing does not occur sitting at a desk or at a computer. Rewriting and editing happen there. Writing occurs when walking with thoughts, between sleep and waking, during sleep, or soaking in a bath. At those times, strands of words congeal significantly to give the threads of writing to follow. I don't know what I am going to write about an artist's work when I begin writing. I find out through the practice of writing. 'How can I tell what I think till I see what I say' (Forster, 1927, p. 99). Writing is not simply the wielding of language as a vehicle to carry pre-thought meaning. Writing practice is, itself, the tool to uncover and reveal meaning. It is a journey into the unknown. 'Art writing isn't only a forum for one's ideas, it's also a process for discovering them' (Mel Bochner, cited in Weiss, 2004, p. 211).

Reading occurs on either side of writing. Before writing begins the writer must 'read' their subject. That might involve close looking at an artwork or site, for instance, or close listening in conversation with an artist or others, alongside research on the topic. I am reading my topic before I begin to write, acting as medium between it and the text I will produce, channelling it. Then I write a text and in turn that text is open to be actively read by a reader, bringing their own associations and understandings to it, each reader reading with different emphases.

Writing is the practice of doing it, of making a text. Language comprises the materials and techniques used in writing. Text is the object produced, that the reader interacts imaginatively with—and that doesn't have to be fixed, as one of my Oxford Brookes students, Eleanor Greenhalgh, demonstrated with her remixable erotica text 'Open Sauce', created for her degree show last year.

I suspect that notions of impromptu, improvisation, spontaneity, may be overrated. We often rehearse our words first in the privacy of our own brains, talking to ourselves, then in conversation perhaps, and then in writing. But, on the other hand, I like to say that sometimes: I open my mouth and words fall out of it, words that take me by surprise. We don't think in fully formed language—in sentences, but in images or words that are short-hand for miles of scrolling other words and meanings.

I often recycle, reuse, appropriate my own texts—putting them through some transformation in the reuse. Just as artists often have one core concern that they return to again and again with different approaches, so too do writers. I frequently revisit a handful of key sources (Bachelard, 1992; Bataille, 1929; Douglas, 1966; Joyce, 1939; James, 1890; Perec, 1997; Scarry, 1985), which are the knot of my influences and concerns around the practice of space and the embodied consciousness in dynamic relationship with its environment. My PhD was called *The Creative Act: A Commodius Vicus of Recirculation—Writing and Curating With Artists*.

Writing needs provocations—a wall, a blank page, a deadline, a commission, a nice notebook and pen. Then writing is generating and spinning out words. It needs procrastination. It cannot be forced—you have to trust that it will come. Then you hone what comes. Sculpting, shaping, reordering, clarifying, cutting, expanding, elaborating, structuring, making it flow, hearing the voice of the text.

Writing doesn't just consist of writing. It also consists of days of thinking unconsciously, of not writing, of waiting. I am capable of being a disciplined writer—of setting myself a schedule to produce one thousand words a day, but I also believe in going with the flow and waiting for the mood to take you if you can. Shifts and extractions from your normal routines—an odd new notebook, a journey on a train, a few days in a hotel room—can shake writing out of you.

The writer enters the topic. The reader enters the text. Misremembered reading is interesting—where you go back to a book to look for a quote you are sure is there, but it isn't, because it is something you added as a reader.

What is on the tip of my tongue—that is what I am chasing and trying to corner when I write. William James has an interesting description of what happens in consciousness when we are trying to remember a forgotten name. He says that the empty space where the name should be is specific to the shape of the name—we can't remember the name, but we know that other names don't fit that space (1890, pp. 251–252).

An example of my own writing practice in the vicinity of art is 'Raw Presence' on Elpida Hadzi-Vasileva's Gloucester Cathedral residency (Warr, 2009a, pp. 15–18). It was speculative in the sense that I had to write it before the artwork was finished and visible, which is often the case when writing an art catalogue essay. Hadzi-Vasileva's work creates beauty out of the disgusting—lard, entrails, skin, bones. Her studio sometimes resembles and smells like a charnel house. This text was the result of close attention to a single conversation with the artist, a visit to her studio and to the site where the works would be installed—Gloucester Cathedral, and then combining that with my own ongoing preoccupations with the *informe*.

I am interested in writing as documentation and its advantages and disadvantages over photographic forms of documentation. One of my students recently used writing instead of images for a project on prostitutes in Oxford. Images would have been prurient and intrusive. Writing as document enabled her to incorporate her own point of view, her empathy and experience. Instead of exposing, writing can protect and cherish its subject. Instead of examining, analysing, carrying out a post-mortem, writing can enable the reader to resuscitate and resurrect what is gone and done.

Writing often functions as a sketch or proposition for art, and most art funding and commissioning focuses on a written speculative account rather than on drawings or models. This is an area of art writing not to be underestimated, where the writer has to engage in the creative act of making something from nothing, conjuring an image in the mind of the reader of a thing that does not yet exist.

Are my texts on art, critical texts or creative writing? 'Sometime in the near future it may be necessary for the writer to be an artist as well as for the artist to be a writer', wrote Lucy Lippard and John Chandler (1968, p. 35). I think my texts are creative writing. I'm not especially interested in judging or explaining in writing, but rather in expanding, imagining, entering my subject. I suppose I have already prejudged by being interested enough to write about something. Text invokes.

30

OPTIK: A MOVING MEDITATION ON A DEAD LINE

2004. First published in *Performance Research*, 8(4), pp. 130–136, DOI: 10.1080/13528165.2003.10871978. *Performance Research* is published by Taylor & Francis: https://www.tandfonline.com/.

interrupted. All the time and eventually irretrievably. Although Bataille sees life disrupting the continuity of death. Continuity and/or caesura. Moving and stopping.

Moving. Going

In October 2001, I went with U.K. performance group, Optik, to Sao Paulo, Brazil (Edwards, 2003). Optik explore moving. And
    walking lying feeling
    running standing focusing
    colliding sitting waiting

rocking seeing deciding
falling looking being
rolling listening stopping.

Walking

Taking a line for a walk. The three Optik performers walk and run in straight lines with Brazilian students in dance studios in Sao Paulo and Campinhas. Their lines are moving sculpture in space. They make fleeting connections and collaborations. They fill a space, a void, gaps, with their moving. They fall into entrainment—walking or running together. They mirror each other. They lie down on the spot where someone else has just stood up. They walk to an internal rhythm—a body clock. They invade or do not invade invisible territories—body space, in your face. They do not go backwards. They do not waver from their straight line. No circling, serpentining or wriggling. I sit on the floor watching, their static recorder. Grounded.

Writing

Taking my line for its walk on the page of my notebook. Filling that void with lines of writing. A line is a purpose. A line is definite. It is a mark, a definition. It is a seam or a zip between one thing and another. A line has continuity, connection, coherence, consecutiveness, duration, a beginning and an end, direction but reversibility. It defines, outlines, manifests invisible and imaginary spaces and things. A line is a border, between one thing and another. A border between self and world. Dead straight. A sign of time on a face. A timeline. A dropped plumb line sounding the depths of consciousness.

Taking a line for a walk through a 'commodius vicus of recirculation' as James Joyce puts it at the beginning, or mid-point, or some point or other, of *Finnegans Wake*. Early in the twentieth century, writers took lines for walks along streams of consciousness, painters took lines for unconscious walks and performers explored the movements of the unchoreographed body in relation to consciousness. The consciousness of Dorothy Richardson's heroine, Miriam, streams along her life as a writer; Joyce's Bloom walks around Dublin for twenty-four hours thinking, mulling it over; Paul Klee takes his line for a walk, dawdling and doodling; the Surrealists do *frottage*, *fumage*, and commit *decalcomania*. Andre Masson's automatic drawings are scrawled lines, graphic apparitions on the paper, pure gesture, rhythm and incantation, and Jackson Pollock is first a still centre of meditation, a vacuum, and then a moving, flinging line of paint. Three mathematicians have analysed Pollock's drip paintings and found that his trance-danced skeins of paint slung with gravity map onto fractals (Taylor *et al.*, 2000, pp. 137–150). They are patterns that replicate the chaotic motion of nature—how snow falls, how forests grow, how turbulence moves in water. Fractals are not detectable or do-able on a conscious level. Of course there is conscious forming operating in all those artists' unconsciousnesses, but still only a tiny proportion of our experience is consciously thought in words or any other symbolic language.

Moving makes a libidinal impact on consciousness. Moving stirs up the contents of consciousness so that as a writer you can find sentences and paragraphs by literally taking your consciousness for a walk. Consciousness is not a thing. It is a process. There is a 'consciousing'. And this consciousing is closely related to movement (Ginsburg, 1999, pp. 79–91), If Optik encounter an obstacle on the line they are moving along—a wall or another body—they may walk or run on the spot, they may embrace the obstacle, they may fall down, they may turn and take their line another way and, if it is a body, they may push the obstacle off their trajectory and continue or they may continue with the obstacle—the body—attached. They may stop.

Stopping

There is a libidinal impact on consciousness of stasis. In stasis there is concentration, focus. No competing bodily data in still meditation. On waking if you can remain still you may remember your dream. If you move your arm or roll over, you are likely to dissipate and lose the memory of the dream through the introduction of competing somatic stimulation (Scarry, 1987, p. 354). The contradiction of seeming to sit still on a train or a plane as the world hurtles past, when in fact you are hurtling through a world that is also moving, but slowly. There is no stopping in consciousness or life until the end of it. There is only focus to hold forms in the flux. The will to sculpt the flux.

> The mind, in short, works on the data it receives very much as a sculptor works on his block of stone. In a sense the statue stood there from eternity, But there were a thousand different ones beside it, and the sculptor alone is to thank for having extricated this one from the rest. Just so the world of each of us, howsoever different our several views of it may be, all lay embedded in the primordial chaos of sensations, which gave the mere matter to the thought of us indifferently. We may, if we like, by our reasonings unwind things back to that black and jointless continuity of space and moving clouds of swarming atoms, which science calls the real world. But all the while the world we feel and live in will be that which our ancestors and we, by slowly cumulative strokes of

choice, have extricated out of this, like sculptors. (James, 1890, pp. 288–289)

Enacting

Carving one reality from the myriad potentials. The mental energy it takes to do anything, go anywhere. Optik's presence in Brazil, for instance, results from the conjunction of the mental energies of the company's director, Barry Edwards, who is actively seeking such connection; Renato Cohen, the Brazilian teacher who invites us; and myself. Wilfully, I create the critical mass of belief that carries us there. Not shy to be an act (Imlah, 1988, p. 35).

Continuing

Anarchic lines of revellers follow carnival floats in Sao Paulo, progressing, processing, shuffling, whirling, dancing. Ravers trance dance and resonate to music that mimics and amplifies the rhythms, thumps and shudderings of the body. Losing conscious-ness in movement. One of the Optik performers actually suffers from narcolepsy. Stopped abruptly in mid-sentence, mid-conscious-ness. Falling to the floor and slumping in a chair, dreaming and moving down streets in sleep like a dog dreaming and twitching its limbs through a dream park. Slipping in and out of consciousness. The stream of consciousness interrupted by sleep or a collapse into unconsciousness. Driving around Sao Paulo at 4 am, sliding in and out of jet-lagged stupor, images of broad avenues, high architecture, topless prostitutes flickering through indistinguishable reality or dream. Performance artists Malcolm and Lily sleepwalking through Hamburg's red-light district, in pyjamas, eyes shut, arms outstretched zombie style (Newman, 2001, p. 22). Somnambulant.

Deciding

Deciding where to draw the line. If the Optik performers stop moving, they must decide when to move again. What is the genesis of movement?

> The precise moment that is the origin of action, the impulse to movement. It is a key point of transition between two polar states of performing, between the desire to move and the desire to rest, between energy conservation and the expenditure of energy. (Edwards, 2003)

The performers try to strip away the usual factors involved in deciding about moving—habit, patterns, aesthetic, rhythm. They try to respond 'unconsciously'—with reflex, urges, temptations, responses, mirroring, entrainment, trajectory, proximity. Everyday interactions, movements and decisions are amplified.

> Engagement in action is a matter of decision, to move or not to move, continuum of potential moments. In this dynamic arena, which is an inner space, the performer can attempt to wait. At this liminal waiting moment, which is a simultaneous experience of movement potential and rest, the body appears not as an image but as an immediate and felt presence. (Edwards, 2003)

Waiting

Waiting for a sense of when to move and what to do. The performer
is both stopping and moving, both the still centre of experience and
the origin of action. There is an anxiety of the actions of others in
relation to yourself, an anxiety of stasis, a pressure from spectators
to act, to resolve the tension of waiting with action. The performers
patiently hold emptiness and inaction, waiting. The difficulty of not
jay-walking. In Germany or Finland, where you should wait for the
lights to change before crossing the road. The difficulty of continuing to wait when there is no perceived physical reason not to move,
only cultural consent. The difficulty is not so much fear of legal
consequence or cultural disapproval. The difficulty is that moving
and bodily actions are on the cusp between entirely unconscious
somatic actions—the heart beating, the lungs breathing, the
stomach digesting—and potential actions that arrive in the
conscious mind requiring attention—thought and decision. When
we live in a city, our navigation of other people, obstacles, routes
and traffic becomes a bodily habituation. After practice, this moving
sinks out of consciously directed action and into the body, into
reflex. The body runs on its own well-worn grooves and ruts.

Running

Marina Abramovic and Ulay run naked in a space, drawn to each
other, colliding with each other, sometimes gently, sometimes
painfully. They want to attach to and hurt each other. Barry Le Va
runs fast in a white space, hitting the walls over and over, leaving
smears of blood from his impacts (Warr, 2000a, p. 121). He wants to
hurt himself and the walls. He wants to escape. Or leave his mark.

An Optik performer is running on the spot, nose up against the wall. Everything I write is on the same subject, running on the same set of ideas.

Seeing

'Seeing is a temporally extended pattern of exploratory activity. Our visual experience includes non-visual components that are vestibular and kinesthetic' (Noe, 2000, p. 131). Balance created in the central cavity of the labyrinth of the inner ear. The beauty of the shape of movement. Myriad invisible lines of potential emanating from or entangling the body in Oskar Schlemmer's drawing of Man. The sensed weight of emotions and moods. Proximity, distance sensed as well as seen. The body sensing invisible magnets that attract and repel. Optik walk straight lines. The *flaneur*, the Situationist walking a derive around a city, meanders in an indeterminate fashion—like a ball in a gentle pinball machine—deflected and impelled by chance. A chance sculpting of experience. 'The curved reality of sense perceptions operates in and out of the straight abstractions of the mind' (Smithson, 1979, pp. 112–113). 'To be an artist is not a matter of making paintings or objects at all. What we are really dealing with is our state of consciousness and the shape of our perception' (Irwin, 1972, cited in Noe, 2000, p. 123).

The Optik performances make emotions, moods, body chemistry, visible. In the dance studio, the relationship between space and performer is stark. There are four walls, the floor, the ceiling, the lighting, sounds, other moving bodies. In Kompanhia Theatre, Optik transgress spatial conventions—they go through doorways, they disappear from view but their footsteps can still be heard, performing invisibly. A performer sits next to a woman in the audience and stares neutrally. She stares back, laughs, breaks away from the stare, reconnects, laughs. The performer waits patiently.

> Am I an actor? A dancer? An object? Or just a projected image? Or shadow? Standing in front of an audience of strangers, of inquisitive/smiling or confused/angry faces? Seeking contact, connection (and disconnection) with other people. It seems like possibilities are endless. When asked what I do in Optik I do not know! I am there, looking for something, some moment, for the audience and myself. (Simon Humm, Optik performer, cited in Edwards, 2003)

The performers' images travel down a phone-line and are performing simultaneously on a screen in London and reappearing re-represented, well travelled, fuzzy at the edges on a screen in Sao Paulo that they sometimes halt in front of and watch. A commodius vicus of recirculation. Listening. They are performing to live music being relayed down the phone-line from London, the image of the musician flickering on a screen. The sound is intermittent and uneven as it travels down the dodgy internet connection. The performers, electronic sound and image, are flowing round the space, round the audience, round each other, round the world.

Walking

Optik perform in Praca de Se, Sao Paulo—a vast crowded busy open rectangle in front of the steps of the high cathedral. The three performers walk and run and stand along their lines carving a performance in the gulf and confusion of this street space. People go about their business, walking momentarily with ladders, buckets, pushchairs or briefcases alongside or through the performance—real life intersecting with art. Or the people form into curves of audience, moving and meandering along the invisible frame that is created around the performance. Hot, heavy air moves around us all, almost visible.

> Being about energy, I have chosen to work in parts of the world where energy (from people) is abundant and freely shared or given; former Soviet countries, as well as North Africa and Brazil. We give back, but also crucially tap in to that energy. (Edwards, 2003)

After the workshops of Optik lines, we are given gifts by our Brazilian hosts. In Sao Paulo we are given and join a circling dance. In Campinhas we join a *Capoeira* masterclass and at the end of the class we stand in a tight ring, shoulder to shoulder, with the *Capoeira* master soothing us, closing our eyes, leaning my whole body weight in trust against my left neighbour as my right neighbour leans on me. Ringsome.

Swaying

In an art bar, two young men with naked torsos stand near the wall, facing into the room, swaying backwards and forwards rhythmically for hours and hours, two inverted pendulums sprouting from the floor (VAIN, 2001). They rock us, they soothe us with their swaying. Existing, in motion, through time. They go on endlessly. They will never stop. They stop.

Stopping

• • •

The full stop. Optik must eventually stop performing although there is no particular reason to do so. Going on a journey, we try to 'finish everything' before we go. Writing to a deadline. I must eventually stop chipping at potential realities, stop thinking, reading, writing and complete, finish, close. End. Start. Life

31
OUT OF CONTROL: CONVERSATIONS ON COLLABORATION

2009. First published in *The Doubt Guardian*, no. 3, np. [Extract]

In the twenty-first century, artistic collaboration has moved from being an aberration to being as commonplace as the individual artist. What are the reasons for this phenomenon?

Collaboration has a long history in the visual arts stretching back to the Pre-Raphaelite Brotherhood and beyond. At the beginning of the twentieth century, artists' and writers' groups were numerous. Dada, Die Brucke, Blue Rider, Futurists, Vorticists, the Surrealists, Bauhaus, Gutai, Fluxus, The Inklings, the New Realists, the Lettrists, the Situationists International and many more groups and collaborations contested the notion of the lone, individual, genius artist and the commodification of the signature artist by the market (see Ades, 1984; Marcus, 1989; Stillinger, 1991). They explored a composite subjectivity and took iconoclastic stances against entrenched and defunct positions. They challenged the canon of art history.

Recent collaborations are numerous and include Abramović and

Ulay, Gilbert and George, and the Christos. The current burgeoning of collaboration has been reflected in a range of exhibitions, events and publications, including *Artistic Collaboration in the Twentieth Century* at the Smithsonian Institute in 1984 (McCabe, 1984), *Team Spirit* in 1990 (Sollins and Sundell, 1990), *Art Lovers* in 2002, a consideration of group practice in *Documenta XI* in 2003, the *Diffusion* symposium at Tate Modern in 2003 and *Collective Creativity* at the Kunsthalle Friedericanium in Kassel in 2005 (What, How & for Whom, 2005).

There are many different types of collaboration with diverse dynamics within them. The psychologists Damon and Phelps developed a distinction between co-operation and collaboration, where the latter had a more fully realised equality in roles and responsibilities (Damon and Phelps, 1989). Sometimes a collaboration is a merger of two or more hands into one, and sometimes it is deliberately manipulating the concept of a signature style itself. Sometimes it is a dyadic exchange. Sometimes collaborations are pseudo-kinship groups reflecting family dynamics. Sometimes they are conversational circles of peers sharing values and goals. Sometimes they are radial networks centred on a single person. A number of critics, including Irit Rogoff (1990), have pointed out that the market and the historical canon can adapt to absorb the group as the author too. Paul O'Neil asks, 'Is the collective just another marketable brand in disguise?' (O'Neil, 2007). Some collaborations, such as Platform or Critical Art Ensemble (Critical Art Ensemble, 1998), are intersections of artistic and activist practice. Some collaborations persist and some have a shelf-life or fizzle out.

Shifts in arts practice to an expanded practice that includes large-scale, site-specific and interdisciplinary work, and the range of skills required to realise that work, is one of the factors driving collaboration. My own work with artist duo, London Fieldworks, has reflected this (*London Fieldworks*, no date). Each of their projects has involved an expanded network of other collaborations with writers, composers, computer programmers, stunt kite flyers, scientists, mountaineers and musicians. They draw on multiple perspectives to approach large themes. Their work also raises the issue of 'collaboration' with sites and with communities. As early as 1957, Duchamp was discussing making meaning as a collaboration between artist, audience and posterity in his seminal text, 'The Creative Act' (Duchamp, 1957). In this text, Duchamp also described the way in which artists generate artworks as a collaboration with context, as opposed to innate self-expressing genius.

Interdisciplinary collaborations often encounter the problem that there is a mutually inexpert and uninformed understanding of the other's work in play. The understanding across disciplines is often a blunt instrument. Like speaking a second language, there is a conversation going on with a paucity of vocabulary. However, sometimes, that very paucity can invoke a more direct, more poetic exchange, free of jargon and ingrained assumptions.

Doubt Guardian's enquiry into collaboration began in York with a meeting of artists and promoters discussing their experiences. This meeting included Kit Monkman and Tom Wexler from KMA. I then interviewed Phelim McDermott from Improbable, one of the most significant long-term collaborations in theatre, and Ackroyd and Harvey, one of the most significant artist duos. They discussed collaboration as an art-making mode and as an urgent subject matter reflecting how we are organised in society today.

Collaboration in the 1970s was ideological as well as pragmatic and many contemporary collaborations are also ideological. The Collaboration Arts website set up in 2005 by Mark Dunhill and Tamiko O'Brien located contemporary art collaborations in an historical context stretching back to the establishment of the Kibbutz Movement in 1909 and the establishment of the Co-operative Movement in 1771 (see *Dunhill and O'Brien*, no date). Contemporary collaborative groups such as Superflex are ostensibly addressing radical modes of social organisation (see Bradley *et al.*, 2006).

The Russian artist duo Komar and Melamid asked what is art? Using a market research process, they produced the person in the street's favourite painting and their least favourite painting. What visual art is and can be has shifted substantially. For example, in this year's *Munster Skulptur Projekt* in Germany, Maria Pask established a self-sufficient food growing and living site and a spirituality research centre in a city park. She then invited a series of art and environmental groups to inhabit the space and maintain it for the next groups coming in over a six-month period. In Gediminas and Nomeda Urbonas' *Pro-Test Lab*, they squatted Vilnius' last large cinema space to save it from indiscriminate developers and to facilitate a space of protest for other people. *Pro-Test Lab* is another example of artists' practice asking questions about how society is organised—how we relate to each other and the environment (*US: Urbonas Studio*, no date).

The problems with collaboration include conflicts over authorship, ownership, competition and rivalry—differential success and recognition, money, editorial control. The advantages of collaboration include the ability to create your own critical research space, your own work context, your own sounding board and your own momentum, rather than having to be passively dependent on someone outside to give that to you. A collaboration can be a self-contained, reflexive artistic entity. Collaboration needn't mean the absorption and loss of individual eccentricities and idiosyncrasies. For many practitioners the advantages of collaboration are clearly outweighing the potential disadvantages. (Also see *Afterimage*, 1999; *Art Journal*, 1993; *Beaux Arts Magazine*, 2007; Billing *et al.*, 2007; Chadwick and de Courtivron, 1993; Farrell, 2001; Steiner, 2000; Watson *et al.*, 2006; Worsdale, 1996.)

Academia, with its need to identify and quantify and its notion of original contributions to knowledge, lags behind the critiques of authorship and origin established in collaborative practice. Instead of a singular authoritative position there is an increasing recognition of intersubjectivity and interdependence. Artists' collaborations are more than simply method. They are also subject. They enact a radical interconnectedness.

32
PICTURE TITLES

2015. Review of Ruth Bernard Yeazell, *Picture Titles: How and Why Western Paintings Acquired Their Names*, first published in *Times Higher Education*, 8 October.

Exploring the 'titular adventures' of paintings, Ruth Bernard Yeazell unearths caricatures, anecdotes and critical responses. One of Paul Cézanne's untitled works acquired the name *Diane et Acteon* because his dealer forgot to remove an old cartouche on the frame. 'Who the hell is Pasiphaë?' asked Jackson Pollock, after a curator gave that name to one of his paintings because the patron Peggy Guggenheim didn't care for Pollock's own title, *Moby Dick*. Mocking James Abbott McNeill Whistler's strategy of giving his paintings musical titles, *Punch* printed a caricature titled *An Arrangement in Fiddle-de-dee*, and *The Examiner* came up with *A Polka-Mazurka in Tartan Plaid*. J.M.W. Turner's titling fared no better. *The Literary Gazette* grumbled that 'it has pleased Mr. Turner...to give a name to a gorgeous assemblage of splendid hues, which has no, or scarcely any, connection with the subject indicated in the title'.

We tend to imagine artwork titles to be the province of the artist, but, as Yeazell's research shows, they were often composed by middlemen, including auctioneers, cataloguers and printmakers. By the eighteenth century, changing conditions of display and marketing required titles. Descriptive accounts created for inventories and identification in public displays gradually morphed into titles. Artists began to title their own works, writing on the back of their canvases. Expository and title labelling in galleries is a modern practice that began with a few experiments in the nineteenth century and was widely adopted in the twentieth century.

Picture Titles is well structured, moving forward effectively in short, well-argued sections. Yeazell's account is based on detailed study of documentary evidence, including *Salon* exhibition guides—the *livrets*, eighteenth-century auction catalogues, and the French *Académie* minutes. The book's first half focuses on titles in relation to middlemen and viewers, and the second presents case studies on the titles of Jacques-Louis David, Turner, Gustave Courbet, Whistler, René Magritte and Jasper Johns.

Yeazell convincingly argues that some artists contribute to theory not only in essays and manifestos but also in their decisions about titling. Titles threaten to short-circuit a viewer's experience and several artists resisted this tendency to render artworks legible. Whistler declared war between the brush and the pen, opposing the popular tendency to read paintings as narrative. The dominance of the written word was increasingly registered as a problem, with George Moore complaining in 1893 that 'painters seemed to have lived in libraries rather than studios'. 'A painting, for me, speaks by itself...A painter has only one language,' declared Picasso, while Clyfford Still asserted, 'My paintings have no titles because I do not wish them to be considered illustrations or pictorial puzzles'. Yeazell's rewarding discussion of Magritte shows how he saw a good title as one that intensified the effect of the image without pretending to explain it.

Yeazell touches only briefly on abstract art and does not venture far into the contemporary period, in which many artists have played with text and image. The book ends rather abruptly, with no conclusion; a bibliography, in addition to references in the Notes, would have been helpful. But only a few other writers, including John Welchman and Leo Hoek, have tackled this subject, and Yeazell's book is a rewarding addition to the literature.

33
MARK ROTHKO: TOWARD THE LIGHT IN THE CHAPEL

2015. Review of Annie Cohen-Solal, *Mark Rothko: Toward the Light in the Chapel*, first published in *Times Higher Education*, 2 April.

From the sorrow wrought by prejudice to envy to malice, the strong emotions that coloured Mark Rothko's life matched the depth and richness of his paintings. Annie Cohen-Solal's engrossing biography follows 'the difficult identity journey' of 'the avant-garde painter [and] the avant-garde Jew', re-examining his work in the historical contexts of both the pogroms in turn-of-the-century Russia and the golden age of capitalism in the United States after the Second World War. In a valuable, detailed account of his life, as well as a vivid portrait of early twentieth-century Europe and America, Cohen-Solal convincingly argues that migration and exile influenced Rothko's pioneering abstract expressionist art.

He was born Marcus Rotkovitch in 1903 in Dvinsk in the Russian Empire (now Latvia's second-largest city, Daugavpils), in the Pale of Settlement where some five million Jews were obliged to live. The youngest child of a German-speaking Jewish mother and a

Lithuanian Jewish pharmacist father, he spent his early years as a Talmud Torah scholar. Jews were conscripted into the Russian army, and as Rotkovitch's two elder brothers neared conscription age, their father decided to move the family to America. He went first in 1910, followed by the two young men, who crossed borders concealed in a sledge. In 1913, ten-year-old Marcus, his mother and sister set out to join them in Portland, Oregon. Upon arrival in New York, they were given tags to wear that read: 'I do not speak English'.

By 1920, more than two million Jews fleeing Russia had entered Ellis Island's 'golden door' to the United States. Although Cohen-Solal's meticulous research reveals warm community support for newly arrived immigrants, the Rotkovitchs lived in the poorer part of town, in marked contrast to their previous life. Marcus' father died not long after their arrival, and the boy soon shed his religious orthodoxy. At high school, indignant that Jewish pupils were excluded from the debating society, he wrote angry polemics for the school magazine. With no early training in art, he looked set instead for a career as a writer. Cohen-Solal offers a vivid picture of Marcus as a newspaper boy, standing on street corners shouting headlines about his former homeland: 'Rasputin Dead! Revolution in Russia!'

In the face of domestic opposition and rising xenophobia, the United States entered the First World War in 1917. In 1921, Rotkovitch won a scholarship to Yale University, but he found himself doubly stigmatised as a 'nebbish' Jew and a poor scholarship boy in an age when, as documents unearthed by Cohen-Solal show, the university's authorities were expressing disquiet at the high number of Jewish students. Once again, Rotkovitch took to his pen, accusing Yale of valuing breeding over merit: 'the whole institution is a lie and serves as a cloak of respectability for a social and athletic club'. Disillusioned, 'wounded by discrimination', he left without completing his degree, went to New York City and slept on relatives' sofas, doing odd jobs. Even if his indignation seems understandable, he comes across as a rather pompous young man. Friends described him as pugnacious, inherently tormented, 'an inveterate crusader'. 'Nothing stimulated him more than a righteous fight', recalled the art historian and curator Katharine Kuh.

Six months before Rotkovitch reached the United States, the *International Exhibition of Modern Art* (known as *The Armory Show*) had introduced an astonished American public to avant-garde European artists, including Duchamp and Georges Braque, drawing scandalised press coverage and unprecedented visitor numbers. Aged twenty-three, Rotkovitch visited a friend at the Art Students League of New York and discovered that radical, misunderstood artists were outcasts he could identify with. He attended classes and became friends with young experimental artists, including Barnett Newman, Jackson Pollock, Adolph Gottlieb, Robert Motherwell and Clyfford Still. He joined, argued with and left groups, such as The Ten (which had nine members), The Artists' Union and The Club, and fulminated against the art world's system of privilege and prestige. Cohen-Solal's account vividly evokes the swirls and eddies of friendship, support, rivalry and resentment in this milieu.

In 1938, Rotkovich became a U.S. citizen; in 1940, he changed his name to Mark Rothko. As Nazi troops marched across Europe, Paris ceded its place at the centre of the art world and New York began its transformation into the world capital of Modernism, bolstered by refugee artists and curators from Europe, including Mondrian, Josef Albers, André Breton, Peggy Guggenheim and Max Ernst.

As Cohen-Solal documents, Rothko's developing career was inspired by Henri Matisse, Joan Miró and André Masson, and by encounters with Greek, Roman and Etruscan art on post-war trips to Europe. In 1948, he co-founded the Subjects of the Artist School, an informal, avowedly non-doctrinaire undertaking that, said one wry commentator, boasted five professors and five students. Rothko's relationships with critics and patrons were often fraught, and his first commission ended in a costly, acrimonious lawsuit. He and Gottlieb wrote to *The New York Times* decrying the critical reception afforded contemporary art, and he was one of the artists dubbed 'The Irascibles', who attacked the Metropolitan Museum of Art for its lack of interest in 'advanced' art. He refused to sell two works to the Whitney Museum of American Art because, he announced, he could not trust it to display them without distorting their meaning. Throughout his career, Rothko was particular about how his works were hung and lit, seeing them as immersive experiences for the viewer.

In 1958, he received a major commission for Mies van der Rohe's new Seagram Building in Manhattan. Rothko's work toured European cities and received a particularly warm reception in London, and he represented the United States at the *Venice Biennale*. But he remained a polarising figure, and Cohen-Solal quotes from letters attacking his work, written around this time by his erstwhile friends, Still and Newman. Increasingly estranged from American capitalist values, Rothko considered buying a medieval chapel near Saint Ives in Cornwall to house his work. Convinced that the Seagram skyscraper's noisy, exclusive restaurant was not the right context for his paintings, he pulled out of the commission, returned the advance, and negotiated with the Tate Gallery to install the murals there instead. John and Dominique de Menil commissioned him to create pieces for a chapel in Houston, and Rothko finished these powerful, dark paintings, his last major works, in 1967. Curator Peter Selz wrote of Rothko's art: 'These silent paintings with their enormous, beautiful, opaque surfaces...deal directly with human emotions, desires, relationships, for they are mirrors of our fantasies and serve as echoes of our experience' (1961).

By 1968, Rothko's health was declining, his heart disease exacerbated by heavy drinking and smoking, and, in February 1970, he took his own life. His children entered a twelve-year legal battle with his estate's executors and the Marlborough Gallery, who would be found guilty of a conflict of interest branded 'manifestly wrong and indeed shocking' by the presiding judge.

Although James E.B. Breslin's 1993 volume has long been considered the standard biography, Cohen-Solal has benefited from the appearance in 2006 of two previously unpublished sets of writings by Rothko himself, *The Artist's Reality: Philosophies of Art* and *Writings on Art*, and she has drawn on material in the archives of the Whitechapel Gallery in London. Her book is both a moving tribute to a great artist and a gripping story. Its strength lies in placing Rothko in the contexts of a Europe devastated by wars and anti-Jewish violence, and America's post-war cultural scene, and the light that Rothko's life sheds on both these tumultuous eras.

34
ALAN SMITH: SILENT RUNNING

2009. First published online on https://www.acart.org.uk/
alansmith-parameter.

[A text created in response to Alan Smith's project *Parameter* in the Smallcleugh lead mine near Nenthead, Cumbria, United Kingdom, November 2009. The other participants were Elpida Hadzi-Vasileva, Andy Wilson, Ged Robinson and Steven Walker. Writer, Emma Cummins, was also part of the group and remained above ground.]

Six of us walked toward the dry-stone walled arch of the old lead mine entrance at 8 pm. We were leaving behind a clear night with a near-full moon haloed in rings of brown and yellow and the smaller bright white circle of Venus. A night-lit roiling blanket of earth and bumpy moss-covered miles of warren-like tunnels beneath. Preparing to go underground, I gulped in the view of the sky.

The entrance to the mine was a steel gate that swung in the middle, so one held the gate and took a bag over the top, while another crouched under and in. We had agreed to stop talking. We would not resume verbal communication for fifteen hours: one hour travelling to and from the mine entrance by car and on foot; four hours walking, wading, crouching, crawling in and out of the tunnels to get to the Ballroom Flat—a large void in the centre of the mine, and then ten hours in the Ballroom itself.

I am wading knee-deep through the first tunnel, through the dramatic subterranean architecture of the miners—excavated caverns and access routes created by stockpiled 'deads' (waste rock stacked to either side).

I am at the back of the group. At the front is Alan who has been going down these mines for ten years. He is the only one who knows the way in and out. It would be pointless for me to try to memorise the way in case Alan is injured since I am dyspraxic and can only navigate with a map. We have no maps apart from the one in Alan's head, no time devices (apart from an alarm Alan carries for the ten-hour marker), no recording devices, no notebooks, no pens and pencils. I am bereft without my pen prosthetic. Will I be able to retain experience if I do not write it down? I decide to use my body and my clothes as a 'text' that I will examine for 'forensic' study when I emerge.

We splash in concert, in wellingtons, through the tunnels. After Alan is Ged, then Elpida, then Steve, then Andy, then me. We are all artists and writers. We have to take care of the person behind us (no one in my case). Andy takes great care of me. I only met him a few hours ago, but thirty minutes into the tunnels and I already know a lot about him. The extremity of the experience is a short-cut to bonding. He is hyperaware of his surroundings, of his tread, of me. He has a deliberate and considered energy and way of moving and being that is very comforting. Warnings are called down the line, our only verbal communication (apart from some swearing and anxious mutterings to ourselves): 'deep shaft to the left!', 'boulder under water!', 'rock protruding from the ceiling!'

'rucksacks off and pass them forward! ', 'don't touch the walls here!'

Three years of frozen shoulders and I have no musculature left in my shoulders and upper arms. Taking my heavy rucksack on and off and dragging it behind me or pushing it ahead of me through the tighter tunnels where I have to crawl becomes harder and harder. Andy takes my bag and then Ged and Steve and Alan pass it up and down the line between them. I know how hard it must be to carry two bags. These negotiations occur in silence. I am mortified to be dependent and anxious not to become a liability for the rest of the group. I realise that I am expending so much emotional energy worrying about my dependency that I am neglecting to look at the astonishing geology around me.

Our helmet lamps light up streaks and nubs of galena and quartz glittering in the dark rock. Every now and then we encounter a spectacular mineral-encrusted rockface: ankerite, calcite, cerussite, chalcanthite, hydrozincite, ktenasite, malachite, melanterite, namuwite, sphalerite, sulphur. Jewels in dirt. We pass the calcifying remains of the historic mineworks: kibbles (wooden buckets that raised the ore), whimseys (winding engines once powered by horse, steam or water) and hoppers (the wooden chutes used to move materials). These old human objects are slowly being absorbed, becoming one with their wet rocky surroundings, part of the so slow flow of rocks. I try to imagine being a thing that always lives in the dark like the microflora and microfauna down here. The adamantine hardness of the rock rubs against the soft fragility of our bodies. There is such a vast expense of energy in mining. The ten miles of these tunnels were mostly carved by hand. A strange relativity of value between precious metal and expendable flesh.

Footing and balance is difficult with the uneven ground and the shifting weight of rucksack, battery pack and helmet lamp. I think of the small bones in the labyrinth of the inner ear that enable us to balance.

When we stop in a flat—an open space—and pass around water, we examine each other's faces in silent communication.

It gets very hot as we squeeze with our gear through tight tunnels where we cannot stand and where we have to avoid touching the walls and ceiling for fear of a cave-in. In places, loose stones litter the floor from previous falls. At some junctions with two tunnels, Alan marks off the wrong tunnel with loose pieces of wood and points this out to us. Eventually, Alan indicates that we have reached the hardest part: ten minutes of very low tunnel where we must crawl and slide on our stomachs, where the air thins with the six of us grunting, pulling bags, kneeling on razor-sharp stones. Then we emerge into a wet tunnel again where we can stand and finally, pass through a tall crevice emerging into the vast cavern of the Ballroom.

The Ballroom is a void left when the miners struck a particularly rich and enormous vein of lead. In 1901 the Masons held a ball down here with an orchestra and chandeliers. We turn off our bouncing helmet lamps and light candles, set up sleeping bags and mats. I feel emotionally exhausted and need to lie down and regroup myself. Slowly, I still and retract my senses that have had to function on full adrenalin for the journey in. Now that we are in this vast space, sweat dries rapidly and my body temperature plummets. I can see my hot breath streaming in the candlelight. I try to imagine the many metres of rock above the ceiling over my head.

I carried down provisional research questions and methods but quickly have to jettison most of them. It is necessary to be totally in the present, to focus on what is happening here and now. We have journeyed into the mine, into the materiality around us, but also into our own interiors, the immateriality of our consciousnesses. Our bodies come into sharp focus as we are intensely confronted with our dependency on them. They are our only reference point and our vulnerability. In darkness, I conduct a study of what seeing consists of. What perceptions of volume are possible? There is only 'paltry information about the environment projected onto the retina' (Noë, 2000, p. 127). I find it difficult to still my senses, to coalesce them to a point where I have enough control to use them for study. I am overwhelmed, disoriented, in turmoil.

The cold, and the warmth of my sleeping bag and layers of clothes, are sucking me into sleep but I want to stay awake to see how dark dark is. Several times I sit up and rock to keep myself awake. My enormous candlelit shadow on the wall looks like a bound mummy, with my arms pinned inside my shaped sleeping bag and the smooth oval of my woolly hat. We have agreed to burn candles or not according to individual preference. Eventually only Andy's candle at the end of the space and Elpida's candle next to me are still alight. Elpida is afraid of the dark. Later she reveals that she feared snakes, rats, ghosts. There is nothing living down here apart from us—and fungi, which Elpida is allergic to.

The air is totally still and silent. Every tiny noise that we make reverberates in the clear acoustics of the space. Someone shifts in their sleeping bag, a sniff, a cough, a fart, a nervous hum, a throat clearing, a tapping of rocks together. Some of these noises are involuntary sounds and some of them seem to be attempts at communication. I walk around the space and slap the rock in the way I saw people in China slapping trees in the People's Park as a meditative exercise. I smear my hands and gloves with material from the floor and walls to take some text out with me.

What is our disposition in the space? Alan is isolated at one end. Andy has set up at the other end. His candle is in a niche and looks to me to be surrounded by stalactites. Steve has arranged a circle of rocks and candles around himself in the middle of the space. Later he tells us that when he arrived in the Ballroom he wept briefly. Ged, then Elpida, then I, are ranged in a line along the far wall.

Elpida's huge shadow is projected onto the opposite wall if she sits up or moves. She is wearing a lovely and strange-shaped hat that turns her shadow into an unknown entity, its every move close in the corner of my eye. The shadows and candlelight alter expected proximities. Opposite and slightly to my left is the tall crevice opening. It is not a man-made shape but rather a fissure of the rock's own making. A few inches below my feet is a mystery boulder. I measure its cube with my hands: about two small hands in each direction. Where has it come from? I cannot see a hole in the ceiling it might have fallen from. It seems to mark the very centre of the space. I would like to move around the space and visit everybody but there are slippery loose rocks underfoot and I am afraid of being injured.

Someone in a white-hooded poncho is walking slowly around the Ballroom. None of us were wearing white. I am mesmerised by the slow, deliberate movement and pauses he makes. Is it Steve? Is it Andy? The candlelight has bleached the colour out of his clothing. He explores slowly, meditatively, drifting like a white ghost. He moves down and stands to Elpida's right. She rolls over and gasps, catching sight of him for the first time, terrified by this white apparition. I snigger, knowing by now it is Andy. I recognise something about him that is not to do with what is visible. Something about the fact that he wants to wander like this. Something to do with the pace of his wandering. Elpida recovers. Perhaps she sees his face. I am cross with myself for sniggering and should be more sympathetic to fear. I don't watch horror films or allow such stuff in my head. I am afraid of things I can't do anything about—death, the happiness of my grown-up daughter. Down here, entombed in sleeping bags and rocks, thoughts of death and burial are inevitable, but I feel surprisingly comfortable. I fear the cessation of consciousness. My last words will be, 'but I haven't finished yet'.

Alan stands up in his sleeping bag and plays with his shadow on the wall. His arm, I hope it's his arm, emerges comically from the bag. He goes off to wander in solitude. He knows the tunnels well. Steve is wandering in the space, in the nearby tunnels. We have agreed limits, but I know that Alan is desperately worried for us all, and for each of us if we leave the space. His anxiety is palpable.

Ged and Elpida stay in their sleeping bags. I visit Alan's space and have a look around at his disposition of things. I go out of the Ballroom, turn on my helmet lamp and walk a short distance down the tunnel to pee. I don't go far for fear of being lost and alone, but I think everyone must hear the noise of my peeing. I vary the flow a little to produce a melody for them if they can hear. I enjoy being alone with the rocks for a while.

I feel the distinctive and varying textures of things in the dark: the rock, the dirt, my sleeping bag, my clothes, my face. The air smells and tastes like cold metal. Elizabethan miners tasted the water in order to assess the mineral content of these sites. Saltiness on my lips. Coldness on my face. Measuring with my hands and arms, the body is a mobile laboratory. I twist my wrists to make cracking noises with my bones wondering if someone will answer in kind. Laughing. Stomach noises.

In darkness it takes twenty minutes for our eyes to adjust from rod vision (day-time) to cone vision (night-time). We have blind-sight. We have latent vision in the back of our hands, the back of our heads and our foreheads. We can feel space and proximity on our faces if we are blindfolded.

I think of hibernation and circadian rhythms: the researchers who spent thirty-two days in Mammoth Cave trying to switch their body rhythms to a twenty-eight-hour cycle, a six-day week. Scientists are trying to develop human hibernation and cryogenics that we might travel to Mars, live forever, be reborn. As a child, I was fearful and then awed each year at the hibernation and reawakening of my dearly loved tortoise. The neolithic burial chambers of Maes Howe and Newgrange were built to be pierced by light once a year at the solstice. The light streamed up the passageway and bathed the disarticulated bones waiting there, waiting for rebirth. As a child, I was afraid of the dark. I thought I could see tiny red aliens climbing up my bedroom curtains. The creaking of the cooling house was the sound of their climbing.

I doze off and when I wake up only Elpida's candle is left burning. I doze off again and wake to total blackness. No candles. Opening and closing my eyes makes no difference at all. Am I even awake? I can see images generated by my own eyes. Marquis d'Hervey de Saint-Denis studied and painted his own hypnagogic images between the state of waking and sleeping. He described 'wheels of light, tiny revolving suns, coloured bubbles rising and falling ... bright lines that cross and interlace, that roll up and make circles, lozenges and other geometric shapes' (d'Hervey de Saint Denis, cited in Coxhead and Hiller, 1976, p. 40). I see short yellow lines emanating from a black void. It seems to turn into an opening that I might rise up and go through. Entoptic phenomena are images generated by the eye itself: slowly drifting blobs of varying size, shape and transparency; tiny bright dots moving rapidly along squiggly lines; subtle bowtie and hourglass shaped patterns. You can see the blood vessels in your own eye appear like a tree (*Entoptic phenomenon*, no date).

I can hear the gentle breathing and shuffling of the others. At one point—am I awake, asleep, in-between—I think I hear two people in conversation coming down the tunnel toward the Ballroom. How surprised they will be to find six silent people here. But then I realise their conversation is very rhythmical and then I realise that it is an auditory hallucination that I have conjured from Alan's gentle snoring.

I sleep for about three hours. This is just a guess. Wafts of cold air seem to grip me, and I shiver uncontrollably for minutes but there are no draughts and no movements in the air. I eat a ginger stem biscuit. Alan wanders in my direction and I give him a biscuit. He goes over to Steve and gives him half. Later I give Elpida a banana. We are all surprised when Alan's ten-hour alarm goes off. It seems too soon.

Preparing to go out, Alan and I have a brief, silent disagreement. He wants me to go in the middle or the front. I know this is good safety procedure but if there is someone behind me I will rush and if I rush I could slip and be injured. Now I am older, I have all kinds of calcifying notions—I don't like anyone behind me, I don't like to rush, I hate being encumbered, I hate being an encumbrance. We are both stubborn old mules. Eventually I get my way. I know the safest way to handle my own body and will stick to it because I am in a potentially life-threatening situation. At one point, I get left behind and come to a junction with two tunnels. 'Hello?' no answer. 'Hello! Hello?' no answer. I cannot hear them moving. They are long gone, and I am alone. I don't panic. I remember the strips of wood Alan placed on the floor to mark the tunnel we should not go down. Now I know. I head up the other tunnel and Steve is on his way back to get me.

There is a difference between going in with Andy ahead of me and coming out with Steve ahead of me. While Andy felt considered and solid like the rocks around us, Steve's energy is more volatile. He points out a fabulous rockface of white and red crystals, a deep red sediment in the wall that we dip our fingertips into, a brilliant cold tiny waterfall that he drinks from, and I follow suit. He picks up a piece of wood, turns it over and finds a finely etched arrow there—a long-gone miner's mark. He shows me all his finds. It is his way of reassuring me and I enjoy these moments of combined experience. After a while he slows down, goes at my pace, unafraid to lose contact with the rest of the group, sure of the way out. I can look about me more now I know I can get out. What goes in must come out.

When we begin to wade through knee-deep water again I know that we are in the last stretch of tunnel before the exit. Steve turns and indicates that I should switch off my helmet lamp. Mine is the last light out and we are plunged into darkness. I touch the wet wall to help me keep my balance, my sense of moving in the right direction. We progress up the tunnel, splashing rhythmically and the white light of the mine entrance begins to emerge. I can see the other five, each silhouetted against the light. The anticipation of emergence and the sun is enormous. Finally, I am the last one out. Alan holds the gate and takes my bag over the top. I crouch under and then hold the gate for him.

We are all outside, up, in the light. The light is extraordinary. We scrabble to rapidly undo and throw off our cumbersome equipment and bags. We are standing in an irregular circle in early morning sunshine that is diffused through white mist or in fact a cloud. The low clouds are hugging the green, so green land that waves and rises and dips like the sea. We gaze in amazement and delight at each other, at the newly vivid world around us. The sound of the stream rushing is loud. Birds. It has been a frosty night. I touch the ice on the surface of a puddle and the frost on a lichened stone. I bury my face in frosted moss and smell it. Slowly we are grinning and shaking hands, hugging. Our faces are smeared with mud and sweat. Our fingers are grimed with the many materials of the mine. Our clothes and bags are covered in grey, green, black, red streaks and smears. My eyes feel stripped, clarified, pinned open. The air smells terrific.

Looking back months later, what traces have I left there? The sweep of my fingers in the dirt to either side of my camping map, a few strands of hair with my DNA, drops of sweat in the tight tunnels, ongoing resonances and vibrations of sounds I made, my energy and thoughts, still there, absorbed and stored by the rocks like a stony library. My absence waits there for me like the negative space left by the mined lead.

35

STILL LIVES: DEATH, DESIRE, AND THE PORTRAIT OF THE OLD MASTER

2015. Review of Maria H. Loh, *Still Lives: Death, Desire and the Portrait of the Old Master*, first published in *Times Higher Education*, 25 June.

Pursuing a selection of Renaissance artists into their studios, bedrooms and even their graves, *Still Lives* is a fresh, audacious examination of self-portraits and portraits of sixteenth- and seventeenth-century artists. Michelangelo, Raphael, Titian and Albrecht Dürer were among the first art stars. The 1568 second edition of Giorgio Vasari's *Lives of the Most Excellent Painters, Sculptors, and Architects*, which included 144 woodcut portraits, was a key turning point when artists became celebrities, and their images became public property. Maria Loh proposes that, as image-makers themselves, artists were in a unique position to contemplate the complexities involved in becoming a representation and the necromantic powers of the portrait. Her discussion focuses on the challenging daily business of being an artist and the survival of artists through their portraits, their immortal avatars. As she observes: 'One's portrait was always at once a companion and a threat'. She vividly writes us into the experience of 'the desperate vitality of the body' (as Pier Paolo Pasolini put it) that knows it will soon be gone. The 'shadow of the tomb', she writes, 'falls upon all portraits'.

Loh illuminates and entertains us with tales of art-world friendship and rivalry. One artist, for example, was poisoned with a spiked salad by an envious competitor. It put the victim out of action for four years. She immerses us in the dust, the pigment-grinding, the bitchiness, the bodily anxieties in an age of plague and syphilis. We find ourselves identifying with one artist rolling his eyeballs at another's pretensions and laughing at Annibale Carracci tricking a cook with *trompe l'oeil* sausages painted on the kitchen wall. She leads us into a world where the artist becomes, in death, a relic, and like the bones of the saints, subject, on occasion, to ludicrous fakery. Raphael's grave in the Pantheon was reverently dug up in the nineteenth century to prove that a skull purported to be his in the *Accademia di San Luca* was in fact somebody else's. Titian's body disappeared in Venice during a plague epidemic and was substituted by a bodiless tomb, described by Jean-Paul Sartre as 'a mountain of sculptured lard' with a representation of the artist that bears no resemblance to any of his self-portraits.

This is a gorgeous book, dazzling us with Loh's evident delight in the text that she is generating, and lavishly illustrated. Among the many paintings, drawings and sculptures included and discussed, the self-portraits by Sofonisba Anguissola, Parmigianino, Jacopo da Pontormo, Nicolas Poussin and the Carracci family are particularly remarkable. Loh's discussion of the contemplation of art-making by early artist-theorists, including Cennino Cennini, Leonardo, Federico Zuccaro and Vasari, makes this a book invaluable for artists, art students and art teachers, as well as for art historians and critics.

Loh's scholarship, her sensitive readings of artworks and her invigorating writing style make this artistic territory relevant for a wide range of readers, from Renaissance scholars to lay readers who are newcomers to the subject. She brings unexpected perspectives to bear on her subject, including an IT user's manual, Roland Barthes, Andy Warhol, Jackson Pollock, Kate Moss and Winnie-the-Pooh. At times, her vivacious text risks veering into incoherence or frivolity, but she successfully lassoes all into order, sweeping the reader along and fulfilling her own demand that the historian should 'find new means to make the beautiful strangeness of the distant past resonate once more'. This volume takes us on a fascinating journey where 'flesh and the image arrive at and depart from each other', as all bodies inexorably become still lives.

36
CHRISTIAN THOMPSON: CAMOUFLAGE, DAZZLE, DISPLAY

2012. First published in *Christian Thompson: We Bury Our Own.* Oxford: Pitt Rivers Museum/Melbourne: Gallery Gabrielle Pizzi, np.

An ambivalence of display and disguise appears in Thompson's new series of photographic self-portraits. Each image is a complex microcosm in which Thompson draws on his training in sculpture and textiles to build a photograph with, as he says, the mindset of a sculptor. The elements of each photograph are carefully selected and posed: clothing, props, backdrop, coloration, and not least himself—the appearance of his hair and hands, the concealment of other aspects of his face. These frontal head-shots conjure associations with the ID photo, the criminal mug-shot, the formal portrait, icons, and colonial photographic studies of indigenous peoples.

The artist tries on and inhabits a range of temporary guises: formal white-tie evening dress combined with a headband made from lumps of white and purple rock crystals, or with a crumpled paper headdress showing a photocopied image of a tree; or the same headdress combined with the ubiquitous lightweight waterproof jacket. In other photographs, he wears a headscarf with a print popular for tourists to Australia, or his head is obscured in a black balaclava. 'I am,' he says, 'the armature for the characters, costumes and various props'. In all these cryptic photographs his eyes are concealed—by crystals, flowers, butterflies, leaves, or hidden behind his hands, decorated with dot paintings, or various props are held up before his face: a Tudor warship, a picture of a bird of prey. In another image his eyes are disappearing beneath a cowl, a swathe, of blooming flowers. The concealment of the eyes makes the other parts of the face—the nose, mouth, cheeks—more visible and vulnerable-looking. We, the viewers are denied access. He does not engage our gaze, but rather his vision is introverted, or he is looking at and through the 'nature' in his eyes.

The work plays with Australian indigenous identity and with indigenous and Western histories and relationships. 'We are not allowed to evolve', writes Marcia Langton. In territory explored by other artists, such as Gómez-Peña, Fusco and Durham, Thompson's work breaks out from Western stereotyping of indigenous cultures as static, traditional, natural, authentic, and also from post-colonial notions of the indigenous victim, and instead allows that identity to escape from aspic and take fluid, contemporary, self-authored, forms. Yet Thompson's work is not limited to issues of identities, histories and geopolitics. His Bidjara heritage also comes into play in a pantheistic vision of the relationship between human and nature.

There are echoes of other (Western) artists in the work: Andy Warhol's video and photographic portraits, Abramović's crystal power-objects, Bruce Nauman's video and photographic works featuring himself, Man Ray's portraits of Duchamp dressed up as Rrose Selavy, Bowery's extraordinary clothing structures. These resonances are combined with evocations of the sensations of the land: the cornucopia of nature, the shimmering mirage, the heat, the smells of the landscapes in the sub-tropical, desert, and temperate zones of Australia. The viewer's gaze is denied in these photographs where the figure defends, protects and owns itself, but also looks beyond identity to ecology.

Camouflage might involve resemblance, concealment or confusion. Naval dazzle camouflage in the First World War, for instance, used strident patterning to confuse the enemy rather than conceal the ships, and was developed by U.K. artists Norman Wilkinson and Edward Wadsworth. In 1935, Roger Caillois published a provocative essay in the Surrealist journal *Minataure*, examining the phenomena of mimetic camouflage in insects and animals and the distinction between an organism and its surroundings. He discusses the insect camouflaged as a leaf, the mantis imitating a flower and the beetle posing as a pebble. After relating mimesis to sympathetic magic—'things once brought into contact remain united, associated by contiguity and resemblance' and considering mimicry as incantation, he goes on to argue that rather than a defensive activity, mimesis is caused by a 'temptation by space', 'the lure of material space', a desire for assimilation, 'to be in everything'.

> The Clolia, Brazilian butterflies, position themselves in a row on small stalks in such a way as to represent bell flowers, in the manner of a sprig of lily of the valley, for example. It is thus a real temptation by space. (Caillois, 1935)

According to Caillois, mimicry is a disturbance in the perception of space. His discussion of blending, blurring, merging, seems pertinent to Thompson's engagement with nature and his response to the temptation of the space of the image.

37
CHRISTIAN THOMPSON: GAZING AT FUTURE HORIZONS

2017. First published in *Lake Dolly*. Sydney: Michael Reid Gallery.

The photographs in Thompson's new series, *Lake Dolly*, are portraits showing the artist crowned with flowers and set amidst the lush plants of Australia. Thompson says the series is 'titled after the lake where my grandfather grew up in Barcaldine in Western Queensland, Australia'. Perhaps there is also a fortuitous *double entendre* in the title, gesturing at how the artist uses himself as a prop, variously dresses himself up as a sort of dolly, the subject of the photographs.

The images are black and white with the exception of the floral headdresses and the eyes of the subject. This contrast between greytone and specific areas bursting with colour creates a startling impact. Are those red eyes glowing, glowering, possessed? Are those sparkling blue eyes the eyes of beauty or ice cold? I will come back to the question of the eyes and the gaze of subject, photographer, and viewer, but focus first on the role of the plants in this photographic series.

The artist reports that:

The headdresses are made of native Australian flowers but are inspired by my Sephardic/Spanish Jewish roots on my mother's side, such as bridal veils and male traditional headdresses. I took them to a florist in Melbourne and these were the creations we came up with, and the wall of native flowers behind. The backgrounds I also captured on journeys around Australia.

Thompson plays with issues of identity, place, and exile. The Sephardic Jews were the Jews of Spain who were persecuted and expelled in 1492. It is interesting to consider the plants used in the photographs along with Thompson's titles.

In *Bitter Nightshade*, the sombre artist is crowned with green cacti and red and pink coral-like plants, standing against a corona of leaves that seems to emanate from the subject's crowned head like holy rays. A sunset or sunrise glows in the subject's eyes. Bitter nightshade is a plant that grows in Australia but is not native. It is an invasive weed, originating in Europe. Its poisonous berries can cause hysteria, hallucinations, and delirium. In Europe in the Middle Ages, it was believed to be good for bruises and was hung around the neck to protect from evil.

In *Devil's Darning Needle*, the subject wears a long, splendid ceremonial headdress of the red coral-like plant. Again, a sunset is reflected in his eyes. The devil's darning needle was a nickname for a dragonfly in American superstition, where it was believed the insect would stitch up the lips of naughty boys. It was also known as the green darner. The titles and the historical associations and characteristics of the plants set up questions about good and bad, about the character of nature, and of the subject of the photographs.

In *Portent Serac*, the subject's floral crown is more like the headdress of a May Queen or something from a Druid's ritual, and, in this photograph, the subject's eyes are lakes of light refracted in blue waters. (My own points of references are necessarily European and there may well be other references to indigenous Australian human-nature histories and practices evoked in these images that I am unaware of.) A serac is a dangerous, unstable column of glacial ice.

In *Purified by Fire*, the subject is literally buried beneath, absorbed within, emergent in, the fecund plant life, so that all we can see are the eyes holding the sun and the horizon. In this image, human and vegetal merge in a representation of the *genius loci*. The image recalls the fruit and vegetable portraits of the sixteenth-century Italian artist Giuseppe Arcimboldo, such as his portrait of the Roman god, Vertumnus, the god of seasons, plant growth and change. The plant life in Thompson's image is sexual, ripe, and his title is a reminder that fire brings about new growth.

In *Sea-Winged Seraph*, the floral headdress is shaped like a bishop's mitre. *Twin Divination* mirrors the *Portent Serac* photograph. In *Twin Divination* the orange flowers and sunset eyes contrast with the glacial blue eyes and pale pink flowers of *Portent Serac*. Thompson's images also recall the Green Man motif—a face surrounded by leaves and other vegetation—which occurs in architecture and sculpture all across Europe and travelled with colonising Europeans to the 'New World'. It is a motif popular among Australian stonemasons. The foliate head of the Green Man was a symbol of rebirth, the cycle of growth each spring, of fertility.

The *Lake Dolly* images celebrate nature and are assertions of power. The words of the titles—portent, divination, seraph, devil, purified—suggest a potent magic. The images also create a sense of doubt. Is the subject represented here good or evil. Are we looking at a joyful celebration of nature or something more sinister? Or is there the possibility of moving beyond such binaries?

'In this series,' Thompson comments, 'I replace my own eyes with landscapes and plant life as a metaphor for the internal emotional landscape, images I have captured on my journeys [around Australia] and then layered with different places and textures.'

Some of Thompson's previous work focused on a photographic reclamation of the indigenous Australian self from the gaze of the colonial photographer and viewer. His exhibition, *We Bury Our Own*, at the Pitt Rivers Museum in Oxford, was created in dialogue with the museum's collection of nineteenth-century photographs of indigenous Australians. Nineteenth-century photographers and collectors, such as Friedrich Dammann, staged studio portraits of Aborigines as the exotic other, as 'savage people', at the same time that around thirty thousand indigenous Australians were dying in wars in Queensland with European settlers. Some one thousand five hundred Europeans also died. The Pitt Rivers Museum gives this apology for the material:

> Some records document research into people and cultures using scientific research models and language from the nineteenth and twentieth centuries and depict people as research subjects in ways which may today be considered offensive. (Morton, 2011)

However, Thompson's work engaging with European anthropological museum collections is not simply a critique of this colonial past. He explores the implicit narratives and voices of the constrained subjects in those historical photographs, using his own biography and ancestry, and the complex, hybridised racial and gender markers of his own appearance (and we should not forget that such complexities apply to all of us).

In images that aspire toward beauty, Thompson's works rupture the zeitgeist and are subversive, inserting alternative narratives of masculinity and Indigenous identity into public discourse. The artist presents his own Native Australian body, which brings with it a range of associations. However, these artworks are not simply autobiographical. Thompson uses his body in the works as a conceptual context and site for drawing, through a process of autoethnography, a relationship between objects and histories that he connects to wider social and cultural understandings. While the photographs resonate strongly with the artist's autobiography, they also transcend ideas of race and gender, embracing iconic symbols of contemporary Australian art, as in his earlier work, the *Black Gum Triptych* from the *Australian Graffiti* series (2007).

The *Lake Dolly* series builds on Thompson's previous work, *Museum of Others*, in which he cut out the eyes of photographs of key colonial Europeans and replaced them with his own eyes. In *Museum of Others* the artist held placards before his face representing the explorer, James Cook; the ethnologist, Augustus Pitt Rivers; the anthropologist, Walter Baldwin Spencer; and the art critic, John Ruskin. The eyes of these European figures were replaced with the artist's own eyes. The skin of his hands, holding the placards, is the only hint in the photographs of the identity of the concealed figure behind the placards. In *Museum of Others*, Thompson steps inside the gaze of those historical Europeans to consider colonial divisions and classifications of the world, the objectification of those who were non-European.

Instead of engaging overtly with colonial division, the *Lake Dolly* series addresses the categories of human and nature and refers to current ecological crisis. The cornucopia of nature, and human life along with it, are under threat from climate change. Nature, in these images, is represented as both generous and ominous, fraught with fecundity and risk. The human is not the opposite of nature, or a separate category from it. We are made up from our environment, just as Arcimboldo's fruit and vegetables construct the faces in his portraits. The exchange between human action and the environment reflected in the eye is dynamic and reciprocal. The human is part of nature, and like other aspects of nature, we might see the human, all humans, as moving with free will on a spectrum of maleficence and beneficence toward one another and toward the nature that surrounds us, that we impact upon, and that we are a part of. Through their alluring beauty, Thompson's works elegantly deliver his message, drawing his audience into a deeper engagement with the work, functioning on both an emotional and conceptual register.

38
JAMES TURRELL: RODEN CRATER

2000. First published in *Contemporary*, 30 September, pp. 42–47.

North-east of the chilled-out and laid-back city of Flagstaff, Arizona, travelling past the settlements of Hopi, Navajo and cowboys, you eventually come to a place where there is just land and sky, with a few cows and eagles. The Painted Desert is 6,000 feet above sea level. The red, grey and black cinder cones of its eight hundred spent volcanoes punctuate the horizon and the muted greens and purples of chaparral and tumbleweed. The volcano field is aptly called Lohavutsotsmo—the testicle hills—by the Hopi. The San Francisco mountains are visible on the horizon and the Grand Canyon lies to the north. Here there is little sign of the human race. Sometimes the sky is a great weight and expanse of blue above; sometimes it is a stormy, lowering presence in a crushing face-off with the land. Then there are the spectacular, lurid striations of sunsets and sunrises when the world seems newborn. Land, eye and mind are bathed in a natural spectacle that beggars belief or description. Here, looking at the sky, you question the nature of materiality—especially your own little span of materiality.

One of the extinct volcanoes in the Painted Desert and one of the millions of such craters throughout the solar system is Roden Crater, where artist Turrell is building a naked-eye observatory. Twenty-eight years ago, Turrell scoured the American landscape in a plane looking for the 'right' volcano. Roden Crater naturally has the kind of symmetry found in a man-made mound such as Silbury Hill. In the seventies, Turrell spent three years persuading the farmer to sell him the land, raising the initial funding from the Dia Foundation and occasionally sleeping and dreaming in the crater bowl. Roden Crater has haunted the artist's imagination for three decades, during which he has produced evocative aquatints of the imagined project, architectural plans and cross-sections, and photographs that meticulously and stunningly record the site and the natural phenomena witnessed there. Twenty-eight years in the making is a long haul for an artwork by any standards.

Turrell has collaborated in archaeological and astronomical research and documentation at the site. Pottery shards found there reveal that Roden Crater was occupied by Sinagua and Anasazi peoples during 1065–1200 AD. At this time, the nearby Sunset Crater was still active, repeatedly erupting up until 1250 AD.

Turrell's *Roden Crater* project has been inspired by the long human tradition of building sacred sites, dream incubators and launch pads for the mind. This tradition has included Stonehenge, the pyramids of Giza, the Mayan temples, the stupas of the Asian jungles and naked-eye observatories such as Jantar Mantar, built in the eighteenth century in Jaipur. In Turrell's other 'skyspaces' (the artist's term for the spaces he creates for the purpose of observing the sky), such as *The Meeting* at PS1 in New York, and in some of his gallery installation works using artificial light, he has explored the induction of alpha brain states via the meditative contemplation of light. Turrell creates opportunities for us to look at the 'seeing' we generate from inside ourselves.

He cites many influences for *Roden Crater*, from the Anasazi underground ceremonial kivas to neolithic structures, such as Newgrange in Ireland or Maes Howe in Scotland, both built around 3,000 BC. During the winter solstice, sunlight streams up a passageway of the Newgrange burial mound and bathes the interior chamber in light for about five hours.

When I visited *Roden Crater* in April this year, a number of chambers and tunnels had already been built. These included a central, circular skyspace; an elliptical skyspace from which one can ascend a stairway into the crater bowl; the great keyhole opening of a sloping, grey tunnel built on a breathtaking, monumental scale; and the sun and moon space, which will project a huge pinhole image of the full moon onto the floor. Another cosmic viewing space in the fumarole (the small secondary cinder cone of the volcano) and a chamber pointing to the North Star were under construction.

Turrell's structure is being built with the materials on site— volcanic obsidian, shale and desert sand. Concrete made from the red and grey cinder ash lines the two tunnels. Turrell has taken on many roles—artist, Quaker, pilot, conscientious objector, antique plane restorer, architect and rancher. Having established the Walking Cane cattle ranch as part of the process of acquiring the land around Roden Crater, he restored the soil and vegetation depleted by earlier farming and has become an award-winning expert on grasses and cattle-raising. When *Roden Crater* is finished, indigenous vegetation will be replanted, and the structure will be almost invisible from the outside. At one point, *Roden Crater* was going to open later this year, but construction continues, and it will open soon—when it's ready. Turrell has designed and built a lodge, semi-buried into the lower slope of the crater, where up to eight people at a time can stay and spend day and night with the phenomena of nature.

Turrell is one of a number of artists who moved out into the Western deserts in the seventies to use the land and natural phenomena as sculptural materials informed by a metaphysical vision of geological time and cosmic space. They were also motivated by a need to evade the limitations of the art world. As Morris put it, 'the static, portable indoor art object can do no more than carry a decorative load that becomes increasingly uninteresting'. De Maria's *Lightning Field* and Charles Ross's *Star Axis* are in *Roden Crater*'s neighbouring state, New Mexico; *Double Negative* by Michael Heizer is in Nevada, while Smithson's *Spiral Jetty* and Holt's *Sun Tunnels* are in Utah to the north. Like *Roden Crater*, Ross's *Star Axis* is a naked-eye observatory nearing completion. It is, he says,

> a place where the earth and sky have equal weight. You get the feeling your feet are on the ground and your head is in the sky, and the horizon cuts you in half ... I'm not trying to direct ... metaphysics, just trying to point out that we're directly plugged into it. (Tiberghien, 1995)

Like other work inspired by non-Western and archaic cosmogonies and techniques, land art seeks to reconnect with a lost spirituality. Suzi Gablik points out that contemporary Western culture lacks a spiritual or transpersonal dimension: 'the faculties with which we might have joined [the gods] have atrophied' (1998, p. 43). Land art is about putting the self in touch with the cosmos.

Turrell's experience as a pilot has influenced his concept of time:

> With the experience of extremely high-altitude flight, new vantage is gained ... Civilizations are buried in the sands of time, then they can become exposed again ... Ancient cultures are revealed through differences in crop water retention, as in the discovery from the air of Woodhenge in England. Other cultures are dissolving back into the surface. (1993, p. 18)

Going into the extinct volcano cone of *Roden Crater,* you are entering geology. Not so long ago, the volcano was a fissure opening into an interior where geology was in violent flux. The site evokes the notion that the earth is an ancient life form. *Roden Crater* is about what is out there—celestial and natural phenomena—and about what is inside you: consciousness, perception, an awareness of the self in a flux of time and space. Entering the crater is a journey both into self and into the earth.

Morris' *Observatory,* built in 1977 near Lelystad in Flevoland, was inspired by neolithic henges. It stands on new land that was until recently the bottom of a shallow inland sea. Tiny shells embedded in the paths leading up to the earthwork remind us that this was once sea and could be again. *Observatory* consists of two concentric rings of earth made from embankments and ditches. Granite and metal 'V' shapes capture the equinox and solstice sunrises. To comprehend this work you have to move around it. Morris describes it as 'a place in which the perceiving self might take measure of certain aspects of its own physical existence ... the terms of this interaction are temporal as well as spatial ... existence is process'. The visitor's own experience of time is placed in direct contrast to the great time spans of human history by the neolithic references, and the imponderable and awesome stretch of astronomical time is gestured at in the solar sight lines.

Roden Crater will be 'an environment of rapture'—a place of encounter with celestial phenomena. Lying supine in the crater bowl, viewers are thrust 400 feet above the horizon into the space of the sky. There they can examine the illusion we create of the sky as a dome—the perceptual phenomenon known as 'celestial vaulting'. But *Roden Crater* is also a subterranean space drawing on associations with prehistoric sites that were strongly connected with death and burial. Turrell is bringing in light to pierce the dark coldness of these interior spaces. *Roden Crater* is a site reconnecting to the sacred and sublime—both above and below. At all the neolithic sites, death was an important component, alongside the celebration, and perhaps invocation, of the seasons. This intertwining of life and death is alien to contemporary Western culture, where death is euphemised, sanitised and removed from view.

At the Getty Research Institute, Margaret Iverson recently lectured on Smithson and the death drive. But the Freudian concept of the death drive depends on a Western individualistic concept of the self as isolated, tragic, terminal. Influenced by Anton Ehrenzweig, Bataille and prehistoric cultures, Smithson seems rather to be concerned with a non-Western concept of life and death, form and formlessness, as a cyclic process, an unending flux. This vision of death, and life, is tough on the individual consciousness but not negative. Smithson's film, *The Spiral Jetty*, makes this clear, with its astronomical and geological references and scenes of the artist running along the spiral floating in a sparkling 'primordial' sea. Eliade writes:

> The West will have to know and to understand the existential situations and the cultural universes of the non-Western peoples ... [It] will come to value them as integral with the history of the human spirit and will no longer regard them as immature episodes or aberrations ... The archaic and Oriental cultures succeeded in conferring positive values on anxiety, death, self-abasement and upon chaos. (Eliade, 1960, p. 14)

Appropriately, Smithson's own work fades back into nature —*Spiral Jetty* has been drowned by rising water levels but is still visible as a coiled shadow under the water. Last year when I visited Smithson's *Broken Circle/Spiral Hill* in Emmen, Holland, some twenty-eight years after its construction, part of this work too had been drowned by the rising water level, and the overall form was fading back into nature. The hyperbole that continues to accrue around both Turrell's position in the art world and the protracted run-up to the opening of *Roden Crater* make the project sound huge and hubristic. Count Giuseppe Panze di Biumo described it as the '*Sistine Chapel* of America'. Astronomer Richard Walker believes it is a new Wonder of the World. But out there in the desert, Nature—with its sheer expanse and the drama of sky and land, together with the timeframe visible in the volcano field itself—has no difficulty whatsoever in upstaging and dwarfing anything human. Big as *Roden Crater* is, intrusive as the construction might seem, it is swallowed up by the cosmic and geological spectacle.

There is an extraordinary capture of immaterial phenomena in Turrell's work. He directs viewers to their own experience, unimpeded by the artist's ego or personality:

the [task] of the Boddhisattva, one who comes back and entices others on the journey, is to some degree the task of the artist ... This is where I began to appreciate an art that could be a non-vicarious act. (1993, p. 18)

The experience of nature in the crater is also unmediated by any visible technology. This is not a work with a techno aesthetic. In many of Turrell's gallery works, and even in some of the skyspaces, technology is evidently spectacularising and mediating experience. But, in the crater, the only evident technology will be the viewer's own consciousness.

Turrell's is a non-symbolic art dealing with an area of consciousness that engages in non-symbolic thought:

First, I am dealing with no object. Perception is the object. Secondly, I am dealing with no image because I want to avoid associative, symbolic thought. Thirdly, I am dealing with no focus or particular place to look. With no object, no image and no focus, what are you looking at? (1993, p. 26)

And how are you thinking, or feeling, about what you are looking at? Your response to the sublime void of light is pre-linguistic:

> Turrell ... sets up a gap between the moment of experience and that of interpretation—a strategy with implications that go against the grain of currently fashionable logocentric philosophies, which generally insist that experience is always already a product of interpretation. (Rugoff, 1999)

Since the land artists first moved into the desert in the seventies, there has been a change in the role of the earth artist. Cleaving the land has been replaced by cleaning and caring for it in, for example, the contemporary 'ecoart' of Dominique Mazeaud or Aviva Rahmani. The American land artists did not walk lightly on this earth like Richard Long or Hamish Fulton. Their motivations were not ecological but metaphysical. Their vision is not anthropocentric but geological and cosmic. Smithson wrote: 'fragments of a timeless geology laugh without mirth at the time-filled hopes of ecology' (1979). Influenced by a vision of unending flux, the works of Turrell and Smithson do not attempt to conquer nature, and despite their apparent differences, all the artists discussed are concerned with the human relationship with nature, sharing the idea that, through nature, the sacred can be revealed.

39
URBONAS STUDIO: WRITING IN WATER

2012. First published online at http://www.vilma.cc/river/.

'riverrun, past Eve and Adams', from swerve of shore to bend of bay' are the opening words of one of the most famous novels in the English language: James Joyce's *Finnegans Wake* (1939). Joyce intended his novel to incorporate everything, and in his earlier novel, *Ulysses*, he described water as an all-encompassing substance, admiring:

> Its universality ... its vastness in the ocean ... the restlessness of its waves ... its hydrostatic quiescence in calm ... its sterility in the circumpolar icecaps ... its preponderance of 3 to 1 over the dry land of the globe ... its slow erosions of peninsulas ... the simplicity of its composition ... its metamorphoses as vapour, mist, cloud, rain, sleet, snow, hail ... its submarine fauna and flora ... its ubiquity as constituting 90% of the human body. (Joyce, 1960, pp. 783–785)

This essay draws together the threads of art-led research by

Urbonas Studio into the human relationship with rivers. For the *River Runs* project, Urbonas Studio consisted of artists Nomeda and Gediminas Urbonas, me—a writer, and architect, Giacomo Castagnola (see *Giacomo Castagnola*, no date; *Urbonas Studio: River Runs*, no date) . Our research began in 2010 and culminated in the 2012 *River Runs* project at Modern Art Oxford. This essay, which knits together quotations and reflective writing on *River Runs*, mimics the organic way in which the project itself unfolded and wove together the knowledges and experiences of many people.

In 2010, I invited artists Nomeda and Gediminas Urbonas to undertake a residency at Oxford Brookes University as part of *The Culture of Rowing and Swimming* event curated by myself and Rob La Frenais. I had worked with Nomeda and Gediminas on and off for over two decades and knew, in a rather tenuous connection to our swimming theme, that they had organised an urban swim art protest against swimming pool closures in Vilnius. More significantly, I knew they were artists with a well-deserved international reputation for creating artworks described as 'devices for action' and for examining invisible emotional infrastructures. During *The Culture of Rowing and Swimming*, Nomeda, Gediminas and I watched dumbfounded as a group of young boys 'tomb-stoned' off Folly Bridge into the Thames in Oxford. (Another young boy tragically died after tomb-stoning from Donnington Bridge during our second residency in 2012.) We were intrigued by the way in which the river was a different and alternative space from the banks on either side —with very few laws, by the way it provoked wildness.

Through a series of residencies, workshops, projects, and symposia in Oxford, United Kingdom and in Cambridge and Boston, United States, we collaboratively developed art-led research focused on water and rivers, hydrophilia, citizenship, climate change. Nomeda and Gediminas arrived in Oxford in 2010 with copies of material from the Massachusetts Institute of Technology (MIT) Archive on György Kepes' 1970s art project for the river Charles in

Boston and Cambridge (*Charles River Project*, no date). They had recently moved to the United States from Lithuania (via Norway) and were searching for their own new citizenship and artistic focus and found it in the role that rivers play in the lives of people. We shape rivers and rivers shape us. We focused our research on the study of freshwater rivers, engaging with a wide range of people interested in rivers from other disciplines and perspectives. Nomeda and Gediminas Urbonas live next to the river Charles in Cambridge, and I live next to the river Thames, in Oxford.

Our research during the 2010 residency led us to the Outdoor Swimming Society and wild swimming and to considering the contemporary 'commons'. We examined riparian rights and discovered that canoeists and swimmers are leading activism to establish the equivalent of the right to roam in Britain's waterways. We investigated the distinctive cultures of the river, including illegally fishing Lithuanians and Poles—fishing for food rather than sport; towpath cyclists; walkers; couples and drinkers; bizarre craft inventions including a bike-boat; and earnest craft manoeuvres—rowing, punts, steamers, the Bangladeshi Boat Club, rowing for mums and children at Falcon Rowing Club, the Oxford University rowing culture—bumps and eights. We ran a rowing workshop for beginners with Oxford Academicals Rowing Club where Gediminas found the drill was an unfortunate and resisted reminder of being in the Soviet Army. Nevertheless, the motley crew of mainly artists and a few architects did succeed in rowing an eight after two days of training. With Kate Rew and the Outdoor Swimming Society, I organised a wild swim in the Thames at Radley with sixty people. We had uncovered a rich area of enquiry and laid plans to continue our collaborative research in 2012.

Are we going to be living with more water in the future? Are we entering a new Water Age? ('The Water Age' was a term I coined; see Warr, 2018a, 2018b, 2018c). What are feasible future scenarios regarding climate change impacts on water levels, supplies, quality? What inspiring inventions and manifestations can artists contribute toward a future Water Age if we will be living with more water? How might we be inspired by aquatic life (fish, mammals, birds, insects, plants) and employ biomimicry to adapt to a future with more water? What role do waterways play in citizenship and belonging to place? Might we have a more amphibian lifestyle in the future and might this impact on the values that we live by? These were some of the questions we began with.

HYDROPHILIA

> To be embraced and sustained by the light green water was less a pleasure, it seemed, than the resumption of a natural condition ... The day was lovely, and that he lived in a world so generously supplied with water seemed like a clemency, a beneficence. (Cheever, 1964)

We examined our affinity with water. Why are many of us hydrophiliacs, unable to stay out of water for long? Although, conversely, some of us are hydrophobics. Water has many benign characteristics, but it also has significant destructive capacities. What impact does immersion in water have on our creativity?

> The warm rain tumbled from the gutter in one of those midsummer downpours as I hastened across the lawn behind my house in Suffolk and took shelter in the moat. Breast-stroking up and down the thirty yards of clear, green water, I nosed along, eyes just at water level ... The best moments were when the storm intensified, drowning birdsong, and a haze rose off the water as though the moat itself were rising to meet the lowering sky... In the water you are immersed in an intensely private world ... I can

dive in with a long face and what feels like a terminal case of depression and emerge a whistling idiot. (Deakin, 2000, pp. 1–4)

Sound travels differently in water and can be experienced through our skulls (*Wet Sounds*, no date). Water is a unique liquid structure.

> Water renders the earth fit as a habitat for life and is involved in life processes at all levels... Water is the only inorganic liquid that occurs naturally on earth... It existed on this planet long before any form of life evolved, and life developed in water. (Franks, 2000)

Water has an extraordinary motility. In the 1960s, Theodor Schwenk developed the 'drop picture method', photographing water to visually manifest its movement and its health. The method shows how the healthy flow of water is immediately affected by the smallest drop of detergent, for instance, with the water movement flattening out, becoming 'dead'. 'The world of water is one of motion, of becoming, and of dissolution, of process. It is impossible to describe the variety of manifestations of water with static concepts' (Wilkens, Jacobi, Schwenk, 2005, p. 25). Water moves in eddies and vortices.

The hydrologic cycle is the continuous circulation of water by evaporation from the hydrosphere and its subsequent precipitation back from the atmosphere. A fixed amount of water turns over in this cycle thirty-seven times every year. Dramatic redistributions of the planet's water have occurred at various points in its long history. A human being synthesises 300 g of water a day (Fishman, 2011). Water presents a thermodynamic paradox and there are still unresolved mysteries about the chemistry of water and many other of its aspects. Since life on this planet first developed in water, it is not surprising that it has remained the basis for all life processes. Water appears abundant, ubiquitous, but there is a finite amount, and it is hypersensitive to what is dissolved and thrown into it. Swimming on my back in the open air, looking up at gathering clouds, I experienced myself in the hydrosphere.

Writing flows like water. Several years ago I made a performance at Penzance Harbour, writing on a long roll of paper into the sea as the tide went out, washing the ink words away as they appeared, writing about sea voyages. I tried writing in a variety of liquids: ink, egg, spit. If I get stuck writing, I get in the bath, my consciousness gets realigned by swishing about in water, and then words flow again. Is the stream of our consciousness beneficially realigned by immersion in water?

Nothing in the world
is as soft and yielding as water
Yet for dissolving the hard and inflexible
nothing can surpass it.

The soft overcomes the hard;
the gentle overcomes the rigid.
Everyone knows this is true,
but few can put it into practice.

(Lao Tzu, 2022, Verse 28).

This quotation and others interspersed through this essay were contributed to the *Future Rivers Symposium* by the participants. This one came from artist Mike Blow. I organised the *Future Rivers Symposium*, a multi-disciplinary dialogue on rivers at the Isis Farmhouse in Oxford in April 2012.

Not only did Joyce's novel *Finnegans Wake* begin and end with the river, it also employed the technique of a 'stream of consciousness', a term invented by the psychologist and philosopher, William James. Consciousness, James wrote, is

> continuous... without breach, crack, or division... Consciousness, then, does not appear to itself chopped up in bits. Such words as 'chain' or 'train' do not describe it fitly as it presents itself ... It is nothing jointed; it flows. A 'river' or a 'stream' are the metaphors by which it is most naturally described. In talking of it hereafter, let us call it the stream of thought, of consciousness, or of subjective life. (James, 1890, pp. 237–239)

CITIZENSHIP

> Besides the sky, the river is the only aspect of our urban environment that has not yet been parcelled out into real estate or butchered by human insensitivity and carelessness. It suggests far-away places and distant memories and thus gives to the urban citizens a most needed sense of freedom. (György Kepes, 1972: np)
>
> (Quotation contributed to the *Future Rivers Symposium* by Nomeda and Gediminas Urbonas.)

In January 2012, we began a series of interdisciplinary engagements pursuing our research on rivers. Our themes and research developed incrementally through each event. At MIT, Gediminas Urbonas and I led a workshop with students: *Learning from the River*. Nomeda and Gediminas Urbonas were developing their ideas relating to citizenship and the river; I developed the idea for a future fiction with the working title of *The Water Age*; Giacomo Castagnola was thinking about mobile and habitation river structures; Mike Blow started devising sound objects for the river; Lily Tran came up with a modular river pontoon, inspired by one of the proposals from Kepes' project in the 1970s (*Charles River Project*, no date).

According to the Environmental Justice Foundation '150 million people's homes will be lost as a result of climate change by 2050' (Vidal, 2009).

> Migration is an adaptation strategy in itself ... and should not be seen as an intrinsically negative outcome to be avoided ... climate change will be experienced very differently around the world and across countries, as the vulnerability to nature is ultimately a product of the socio-economic forces that shape all societies. (Piguet, Pécoud and de Guchteneire, 2011)

During our research in Boston we visited curator Kurt Hasselbach at the MIT Museum and he asked: How can we expect people to care about the environment if they can't be in it? Hasselbach was talking specifically about the river Charles and the fencing, walling, inaccessibility and pollution from its industrial past, which meant that it was very difficult for people to be in the environment of the river. Working with Nader Tirani, Nomeda and Gediminas developed proposals for the *FAST Festival* celebrating the MIT centenary. Their proposals found ways for people to get in the river and they projected the Kepes archive images onto an inflatable floating screen. Gediminas ran classes with his MIT students on river inventions, which included Song Woo's ingenious water wheel for river mobility, drawing on the history and present of Boston's Chinese community.

FUTURE RIVERS SYMPOSIUM

The *Future Rivers Symposium* was held at the Isis Farmhouse in Oxford in March 2012, asking: What is a river and why are rivers important to you? The *Future Rivers Symposium* brought together a small group of people working in different disciplines to discuss rivers from a range of perspectives. There were presentations by me;

Alan Boldon, who spoke about his research on what makes a good place; and Richard Bailey, who spoke about his experiences of Venetian rowing on the Thames in Oxford. A consideration of the future of rivers raises a host of issues, including their impacts on human quality of life and well-being, water quality for drinking and swimming, water shortages, rising water levels, climate change and climate justice, public access, management versus adaptation, high tech versus low tech and aquatic biomimicry solutions, river-based structures and mobilities, aquatic wildlife and habitats, river-based leisure, sport, transport and more. 'The Thames is liquid history' (John Burns, in Knowles, *Oxford Dictionary of Quotations*, 2014). (Quotation contributed to the *Future Rivers Symposium* by artist Colin Priest.)

The other symposium participants were Mark Davies—a local historian, Colin Priest—an architect and artist, Elizabeth Price—a climate change researcher, Cookie Scotton—a curator at the River and Rowing Museum in Henley, Laura Degenhardt—an artist, Jane Wafer—an artist and Mike Blow—an artist. We discussed the significances of rivers to each of us and our concerns and knowledges about the possible future scenarios for rivers and for us in relation to them.

> There are bits and pieces of the Thames all over Oxford, runnels and reaches and backwaters—'more in number than your eyelashes', Keats said—and beneath the very centre of the city runs the Trill Mill stream, a gloomy underground waterway in which was discovered, one day in the 1920s, a rotted Victorian punt with two Victorian skeletons in it.... The early inhabitants of Oxford must have considered themselves river people, like Mississippi mudlarks, and the very names of the western districts—Osney, Binsey, Hinksey—recall old island settlements in the swamp. (Morris, 2001, p. 17)

(Quotation contributed to the *Future Rivers Symposium* by artist Laura Degenhardt.)

Jane Wafer remarked:

I studied biology many years ago, before turning to fine art as a complementary way of engaging with the world, and I find my interest in rivers spans both these disciplines. I walk by the Cherwell every morning and I find this has the same effect on me as a really good artwork. It fills my senses, opens a space for creative thinking and sharpens my powers of observation. I see rivers as a living, breathing thing and a measure of the health of our environment. (*Future Rivers Symposium*, 2012)

CLIMATE CHANGE

The majority of scientists agree that water levels are rising and will continue to do so for centuries, due to the thermal expansion of the oceans and melting ice sheets. The Intergovernmental Panel on Climate Change estimates a 7-inch to 2-foot rise in water levels by 2099 (2013). The U.S. Climate Action Report claims that is conservative and estimates instead a 2-foot to 6.5-foot rise (2014). The Netherlands are planning for a 4-foot rise by 2100 and a 13-foot (4-metre) rise by 2200 (European Environment Agency, 2012).

Rising water levels will create climate refugees—displaced homeless populations. Six hundred and thirty-four million people live in coastal areas. Low-lying countries and islands, including the Maldives, Tuvalu and Bangladesh and the east coast of the United States, will be most affected. There is disagreement about how much water levels will rise, when, and whether it will be sudden and catastrophic, or gradual (Lynas, 2008).

We have already experienced extreme flooding all around the world in the last few years. And we can see then that rising water levels are not just about coastal areas, because of the interconnected nature of the whole system, so rivers are affected along their entire length. The water table and subterranean water levels are affected. Eventually these waters recede but eventually some of them will not. Predictive maps exist showing where we might attempt to hold back the sea and where we would have to allow the land to be inundated, and this includes areas with major cities and communities (see *Climate Central*, no date).

So how might we react to rising water levels? Coastal retreat is one option but migration on that scale would significantly impact on population densities inland. There might be a role for sea and flood defences and water management, but given the scale of the issue, the degree of futility in that, the enormous cost and our current economic crises, this may not be the solution.

Instead of a dystopic disaster scenario we could try to imagine solutions and adaptations. It is well-established that science fiction influences technological developments (Battrick, 2001). Artists can propose what appear to be unfeasible solutions that nevertheless inspire future development. We could imagine living happily with more water, going with the flow, and the possibility that such change could have beneficial impacts on our values and the ways we live our lives. The eleventh-century Danish king of England, Canute, sat on the beach on a throne commanding the sea to stay back, to demonstrate to fawning courtiers his impotence in the face of the incoming tide. This is an interesting story if we consider that the Vikings were perhaps the closest humans have come to being amphibian.

Drought and water shortages are the other face of a future Water Age.

England's drought draws attention to the condition of England's rivers. And England's rivers—with those in Scotland and Wales— have ancient names, often conferred before the Roman legions came, and passed down almost unchanged to the present. A *Daily Mail* spread on the misery that will last all summer featured the Bewl, the Chess and the Pang. But these are just the start. What about the Mease, the Tees, the Dee, the Cree, the Nar, the Ter and the Ver? Or the Box, the Yox and the Axe? Or the Neet, the Fleet and the Smite? Do not forget, either, the Ebble, the Piddle, the Polly, the Nadder or the Wandle. Or the Feshie, the Mashie and the Wissey. Then there are the Lugg, the Ugie, the Meggat, the Tud, the Lud and the Irt. Like these other rivers, the Wampool, the Snizort, the Skirfare, the Deveron, the Cocker and the Stinchar speak of a deep Britain, to which we are more connected than we realise. Or would be, if it rained. ('In Praise of the Names of Rivers', 2012)

(Quotation contributed to the *Future Rivers Symposium* by environmental planner Elizabeth Wilson.)

AQUATIC BIOMIMICRY

We introduced aquatic biomimicry as an aspect of our research at MIT and I was fascinated by the glass sculptures of aquatic flora and fauna by Leopold and Rudolph Blaschka displayed in the Harvard Museum (Rossi-Wilcox and Whitehouse, 2007). With Kurt Hassel-bach at MIT Museum, we discussed 'Robofish', researchers' creation of a robotic fish, which is trying to figure out how fish use the fluid dynamics of the water, how they turn on a sixpence. Victor Schauberger said that a fish did not swim, it was swum by the river (Alexandersson, 2002, p. 85).

In January 2012, at an Oxford Visual Arts Development Agency *Stammtisch* event at The Port Mahon pub in Oxford, I led a workshop with artists asking them to draw inventions in response to the proposition that we would be living in a future Water Age. They envisaged things for daily life, to cope with an increased aquatic environment, and then drew these inventions on their tablecloths.

What daily technologies might we need for amphibian conditions: clothing, housing, food and drinking water, warmth, mobility, but also recreation—what happens to art, books or cats? How do we keep things dry that have to be dry? Do we sleep in water?

How are aquatic flora and fauna adapted to their environment? Might we learn ways to adapt to living with more water by looking at them? Lilypads are waxy and repel water; otters have a long tail to balance when swimming, closable nostrils and ears, and dense fur to create a waterproof surface; ducks have a gland producing oil to preen their feathers and keep them waterproof, under the waterproof layer is a downy layer for warmth, their webbed feet help them paddle; frogs breathe and absorb water through their skin, their bulging eyes see in all directions and their sticky tongues flick out to catch insects, their skin is slimy; salmon leap out of the water over weirs and falls. (I am indebted to Julie Turley for some of the research on aquatic fauna that we drew upon for the *River Runs* project. She ran the project's workshop for children at Modern Art Oxford.) Syndactyly—webbed toes or fingers—is a recognised condition that one in two thousand people have.

Will our bodies evolve to cope with an aqueous world? In the meantime, can we imagine other ways of living with liquid? Biomimicry looks at natural forms but also at the amazing functions and technologies that animals and plants have evolved to survive in their environments. Just a few examples of biomimicry are camouflage, velcro inspired by the burdock burr, biomimetic swimsuits based on shark skin, fibre-optic cable inspired by sea sponges, the Shinkansen bullet train influenced by diving kingfishers, tape imitating gecko suckers, wind turbine design influenced by humpback whales, sensors imitating rats' whiskers (Lee, 2011; Pawlyn, 2011). Underwater search vehicles are based on fish, earthquake search robots are based on snakes that can wiggle through rubble, mimicking dolphin sounds has enhanced long-distance underwater transmissions.

RIVER RUNS RESIDENCY AT MODERN ART OXFORD

For several weeks before our 2012 *River Runs* residency at Modern Art Oxford began, I embarked on a daily immersion—first in the river Viaur in southern France and then in Barton indoor and Hinksey outdoor pools in Oxford. Swimming in the open-air is vastly superior to swimming indoors, but the river is easily the most wonderful of immersions. Swimming upriver you see its green-edged channel opening onwards before you, beckoning you into the unknown. You experience the changing of the water, the weather, the sky and the banks. Bioprene—a layer of fat—is good for buoyancy and insulation in the open water.

Nomeda and Gediminas Urbonas meanwhile had been experimenting with fog screens that might hover over the surface of the river to project films onto. We observed the glee of the summer river —teenagers' river raves, picnics, dog walks and runners, and then the threat of the fast brown waters of the spring spate, the river running down roads, swamping allotments, inventing new lakes swiftly inhabited by swans and waders, redesigning landscapes and neighbourhoods, according to its own needs.

During our open studio days at Modern Art Oxford, our experiments with hydrophones in the project room sounded like whales calling and seduced visitors away from the Jenny Saville exhibition in the main galleries. Our open studio was a welter of computer and camera cables, books, half-finished texts, half-finished films, a lab structure with pool and waterfall, model rafts, sketches, displays of the outcomes of the workshops we ran with children and adults.

Nomeda and Gediminas were swimming most mornings at Port Meadow near The Perch in Binsey. There are a lot of myths and irrational fears around the quality of river water. In the past, rivers were used as the sewers of cities—everything from dead dogs to human and industrial waste were thrown into them, but now English rivers are significantly cleaner.

We made sixteen research films, interviewing people who live, work and play on and in the river, including Will McCallum, Mark Davies and Liz Lake who live on boats. Will is an environmental activist, Mark a Thames local historian (see Davies and Robinson, 2012) and Liz an artist. We also interviewed Richard Bailey—Venetian rower, Russell Robson from the Environment Agency, Sarah Markham—the Iffley lockkeeper, Chris Perrins—the Queen's Swankeeper at Port Meadow, Mike Bedwell a rowing inventor, Vicky Sweetlove—a dowser, and staff at Salters' Steamers. On the Cherwell with Richard Bailey in his Venetian sandolo, we glimpsed the traffic of the High Street and Magdalen Bridge through the trees, but its stressful, inexorable noise was damped down and almost inaudible. The maximum speed of four miles per hour on the river means that everything slows down—you included.

I had been test-swimming with Kate Rew in the Thames at Port Meadow and my fountain pen rolled off a pontoon into the water. When curator Rob La Frenais visited us, he leant over to examine the Venetian boat and dropped his reading glasses from his top pocket into the river. We became interested in all the things over centuries that had deliberately or accidentally been lost to the river. We interviewed river archaeologist, Zena Kamash, and looked at objects in the Ashmolean Museum that had been found in the river. Later we used a high-powered magnet towed behind our raft to dredge and garner various objects rusted and transformed by the river—forks, nails, a penknife looking like the carapace of an unknown insect. With genetic scientist, Ryan Pink, we discussed river genes—what makes the river green, why does being near and in sight of water make us feel good. We immersed ourselves in river culture looking for answers to our questions.

Using recycled materials from Orinoco and borrowed materials from fruit farms and the Covered Market in Oxford, we built a model river, waterfall and lake environment in our Modern Art Oxford studio. During the workshops, children and adults tried out their biomimetic designs for living in a future Water Age in the model landscape. And, in turn, we used it for our first tests with maquettes of our device for action, the *Jellypad Lilyfish*.

JELLYPAD LILYFISH

We were working toward a device for action for a future Water Age, drawing inspiration from biomimicry of aquatic flora and fauna and were interested in something that was flexibly about wearability and habitation. We envisaged a raft with multiple functions—a platform or water station, a water lab. We looked to historical examples of living with water, including the Vikings, and contemporary floating fishing villages and markets, long-established communities that exist entirely on, and from, the water. Giacomo researched underwater wearables, including diving suits from various times. We were interested in building a sculpture, a pontoon-boat, a hybrid laboratory/playground imaging the future of rivers in the Modern Art Oxford Project Space. I sent off a registration form to the Environment Agency to get a license for this boat that did not yet exist but was emerging in our imaginations.

Building the raft was a materials-led research process. There was an irresistible large roll of white neoprene hanging around in the Modern Art Oxford workshop, left over from a previous artist's project, which was immaculately stitched and seamed into lilypads for us by Stephanie Turner. At Kingcraft Chandlery in Abingdon, we were inspired by the materials and gadgets of river life: a waterproof box to keep your mobile phone in, plastic and rope fenders like underwater flora, ships' bells, a lifejacket for a dog, but most of our materials came from the Orinoco recycling centre.

Our method of propulsion came through serendipity. From the towpath at Port Meadow, we witnessed a curious craft being steered by inventor, Mike Bedwell, with his friend, Duncan Grant. Mike generously shared his ideas with us and Giacomo recreated Mike's yuloh oar for our craft. Instead of effortful pulling against the water, the yuloh rocks from side to side, gently stirring the water and propelling the craft forward. In the 1930s, Victor Schauberger wrote:

> Nature works in a spiral ... It is not a question of harnessing this energy, but of releasing it from its confines ... if craft are to be designed to be able to use vortexian energy as a motive force, they would do so not because of power generated to overcome gravity and other forms of resistance, but because a frequency was set up which was in total harmony with the energies that lie at the heart of all matter. (Alexandersson, 1990, pp. 141–142)

The *Jellypad Lilyfish* got its first unplanned outing from Port Meadow to Osney Lock, crewed by Gediminas Urbonas and Giacomo Castagnola, with me along as a passenger, Scot Blyth acting as human anchor, Nomeda Urboniene dashing along the riverbank documenting the maiden voyage, Laura Degenhardt providing van support, and the assistance of various other helpers, including Emily Korchmaros. We had planned to simply construct the raft near the bank at Port Meadow at dawn to see how it held water, but once it was put together, the river wanted to take it for a journey and so we went with the flow, amazing boat traffic and passers-by (one passer-by couldn't resist jumping into one of the lilypads himself). The neoprene pads were surprisingly warm and dry, but created an intimate, sculptural relationship with the water for their human freight. The lilypads enabled the traveller to be both on and in the river, drifting and flowing with the slow, inexorable movement of the water, enclosed in a green world reflecting light.

THE WET SYMPOSIUM

The following month, in August, I organised *The Wet Symposium*, supported by the Canal and River Trust and the Outdoor Swimming

Society. On a boat from Folly Bridge to Port Meadow, Tim Eastop introduced the day; Bridget Anderson from Oxford University talked about citizenship and water; Jake Piper from Oxford Brookes University spoke about climate change; and I described my future fiction novel, *The Water Age*, based on the idea of an adaptive future (not dystopic) of living with more water (Warr, 2018a). Then all the symposium participants got into the river to debate the papers that had been presented. From Archimedes to Roger Deakin's *Waterlog*, immersion in water has a demonstrable track record of impacting on our creative ideas. Being in the river caused adrenalin to flow and excited thought and dialogue.

The *Jellypad Lilyfish* made a second voyage for *The Wet Symposium*, travelling from Godstow Lock to Port Meadow where it was tested by the symposium participants. The day ended with a discussion led by Gediminas Urbonas and Russell Robson, at the Old Bookbinders pub on the Oxford Canal. The discussion addressed the river as cultural space and the future challenges for waterways policy makers.

Rivers and canals were once the highways of the world and may be again in the not-too-distant future when standing by the river gongoozling may become something more than watching the world float by.

TEXTS NOT INCLUDED

I have not included the following essays, which continue to be available in book form:

Warr, T. (2010) 'Texts from the Body: Bruce Gilchrist', in S. Broadhurst and J. Machon (eds) *Sensualities/Textualities and Technologies: Writings of the Body in 21st Century Performance*. London: Palgrave Macmillan, pp. 23–37.

Warr, T. (2012) 'The Body in your Lap', in R. Zerihan and M. Chatzichristodoulou (eds) *Intimacy Across Visceral and Digital Performance*. London: Palgrave Macmillan, pp. 15–25.

Warr, T. (2015) 'Finding a Different Way Home: Misha Myers in conversation with Tracey Warr', in M. Merskimmon and D. Row (eds) *Women, The Arts and Globalization*. Manchester: Manchester University Press, pp. 67–84.

Warr, T. (2015) 'Geo-Graphy', in B. Gilchrist, J. Joelson, and T. Warr (eds) *Remote Performances in Nature and Architecture*. London: Routledge, pp. 43–54.

Warr, T. (2018) 'Midden Lapidescence', in J. Nurmenniemi and T. Warr (eds) *The Midden*. Helsinki: Garret, pp. 114–153.

Warr, T. (2018) 'Compost and Life', in H. Curtis and M. Hargreaves (eds) *Kira O'Reilly: Untitled (Bodies)*. Bristol: Intellect/Live Art Development Agency, pp. 36–47.

My fiction texts created in the context of art exhibitions and residencies are also not included:

Warr, T. (2018) *The Water Age and Other Fictions*. London: Meanda Books. Includes 'Meanda', created for the exhibition *Exoplanet Lot*, Maison des Arts Claude et Georges Pompidou, Cajarc; 'The Extraterrestrial', created for *As Above So Below*, Allenheads Contemporary Arts; and 'Asbru', created for *Frontiers in Retreat*, HIAP, Helsinki.

Warr, T. (2019) 'Remolino', in A.P. González and M. Hoff (eds) *Corazón Pulmones Higado*. Madrid: Matadero, pp. 90–96. [Spanish]

COMING SOON IN WRITING IN THE VICINITY OF ART VOLUME 2

- Artscape Nordland
- Bauhaus University: Wanderlust
- Creative Acts: Curatorial Commentaries, including the Edge biennales
- Earth Art, Consciousness and the Thing Itself
- *Frontiers in Retreat* Interviews
- A Hysterical Sense of Leaking: Women's Body Art Now
- Cyril Lepetit: Consensual Art
- London Fieldworks: Outlandia
- Met Office: Weathering
- NVA: Contemporary Metaphysics
- Oskar Schlemmer and Trisha Brown: Bodies in Space
- Carolee Schneemann: Interview
- Alan Smith: Taking a Line for a Walk
- A Study Room Guide to Remoteness
- Urbonas Studio: Kukarkin Emerging
- Urbonas Studio: Zooetics
- and more.

BIBLIOGRAPHY

Abramović, M. (1995a) *Marina Abramović: Cleaning the House*. London: Academy Editions.

Abramović, M. (1995b) *Marina Abramović: Objects, Performance, Video, Sound*. Oxford: Museum of Modern Art.

Ackroyd, H., Harvey, D. and Thomas, H. (2000) 'The ephemeral in focus', Royal Society Lecture delivered at *Creating Sparks*, Victoria & Albert Museum, 17 September.

Ades, D. (ed) (1984) *Dada and Surrealism Reviewed*. London: Hayward Gallery.

Afterimage (1999) Special issue on artistic partnerships, 27(3), November/December.

Alexandersson, O. (2002) *Living Water: Viktor Schauberger and the Secrets of Natural Energy*. Translated by C. Zweigbergk and K Zweigbergk. London: Gateway.

Allenheads Contemporary Arts (no date). Available at https://www.acart.org.uk.

The Alpine Club (1862) *Peaks, Passes and Glaciers*. London: Longman, Green, Longman and Roberts.

Amino (no date). Available at http://www.amino.org.uk.

Armstrong, E. and Rothfuss, J. (eds) (1993) *In the Spirit of Fluxus*. Minneapolis: Walker Art Center.

Art Journal (1993) Special issue on collaborations between artists and writers, 52(4), (Winter).

Artaud, A. (1974) 'The theatre of cruelty: First manifesto', in *Collected Works*, vol. 4. Translated by V. Corti. London: Calder and Boyars, pp. 68–76.

Artitudes (1972–1974). Saint Jeannet: SPEB.

Ashcroft, F. (2001) *Life at the Extremes*. London: Flamingo.

Atlas, C. (2004) *The Legend of Leigh Bowery*, DVD. London: Palm Pictures.

Avalanche (1970–1976). New York: Center for New Art Archives.

Bacon, F. (1955) 'Statement', in A.C. Ritchie (ed) *The New Decade: 22 European Painters and Sculptors*. New York: Museum of Modern Art. Reprinted in H.B. Chipp (1968) *Theories of Modern Art*. London: University of California Press, p. 621.

Bachelard, G. (1969) *The Poetics of Space*. Boston: Beacon Press.

Ball, H. (1996) *Flight Out of Time: A Dada Diary*. Edited by J. Elderfield. Translated by A. Raimes. Berkeley and London: University of California Press.

Barnard, A. (1890) *The Noted Breweries of Great Britain and Ireland*. London: Sir Joseph Causton & Sons.

Barnes, M. and Berke, J. (1973) *Mary Barnes: Two Accounts of A Journey Through Madness*. Harmondsworth: Penguin.

Barthes, R. (1964) 'Rhetorique de l'image', *Communications*, 4(1), pp. 40–51.

Bataille, G. (1929) 'A critical dictionary: L'informe', *Documents*, 1(7), p. 382. Reprinted in Bataille, G. (1970) *Oeuvres Completes*, vol. 1. Paris: Gallimard, p. 217 and in Stoekl, A. (ed) (1985) *Georges Bataille: Visions of Excess: Selected Writings 1927–1939*. Minneapolis: University of Minnesota Press, p. 31. *Documents* are reprinted in a facsimile bound edition (1991). Paris: Jean-Michel Place.

Bataille, G. (1962) *Death and Sensuality: A Study of Eroticism and the Taboo*. New York: Walker.

Battrick, B. (ed) (2001) *Innovative Technologies from Science Fiction for Space Applications*. Paris: European Space Agency. Available at https://www.esa.int/esapub/br/br176/br176.pdf.

Beaux Arts Magazine (2007) Special issue on artistic partnerships, 272, February.

Becker, E. (1973) *The Denial of Death*. New York: The Free Press.

Beeber, S. (2006) *The Heebie-Jeebies at CBGB's: A Secret History of Jewish Punk*. Chicago: Chicago Review Press.

Bennett, O. (ed) (1990) *Edge 90: Art and Life in the Nineties*. London/Amsterdam: Edge Biennale Trust/Stichting Mediamatic Foundation.

Billing, J., Lind, M. and Nilsson, L. (2007) *Taking the Matter into Common Hands*. London: Black Dog.

Blazwick, I. (ed) (1989) *An Endless Adventure—An Endless Passion—An Endless Banquet: A Situationist Scrapbook: The Situationist International Selected Documents from 1957–1962: Documents Tracing the Impact on British Culture from the 1960s to the 1980s*. London: ICA/Verso.

Blueprint (1983–2020). London: Wordsearch.

The Body in Communism (1995) Symposium, Literaturhaus, Berlin, March. Unpublished.

Bourneuf, A. (2015) *Paul Klee: The Visible and the Legible*. Chicago: University of Chicago Press.

Bradley, W., Hannula, M., Ricupero, C. and Superflex (2006) *Self-Organisation/Counter-Economic Strategies*. Berlin: Sternberg Press.

Bracewell, M. (1994) 'Leigh Bowery's immaculate conception', *Frieze*, 19, November/December, pp. 38–43.

British History Online (no date). Available at https://www.british-history.ac.uk.

Broeke, L. (tr. and ed.) (2015) *Cennino Cennini, Il libro del arte*. London: Archetype.

brook & black (no date). Available at https://www.brookandblack.co.uk.

Buckingham, M. (2003) 'Muhheakantuck: Everything has a name', in *This Storm is What we Call Progress*. Bristol: Arnolfini.

Burden, C. (1975) 'Bed Piece, 1972', in *Chris Burden: Documentation of Selected Works 1971–74*. Video, 35 mins, b&w and col. New York: Electronic Arts Intermix.

Butterfield, J. (1975) 'Chris Burden: Through the night softly', *Arts Magazine*, March, pp. 68–72.

Caillois, R. (1935) 'Mimicry and legendary psychaesthenia', originally published in *Minataure*, 7. Translated by J. Shepley (1984) in *October*, 31.

Caillois, R. (1938) *Le Myth et L'Homme*. Paris: Idees/Gallimard.

Calas, N. (1978) 'Bodyworks and porpoises', *Artforum*, January, pp. 33–37.

Calvin, W. (1998) *How Brains Think: Evolving Intelligence, Then & Now*. London: Phoenix.

Cat Cairn—The Kielder Skyspace (no date). Available at http://www.visitkielder.com/great-outdoors/cat-cairn-the-kielder-skyspace-james-turrell-2000.

Chadwick, W. and de Courtivron, I. (eds) (1993) *Significant Others: Creativity and Intimate Partnership*. London: Thames and Hudson.

Chalmers, D. (1996) *The Conscious Mind*. Oxford: Oxford University Press.

Chalupecky, J. (1978) 'Art and sacrifice', translated by J. Mladejovsky, *Flash Art*, 80–81, pp. 33–35.

Charles River Project (no date), Center for Advanced Visual Studies Special Collection, MIT http://act.mit.edu/cavs/group/5JQf8Sg0Qiy6YZWj7noZ9t.

Cheever, J. (1964) 'The swimmer', *The New Yorker*, 10 July. Available at https://www.newyorker.com/magazine/1964/07/18/the-swimmer.

Chipp, H.B. (1968) *Theories of Modern Art*. Berkeley: University of California Press.

Cixous, H. (1975) 'The Laugh of the Medusa', reprinted in L. Burke, T. Crowley and A. Girvin (eds) (2000) *The Routledge Language and Cultural Theory Reader*. London: Psychology Press, pp. 161–166.

Claire Coté (no date). Available at https://www.clairecote.com/radio-dreaming.

Clark, L. (1973) 'De la suppression de l'objet', *Macula*, 1, p. 118.

Clausen, B. (2003) 'Drawing languages', in V. Smith and W. Niesluchowski (eds) *Joan Jonas: Five Works*. New York: Queens Museum of Art, pp. 113–116.

Climate Central (no date) 'Coastal Risk Screening Tool'. Available at https://coastal.climatecentral.org.

Coates, M. (ed) (2002) *Marcus Coates*. Ambleside: Grizedale.

Cohen-Solaal, A. (2015) *Mark Rothko: Toward the Light in the Chapel*. New York: Yale University Press.

Cowley, S. (2005) ' The electric universe: An essay on the scientific life, times, and legacy of Kristian Birkeland', in B. Gilchrist and J. Joelson (eds) *Little Earth*. London: London Fieldworks, pp. 64–93.

Cox, L. (2001) 'Anagrammatical "Unsods"', *Podomatic*. Audio Work. Available at https://www.podomatic.com/podcasts/podcastanagrammaticalunsods/episodes/2012-09-07T09_52_22-07_00.

Coxhead, D. and Hiller, S. (1976) *Dreams: Visions of the Night*. London: Thames and Hudson.

Crimp, D. (ed) (1983) *Joan Jonas: Scripts and Descriptions 1968–1982*. Berkeley: University of California Art Museum/Eindhoven: Stedelijk van Abbemuseum.

Critical Art Ensemble (1998) 'Observations on collective cultural action', *The Art Journal*, 57(2), (Summer), pp. 73–85.

Cross, D. (1996) *even: Dorothy Cross*. Bristol: Arnolfini.

Daily Mirror (1996) 'You couldn't make it up special', 6 August.

Damasio, A. (1999) *The Feeling of What Happens: Body, Emotion and the Making of Consciousness*. London: Heinemann.

Damon, W. and Phelps, E. (1989) 'Critical distinctions among three approaches to peer education', *International Journal of Educational Research*, 58(2), pp. 9–19.

Davies, M.J. and Robinson, C.M. (2012) *A Towpath Walk in Oxford: The Canal and River Thames Between Wolvercote and the City*. Oxford: Oxford Towpath Press.

Deakin, R. (2000) *Waterlog: A Swimmer's Journey Through Britain*. London: Vintage.

Debord, G. and Jorn, A. (1959) *Mémoires*. Paris: Situationist International.

DeLanda, M. (1991) *War in the Age of Intelligent Machines*. New York: Zone Books.

DeLanda, M. (1992) 'Nonorganic life', in J. Crary and S. Kwinter (eds) *Incorporations*. New York: Zone Books, pp. 129–167.

Deleuze, G. and Guattari, F. (1987) *A Thousand Plateaus*. Translated by Brian Massumi. Minneapolis: University of Minnesota Press.

Deleuze, Gilles (1981) *Francis Bacon*. Paris: Editions de la difference.

de Loisy, J. (ed) (1994) *Hors Limites: L'Art et La Vie 1952–1994*. Paris: Centre Georges Pompidou.

Dennett, D. (1992) *Consciousness Explained*. London: Allen Lane.

Dennett, D. (1995) *Darwin's Dangerous Idea*. London: Allen Lane.

de Zegher, C.M. (1996) *Inside the Visible: An Elliptical Traverse of Twentieth-Century Art in, of, and from the Feminine*. Cambridge, Mass. and London: MIT Press.

Didi-Huberman, G. (1984) 'The index of the absent wound (monograph on a stain)', translated by Thomas Repensek, *October*, 29, Summer, pp. 63–81.

Dixon, J.W. Jnr. (1982) 'Towards an aesthetic of early earth art', *Art Journal*, Fall, pp. 195–199.

Douglas, M. (1966) *Purity and Danger: An Analysis of Concepts of Pollution and Taboo*. London: Routledge and Kegan Paul.

Douglas, M. (1978) 'Do dogs laugh?: A cross-cultural approach to body symbolism', in T. Polhemus (ed) *The Body Reader: Social Aspects of the Human Body*. New York: Pantheon Books, pp. 295–301. Originally published in *Journal of Psychosomatic Research* (1971), 15, pp. 387–390.

Dreaming Place (no date). Available at http://dreamingplaceproject.wordpress.com/radio-dreaming/episodes/.

Duchamp, M. (1957) 'The creative act', in M. Sanouillet and E. Peterson (eds) (1973) *The Writings of Marcel Duchamp*. New York: Da Capo, pp. 138–140.

Dunhill and O'Brien (no date). Available at http://www.dunhillandobrien.co.uk/info/.

Eco, U. (1989) *The Open Work*. Translated by A. Cancogni. Cambridge, Mass.: Harvard University Press.

Ede, S. (2000) *Strange and Charmed: Science and the Contemporary Visual Arts*. London: Calouste Gulbenkian.

Edwards, B. (2003) *Optik*. Unpublished. Available at http://www.barryedwards.net/international-projects.

Einzig, B. (1996) *Thinking About Art: Conversations with Susan Hiller*. Manchester: Manchester University Press.

Eliade, M. (1960) *Myths, Dreams and Mysteries*. London: Harvill Press.

Eliade, M. (1963) *Aspects du mythe*. Paris: Gallimard.

Eliade, M. (1964) *Shamanism: Archaic Techniques of Ecstasy*. Translated by Willard R. Trask. Henley-on-Thames: Routledge & Kegan Paul.

Elliott, D. (1978) 'The Museum of Modern Art', *Oxford Art Journal*, pp. 57–58.

Emotional Rescue (2007) Exhibition, Kunsthalle Nurnberg.

Endurance (1995) Exhibition, Exit Art, New York and Video Programme, Video Data Bank. Available at http://www.vdb.org.

Exit Art (1996) 'Endurance art', *Performing Arts Journal*, 18(3), September, pp. 66–70.

Entoptic phenomenon (no date). Available at http://en.wikipedia.org.

European Environment Agency (2012) *Climate Change, Impacts and Vulnerability in Europe*. Available at https://www.eea.europa.eu/publications/climate-impacts-and-vulnerability-2012.

Export, V. and Justessen, K. (1996) *Jayne Parker: Body as Membrane*. Odense: Kunsthallen Brandts Klaedefabrik.

The Face (1980–2004). London: s.n.

Farrell, M.P. (2001) *Collaborative Circles: Friendship Dynamics and Creative Work*. Chicago: University of Chicago Press.

Feaver, W. (1996) 'And there's no silver lining', *Observer*, 1 September.

Ferguson, R. (ed) (1998) *Out of Actions: Between Performance and the Object 1949–1979*. London: Thames & Hudson.

Fishman, C. (2011) *The Big Thirst: The Secret Life and Turbulent Future of Water*. New York: Free Press.

Forster, E.M. (1927) *Aspects of the Novel*. Harmondsworth: Penguin.

Foster, H. (1993) *Compulsive Beauty*. Cambridge, Mass.: October/MIT Press.

Fox, T. (1982) *Metaphorical Instruments*. Essen: Museum Folkwang.

Frank, P. (1976) 'Auto-art: Self-indulgent? And how!', *Art News*, September, pp. 43–48.

Franks, F. (2000) *Water: A Matrix of Life*. London: Royal Society of Chemistry.

Freud, S. (1930) *Civilization and its Discontents*, translated by J. Riviere, in *The Standard Edition of the Complete Psychological Works of Sigmund Freud*, Volume 21. London: Hogarth Press, pp. 64–145.

Future Rivers Symposium (2012). Unpublished.

Gablik, S. (1998) *The Re-enchantment of Art*. London: Thames and Hudson.

Gamwell, L. (2002) *Exploring the Invisible: Art, Science and the Spiritual*. Woodstock: Princetown University Press.

George, A. (ed) (2003) *Art, Lies and Videotape*. Liverpool: Tate.

Giacomo Castagnola: River Runs (no date). Available at http://giacomocastagnola.com/en/projects/river-runs

Gilchrist, B. (1995) 'Divided by resistance: Dream research and neural networks'. Unpublished essay.

Gilchrist, B. (1996) 'Prepared pages', *Performance Research* 1(2), between pp. 19 and 20.

Gilchrist, B. (2001) 'KnoWhere', *Navigations* CD published in *Performance Research*, 6(3), Winter.

Gilchrist, B. and Joelson, J. (eds) (2001) *Syzygy/Polaria*. London: Black Dog.

Gilchrist, B. and Joelson, J. (eds) (2005) *Little Earth*. London: London Fieldworks.

Gilchrist, B. and Warr, T. (2000) 'Art as a first-person methodology in consciousness research', in K. Sutherland (ed) *Consciousness Research Abstracts: Toward a Science of Consciousness 2000*. Thorveton/Tucson: Journal of Consciousness Studies/University of Arizona, p. 162.

Gilchrist, B., Joelson, J. and Warr, T. (eds) (2015) *Remote Performances in Nature and Architecture*. Abingdon on Thames: Routledge.

Ginsburg, C. (1999) 'Body-image, movement and consciousness', *Journal of Consciousness Studies*, 6(2–3), pp. 79–91.

Goguen, J.A. (ed) (1999) *Journal of Consciousness Studies: Art and the Brain*, vol. 6, June/July. Thorveton: Imprint Academic.

Graham, D. (ed) (1979) *The Complete Poems of Keith Douglas*. Oxford: Oxford University Press.

Grant, C. (2002) 'Private performances: Editing performance photography', *Performance Research*, 7(1), pp. 34–44.

Green, C. (2001) *The Third Hand: Collaboration in Art from Conceptualism to Postmodernism*. Minneapolis: University of Minnesota Press.

Gropius, W. (ed) (1961) *The Theater of the Bauhaus*. Middletown, Connecticut: Wesleyan University Press.

Gysin, B. and Burroughs, W.S. (1978) *The Third Mind*. New York: Viking.

Hadzi-Vasileva, E. (2009) *Motectum*. Gloucester: University of Gloucestershire.

Hameroff, S. R., Rasmussen, S. and Mansson, B. (1988) 'Molecular automata in microtubles: Basic computational logic of the living state?', in C. Langton (ed) *Artificial Life: SF! Studies in the Sciences of Complexity*. New York: Addison-Wesley.

Haraway, D. (1989) *Primate Visions: Gender, Race and Nature in the World of Modern Science*. London: Routledge.

Harrison, C. and Wood, P. (eds) (1992) *Art in Theory 1900–1990*. Oxford: Blackwell.

Higgins, D. (1966) 'Statement on Intermedia', reprinted in E. Armstrong and J. Rothfuss (eds) (1993) *In the Spirit of Fluxus*. Minneapolis: Walker Art Center.

Hollinghurst, A. (1983) 'Robert Mapplethorpe', in S. Nairne (ed) *Robert Mapplethorpe 1970–1983*. London: Institute of Contemporary Arts.

Hopkins, T. (1989) *Pennine Way North*. London: Aurum Press.

Horvitz, R. (1976) 'Chris Burden', *Artforum*, 14 May, pp. 24–31.

Hynes, N. (2003) 'Joan Jonas: Lines in the sand', *n.paradoxa*, 11, pp. 6–13.

i-D (1980–). London: T.J. Informat Design.

Iffley History Society (no date). Available at http://www.iffleyhistory.org.uk.

IGER (2000) 'Something special happens when the human eye and green leaves meet', in H. Ackroyd and D. Harvey (eds.) (2001) *Afterlife*. London: Beaconsfield/Arts Admin, np.

Imlah, M. (1988) *Birthmarks*. London: Faber & Faber.

Improbable (no date). Available at https://www.improbable.co.uk.

'In praise of the names of rivers' (2012) *The Guardian*, 13 March. Available at https://www.theguardian.com/commentisfree/2012/mar/13/in-praise-of-the-names-of-rivers.

Intergovernmental Panel on Climate Change (2013) *Climate Change 2013: The Physical Science Basis*. Available at https://www.ipcc.ch/report/ar5/wg1/.

James, W. (1890) *The Principles of Psychology*, Vols. 1 & 2. New York: Dover.

Jones, A. (1994) 'Dis/playing the phallus: Male artists perform their masculinities', *Art History*, 17(4), December, pp. 546–584.

Jones, A. (1998) *Body Art/Performing the Subject*. Minneapolis: University of Minnesota Press.

Joyce, J. (1939) *Finnegans Wake*. London: Faber & Faber.

Joyce, J. (1960) *Ulysses*. London: Bodley Head. First published 1920.

Johnston, J. (1984) 'Hardship art', *Art in America*, September, pp. 176–179.

Jonas, J. (1994) *Joan Jonas Works 1968–1994*. Amsterdam: Stedelijk Museum.

Kaprow. A. (1966) *Assemblage, Environments and Happenings*. New York: Harry N. Abrams.

Kastner, J. (ed) (1998) *Land and Environmental Art*. London: Phaidon.

Kauffman, L. (1998) *Bad Girls and Sick Boys: Fantasies in Contemporary Art and Culture*. Berkeley: University of California Press.

Kavanagh, P.J. (ed) (1982) *Collected Poems of Ivor Gurney*. Oxford: Oxford University Press.

Keidon, L. (ed) (1996) *Totally Wired*. London: Institute of Contemporary Arts.

Keleher, A. and Coté, C. (2016) *Dreaming Place: An Irish Adventure*. London: KDP.

Kelly, M. (1984) 'Woman— desire— image', in L. Appignanesi (ed) *Desire*. London: Institute of Contemporary Arts, pp. 30–31.

Kepes, G. (1972) 'Unpublished letter', in *György Kepes Papers* https://archivesspace.mit.edu/repositories/2/resources/1358.

Klocker, H. (1989) 'The dramaturgy of the organic', in H. Klocker, (ed) *Vienna 1960–1971: The Shattered Mirror*. Klagenfurt: Ritter, pp. 41–55.

Knowles. E. (2014) *Oxford Dictionary of Quotations*. Oxford: Oxford University Press.

Koerner, J.L. (2016) *Bosch and Bruegel: From Enemy Painting to Everyday Life*. New York: Princeton University Press.

Kosuth, J. (1969) 'Art after philosophy', *Studio International*, October, pp. 134–137.

Kozloff, M. (1975) 'Pygmalion reversed', *Artforum*, November, pp. 29–37.

Krauss, R.E. (1977) 'Notes on the index: Seventies art in America, Part 2', *October*, 4, Autumn, pp. 58–67.

Krauss, R.E. (1985) *The Originality of the Avant-Garde and Other Modernist Myths*. Cambridge Mass.: MIT Press.

Krauss, R.E. (2016) *Willem de Kooning Nonstop: Cherchez La Femme*. Chicago: University of Chicago Press.

Kuhn, T.S. (1962) *The Structure of Scientific Revolutions*. Chicago: University of Chicago Press.

La Berge, S. and Gackenbach, J. (eds) (1988) *Conscious Mind, Sleeping Brain: Perspectives on Lucid Dreaming*. New York: Plenum.

La Frenais, R. (1994) '*Earth Wire*: Taking the alien exam', *Mute*, Winter, p. 1 & p. 6.

Lao Tzu (2022) *Tao Te Ching*. Translated by D. Hinton. London: Macmillan.

Lee, D. (2011) *Biomimicry: Inventions Inspired by Nature*. Toronto: Kids Can Press.

Lefebvre, H. (1991) *The Production of Space*. Translated by D. Nicholson-Smith. Oxford: Blackwell.

Libet, B. (1999) 'Do we have free will?', in B. Libet, A. Freeman and K. Sutherland (eds) *The Volitional Brain: Towards a Neuroscience of Free Will*. Thorveton: Imprint Academic, pp. 47–58.

Lippard, L.R. and Chandler, J. (1968) 'The dematerialization of art', *Art International*, 12(2), February, pp. 31–36.

Lippard, L.R. (1973) *Six Years: The Dematerialization of the Art Object*. New York: Praeger.

Lippard, L.R. (1976) 'The pains and pleasures of rebirth: Women's body art', *Art in America*, 69: 3, May—June, pp. 73–81.

Lippard, L.R. (1983) *Overlay: Contemporary Art and the Art of Prehistory*. New York: Pantheon.

Loh, M. (2015) *Still Lives: Death, Desire, and the Portrait of the Old Master*. New York: Princeton University Press.

London Fieldworks (no date). Available at https://londonfieldworks.com.

Lundy Island (no date). Available at https://www.landmarktrust.org.uk/lundyisland/.

Lynas, M. (2008) *Six Degrees: Our Future on a Hotter Planet*. London: Harper Perennial.

McCabe, C.J. (ed) (1984) *Artistic Collaboration in the Twentieth Century*. Washington: Smithsonian Institute.

McEvilley, T. (1983) 'Art in the dark', *Artforum*, Summer, pp. 62–71.

Macey, D. (1993) *The Lives of Michel Foucault*. New York: Pantheon.

Macfarlane, R. (2003) *Mountains of the Mind: A History of a Fascination*. London: Granta.

Macfarlane, R. (2008) *The Wild Places*. London: Granta.

McLuhan, E. and Zingrone, F. (eds) (1997) *Essential McLuhan*. London: Routledge.

Manzoni, P. (1962) 'Some realisations, some experiments, some projects', self-published pamphlet, Milan. Translated by C. Tisdall and A. Bozzola. Reprinted in G. Celant (ed.) (1974) *Piero Manzoni: Paintings, Reliefs and Objects*. London: Tate Gallery, pp. 84-85.

Marcus, G. (1987) 'The dance that everybody forgot', *New Formations*, 2, Summer, pp. 37–50.

Marcus, G. (1989) *Lipstick Traces: A Secret History of the Twentieth Century*. Cambridge, Mass.: Harvard University Press.

Massey, D. (2005) *For Space*. London: Sage.

Martin, T. (1994) 'Trois hommes et un bébé: Avec Burden, Kelley et McCarthy, balancer le canot de sauvetage', in J. de Loisy (ed), *Hors Limites: L'Art et La Vie 1952–1994*. Paris: Centre Georges Pompidou, pp. 268–285.

Mauss, M. (1934) 'Techniques of the body', reprinted in J. Crary and S. Kwinter (eds) (1992) *Incorporations*. New York: Zone Books, pp. 455–472.

Mauss, M. (1972) *A General Theory of Magic*. Translated by Robert Brain. London: Routledge & Kegan Paul.

Mehta, V. (1987) *Sound Shadows Of The New World*. New York: Norton.

Melzer, A. (1994) *Latest Rage the Big Drum: Dada and Surrealist Performance*. Baltimore: John Hopkins University Press.

Merleau-Ponty, M. (1964) *The Primacy of Perception and other Essays*. Evanston, IL: Northwestern University Press.

Meschede, F. (ed.) (1993) *Marina Abramović*. Berlin: Editions Cantz.

Metal (no date). Available at https://metalculture.com.

Miller, J. (2003) 'Lines in the sand', in V. Smith and W. Niesluchowski (eds) *Joan Jonas: Five Works*. New York: Queens Museum of Art, pp. 123–126.

Molesworth, H. (1993) 'Before bed', *October*, 63, Winter, pp. 69–82.

Moravec, H. (1988) *Mind Children: The Future of Robot and Human Intelligence*. Cambridge, Mass.: Harvard University Press.

Morris, J. (2001) *Oxford*. Oxford: Oxford University Press.

Morton, C. (2011) 'Object biographies: Ten Queensland photographs in the founding collection of the Pitt Rivers Museum', *Rethinking Pitt-Rivers*. Available at http://web.prm.ox.ac.uk/rpr/index.php/objectbiographies/72-10-queensland-photographs.html.

Nagel, T. (1974) 'What is it like to be a bat?', *Philosophical Review*, 83, 4 October, pp. 435–450.

Nairne, S. (ed) (1983) *Robert Mapplethorpe 1970–1983*. London: Institute of Contemporary Arts.

Narby, J. (1999) *The Cosmic Serpent: DNA and the Origins of Knowledge*. London: Wiedenfeld & Nicolson.

Nemser, C. (1971) 'Subject-object: Body art', *Arts Magazine*, September, pp. 14–17.

Newman, H. (1999) *Performancemania*. London: Matt's Gallery.

Noë, A. (2000) 'Experience and experiment in art', *Journal of Consciousness Studies*, 7(8–9), pp. 123–136.

O'Dell, K. (1998) *Contract with the Skin: Masochism and Performance Art and the 1970s*. Minneapolis: University of Minnesota Press.

Oiticica, H. (1969) *Eden*. London: Whitechapel Art Gallery.

O'Neil, P. (2007) 'Group practice', *Art Monthly*, no. 304, March, pp. 7–10.

Open Space World (no date). Available at https://openspaceworld.org/wp2/.

Orlan (1995) 'I do not want to look like …', *Women's Art Magazine*, pp. 5–10.

Orton, F. and Pollock, G. (1996) 'Jackson Pollock, painting and the myth of photography', in *Avant-Gardes and Partisans Reviewed*. Manchester: Manchester University Press, pp. 165–176.

Outlandia (no date). Available at https://outlandia.com.

Oxford History (no date). Available at http://www.oxfordhistory.org.uk.

Pawlyn, M. (2011) *Biomimicry in Architecture*. London: RIBA.

Pejic, B. (1993) 'Being in the body: On the spiritual in Marina Abramović's art', in F. Meschede (ed) *Marina Abramović*. Berlin: Editions Cantz.

Penrose, R. (1990) *The Emperor's New Mind*. London: Vintage.

Penrose, R. (1995) *Shadows of the Mind*. London: Vintage.

Perec, G. (1997) *Species of Spaces and other Pieces*. London: Penguin.

Perry, M. (2000) *Sniffin Glue: The Essential Punk Accessory*. London: Sanctuary House.

Phelan, P. (1993) *Unmarked: The Politics of Performance*. London: Routledge.

Piguet, E., Pécoud, A. and de Guchteneire, P. (2011) 'Migration and climate change: An overview', *Refugee Survey Quarterly*, 30(3), pp. 1–23.

Pijnappel, J. (ed) (1995) *Marina Abramovic: Cleaning the House*. London: Academy Editions.

Piper, A. (1976) 'Catalysis', in L.R. Lippard, *From the Center: Feminist Essays on Women's Art*. New York: E.P. Dutton & Co., pp. 167–171.

Pluchart, F. (1975) *L'Art Corporel*. Paris: Editions Rodolfe Stadler.

Pluchart, F. (1978) 'Risk as the practice of thought', *Flash Art*, pp. 80–82 and pp. 39–40.

Pollock, G. (1980) 'Artists, mythologies and media: Genius, madness and art history', *Screen*, 21(3), Autumn, pp. 57–96.

Price, R.F. and Cohen, D.B. (1988) 'Lucid dream induction: An empirical evaluation', in

S. La Berge and J. Gackenbach (eds) *Conscious Mind, Sleeping Brain: Perspectives on Lucid Dreaming*. New York and London: Plenum.

Pro-Test Lab (no date). Available at http://nugu.lt/KIT/archives/category/workshops/pro-test-lab-vilnius.

Punk (1976–1979). New York: Punk Publications.

Remote Performances (a) (no date). Available at https://www.remoteperformances.co.uk.

Remote Performances (b) (no date). Available at https://www.mixcloud.com/lfw/.

Rendell, J. (2006) *Art and Architecture: A Space Between*. London: I.B. Tauris.

Richard, N. (1986) 'The rhetoric of the body', *Margins and Institutions: Art in Chile since 1973/Art and Text*, 21, pp. 64–73.

Rimmer, D. (1985) *Like Punk Never Happened: Culture Club and the New Pop*. London/Boston: Faber & Faber.

Roden Crater (no date). Available at https://rodencrater.com/about/.

Rogoff, I. (1990) 'Production Lines', in S. Sollins and N.C. Sundell (eds) *Team Spirit*. New York: Independent Curators Incorporated.

Rosenberg, H. (1952) 'The American action painters' (1952), *Art News*, 51(8), September, p. 22. Reprinted in H. Geldzahler (1969) *New York Painting and Sculpture 1940–1970*. London: Pall Mall Press and New York: Metropolitan Museum of Modern Art, pp. 342–349.

Rosenfeld, K. (1999–2000) 'The end of everything was 20 years ago today: Punk nostalgia', *New Art Examiner*, 27(4), December–January, pp. 26–29.

Rossi-Wilcox, S.M and Whitehouse, D. (2007) *Drawing Upon Nature: Studies for the Blaschkas' Glass Models*. Edited by R.W. Price. New York: Corning Museum of Glass.

Roy, M. (2004) *The Weathermen of Ben Nevis 1883–1904*. Fort William: Royal Meteorological Society.

Roy, M. (2005) 'C.T.R. Wilson and the Ben Nevis Observatory', in B. Gilchrist and J. Joelson (eds) *Little Earth*. London: London Fieldworks, pp. 50–57.

Rugoff, R. (1996) 'Mr McCarthy's neighborhood', in R. Rugoff, K. Stiles and G. Di Pietrantonio (eds) *Paul McCarthy*. London: Phaidon, pp. 32–87.

Rugoff, R. (1999) 'Lost horizons', *Tate etc.*, 18, Summer, pp. 23–29.

Rugoff, R., Stiles, K. and Di Pietrantonio, G. (1996) *Paul McCarthy*. London: Phaidon.

Saggese, J.M. (2014) *Reading Basquiat: Exploring Ambivalence in American Art*. Berkeley: University of California Press.

Sally Booth Projects (no date). Available at https://sallybooth.co.uk/projectArchive/lundyIsland/index.html.

Sarduy, S. (1975) 'The transvestites. Kallima on a body: Painting, Idol', *Art Press*, 20, September, pp. 12–13. Translated in T. Warr (ed) (2000) *The Artist's Body*. London: Phaidon, p. 250.

Sayre, H. (1990) *The Object of Performance*. Chicago: University of Chicago Press.

Scarry, E. (1985) *The Body in Pain: The Making and Unmaking of the World*. Oxford: Oxford University Press.

Schilder, P. (1950) *The Image and Appearance of the Human Body: Studies in the Constructive Energies of the Psyche*. New York: International University Press.

Schmidt, J. (1995) 'Scenes and variations: An interview with Joan Jonas', *Art in America*, July, pp. 72–79 and pp. 100–101.

Scholder, A. (ed) (1999) *Fever: The Art of David Wojnarowicz*. New York: Rizzoli/New Museum of Contemporary Art.

Selz, P. (1961) *Mark Rothko*. New York: Museum of Modern Art.

Sharp, W. (1970) 'Body works: A pre-critical non-definitive survey of very recent works using the human body or parts thereof', *Avalanche* (Autumn), pp. 14–17.

Sharp, W. (1971) 'Interview with Terry Fox', *Avalanche*, Winter, pp. 70–81.

Shiff, R. (2011) *Between Sense and de Kooning*. London: Reaktion Books.

Sharp, W. and Bear, L. (1973) 'Chris Burden: The Church of Human Energy', *Avalanche*, Fall, pp. 52–61.

Smith, B. (1979) 'Paul McCarthy', *Southern California Art Magazine*, 21, January–February, pp. 45–50.

Smith, V. and Niesluchowski, W. (eds) (2003) *Joan Jonas: Five Works*. New York: Queens Museum of Art.

Smithson, R. (1968) 'A museum of language in the vicinity of art', in J. Flam (ed) (1996) *Robert Smithson: The Collected Writings*. Berkeley: University of California Press, pp. 78–94.

Smithson, R. (1979) 'A sedimentation of the mind: Earth projects', in N. Holt (ed) *The Writings of Robert Smithson*. New York: New York University Press, pp. 82–91.

Sniffin Glue (1976–1977). London: Mark Perry.

Soja, E.W. (1989) *Postmodern Geographies: The Reassertion of Space in Critical Social Theory*. London: Verso.

Sollins, S. and Sundell, N.C. (eds) (1990) *Team Spirit*. New York: Independent Curators Incorporated.

Solnit, R. (2001) 'After the ruins', *Art Issues*, 70, November/December, pp. 18–22.

Stankevicius, E. (ed) (1998) *Twilight/Sutemos*. Vilnius: Contemporary Art Centre. [Lithuanian and English.]

Steiner, G. (1978) *Has Truth a Future?: Bronowski Memorial Lecture*. London: BBC Books.

Steiner, V.J. (2000) *Creative Collaboration*. Oxford: Oxford University Press.

Stelarc (1997) 'From psycho to cyber strategies: Prosthetics, robotics and remote existence', *Cultural Values*, 1(2), pp. 241–249.

Stelarc and Paffrath, J.D. (eds) (1984) *Obsolete Body/Suspensions/Stelarc*. Davis, Calif.: JP Publications.

Stephano, E. (1973) 'Performance of concern', *Art & Artists*, 8, April, pp. 20–27.

Stevens, M. and Swan, A. (2004) *de Kooning: An American Master*. New York: Alfred A. Knopf.

Stiles, K. (1992) 'Survival ethos and destruction art', *Discourse*, 14(2), Spring, pp.

74–102.

Stillinger, J. (1991) *Multiple Authorship and the Myth of Solitary Genius*. Oxford: Oxford University Press.

Studio International (1964–1993). London: Studio Trust.

Taylor, R.P., Micolich, A.P. and Jonas, D. (2000) 'Using science to investigate Jackson Pollock's drip paintings', *Journal of Consciousness Studies*, 7(8–9), pp. 137–150.

Texte zur Kunst (2007) Special edition on Romanticism, March.

Third Text (2004) Special issue on collaboration, 18(6).

Tiberghien, G.A. (1993) *Land Art*. London: Art Data.

Tisdall, C. (1976) 'Beuys: Coyote', *Studio International*, 192(982), Jul-Aug, pp. 36–40.

Toward a Science of Consciousness (no date). Conferences, University of Arizona. Available at http://www.consciousness.arizona.edu

Troy, N.J. (2014) *The Afterlife of Piet Mondrian*. Chicago: University of Chicago Press.

Turner, V. (1982) *From Ritual to Theatre: The Human Seriousness of Play*. New York: PAJ.

Turrell, J. (1993) *Air Mass*. London: Hayward Gallery.

Tyler, C. (2000) 'Metaphors for the emergent properties of consciousness', in *Toward a Science of Consciousness Research: Consciousness Research Abstracts*. Thorveton: Journal of Consciousness Studies/Imprint Academic, p. 30.

Ulay/Abramovic (1983) *Nightsea Crossing*. Amsterdam: Sonesta Koepelzaal.

United States Climate Action Report (2014) *2014 CAR*. Available at https://unfccc.int/files/national_reports/annex_i_natcom/submitted_natcom/application/pdf/2014_u.s._climate_action_report%5B1%5Drev.pdf.

Urbonas Studios: River Runs (no date). Available at http://www.vilma.cc/river/.

Urbonas, G., Lui, A. and Freeman, L. (eds) (2017) *Public Space?: Lost and Found*. Cambridge, Mass. SA+P Press.

US: Urbonas Studio (no date). Available at https://nugu.lt/us/.

VAIN (2001) Kier Williams and Roly Carline Performance at *VAIN 2001*, Freud's Art Cafe, Oxford.

Varela, F.J. (1999) 'The portable laboratory', in H.U. Obrist and B. Vanderlinden (eds) *Laboratorium*. Antwerp: Provincaal Museum voor Fotografie, np.

Velmans, M. (2000) *Understanding Consciousness*. London: Routledge.

Vergine, L. (1974) 'Bodylanguage', *Art and Artists*, September, pp. 22–100.

Vergine, L. (2000) *Body Art and Performance: The Body as Language*. Milan: Skira.

Vidal, J. (2009) 'Climate crisis', *The Guardian*, 3 Nov. Available at https://www.theguardian.com/environment/2009/nov/03/global-warming-climate-refugees.

Viola, B. (1995) *Reasons for Knocking at an Empty House: Writings 1973–1994*. London: Thames and Hudson.

Virilio, P. (1991) *The Aesthetics of Disappearance*. Translated by P. Beitchmann. New

York: Semiotext(e).

von Drathen, D. (1993) 'World unity: Dream or reality, a question of survival', in F. Meschede (ed) *Marina Abramović*. Berlin: Editions Cantz.

Wagner, A.M. (2000) 'Performance, video and the rhetoric of presence', *October*, 91, Winter, pp. 59–80.

Walwin, J. (1997) *Low Tide: Writings on Artists' Collaborations*. London: Black Dog.

Ward, F. (1999) 'Chris Burden transfixed: Between public and private', *Collapse*, 4, May, p. 15.

Warner, M. (2003) 'On oracles and treacle: Some reflections on the art of Joan Jonas', in V. Smith and W. Niesluchowski (eds) *Joan Jonas: Five Works*. New York: Queens Museum of Art, pp. 89–93.

Warr, T. (1994) 'Earth Wire', *The Message*, pp. 4–5.

Warr, T. (1995a) 'To Rupture is to Find', *Women's Art Magazine*, May/June, pp. 11–13.

Warr, T. (1995b) 'Interview with Marina Abramović'. Unpublished.

Warr, T. (1996a) 'Sleeper', *Performance Research*, 1(2), pp. 1–19. DOI: 10.1080/13528165.1996.10871484.

Warr, T. (1996b) 'Udders, drills, and x-rays', *Women's Art Magazine*, 70, June/July, pp. 20–21.

Warr, T. (1998a) 'The Informe Body', *Performance Research*, 3(2), pp. 118–121.

Warr, T. (1998b) 'In the dark about art', in E. Stankevicius (ed) *Twilight/Sutemos*. Vilnius: Centre for Contemporary Art, pp. viii–xv. [Lithuanian and English.]

Warr, T. (ed) (2000a) *The Artist's Body*. London: Phaidon.

Warr, T. (2000b) 'The informe body', *Body, Space and Technology*, 1(1), July.

Warr, T. (2000c) 'Roden Crater', *Contemporary*, 30 September, pp. 42–47.

Warr, T. (2001a) 'Book review: Linda Kauffman, Kathy O'Dell', *Performance Research*, 6(1), pp. 127–131.

Warr, T. (2001b) 'Being something', in M. Coates, *Marcus Coates*. Ambleside: Grizedale Books.

Warr, T. (2001c) 'Circuitry', *Performance Research*, 6(3), pp. 8–12, DOI: 10.1080/13528165.2001.10871800.

Warr, T. (2002a) 'Tuning in', in B. Gilchrist and J. Joelson (eds) *Syzygy/Polaria*. London: Black Dog, pp. 6–11.

Warr, T. (2002b) 'Passing Presence', in H. Ackroyd and D. Harvey (eds) *Afterlife*. London: Beaconsfield/Arts Admin, np.

Warr, T. (2002c) 'Materialisation', in T. Bech and A. Damgaard, *The Inbetween: Plus & Pulse*, Arhus: Arhus Kunstbygning, np.

Warr, T. (2003) 'Image as icon: Recognising the enigma', in A. George (ed) *Art, Lies and Videotape: Exposing Performance*. Liverpool: Tate, pp. 30–37.

Warr, T. (2004a) 'A moving meditation on a dead line', *Performance Research*, 8(4), pp. 130–136, DOI: 10.1080/13528165.2003.10871978.

Warr, T. (2004b) 'What a performance is', in S. Foster (ed) *Joan Jonas*. Southampton: John Hansard Gallery, pp. 17–24.

Warr, T. (2005) 'Measuring beauty in the upper ice-world', in B. Gilchrist and J. Joelson (eds) *Little Earth*. London: London Fieldworks, pp. 11–19.

Warr, T. (2006) *Creative Acts: Curating and Writing with Artists*. Unpublished PhD thesis. University of Plymouth/Dartington College of Arts.

Warr, T. (2007) 'Feral city', in M. Sladen and A. Yedgar (eds) *Panic Attack!: Art in the Punk Years*. London: Barbican Art Gallery/Merrell, pp. 116–121.

Warr, T. (2008a) 'Dear body', in D. Kermode (ed) *Endurance*. Birmingham: Vivid, np.

Warr, T. (2008b) '*The Incident*', *Mute*, 1(3), October.

Warr, T. (2009a) 'Raw presence', in E. Hadzi-Vasileva (ed) *Motectum*. Gloucester: University of Gloucester, pp. 15–18.

Warr, T. (2009b) 'Place', in T. Warr, H. Ratcliffe, A. Smith and E. Carpenter (eds) *Setting the Fell on Fire: Allenheads Contemporary Arts: Art in a Rural Context*. Sunderland: Editions North, pp. 13–15.

Warr, T. (2009c) 'Green road', in T. Warr, H. Ratcliffe, A. Smith and E. Carpenter (eds) *Setting the Fell on Fire: Allenheads Contemporary Arts: Art in a Rural Context*. Sunderland: Editions North, pp. 29–34.

Warr, T. (2009d) 'Watery looks', in *Bech/Nacha*, Toronto: Open Studio.

Warr, T. (2009e) 'Out of control: Conversations on collaboration', *The Doubt Guardian*, no. 3, np.

Warr, T. (2009f) 'Silent running'. Available at https://www.acart.org.uk/alansmith-parameter.

Warr, T. (2010) 'Texts from the body: Bruce Gilchrist', in S. Broadhurst and J. Machon (eds) *Sensualities/Textualities and Technologies: Writings of the Body in 21st-Century Performance*. London: Palgrave Macmillan, pp. 23–37.

Warr, T. (2012a) 'Camouflage, dazzle, display', in *Christian Thompson: We Bury Our Own*. Oxford: Pitt Rivers Museum/Melbourne: Gallery Gabrielle Pizzi, np.

Warr, T. (2012b) 'Writing in water'. Available at http://www.vilma.cc/river/.

Warr, T. (2013a) 'Mellow Fruitfulness', in *Brook & Black, Plot 16: The Fermenting Room*. IXIA.

Warr, T. (2013b) 'The Practice of Space'. Available at http://www.castlefieldgallery.co.uk/event/hayley-newman-emily-speed/.

Warr, T. (2013c) 'On the tip of my tongue', *Journal of Writing in Creative Practice*, 6:1, pp. 107–125.

Warr, T. (2014a) 'Under the blanket of the earth', *a-n*, March.

Warr, T. (2014b) 'Book Review: *The Afterlife of Piet Mondrian*', *Times Higher Education*, 7 April.

Warr, T. (2014c) 'Book Review: *Reading Basquiat*', *Times Higher Education*, 25 September.

Warr, T. (2015a) 'Book Review: *Mark Rothko: Toward the Light in the Chapel*', *Times Higher Education*, 2 April.

Warr, T. (2015b) 'Book Review: *Still Lives*', *Times Higher Education*, 25 June.

Warr, T. (2015c) 'Book Review: *Paul Klee: The Visible and the Legible*', *Times Higher Education*, 3 September.

Warr, T. (2015d) 'Book Review: *Picture Titles*', *Times Higher Education*, 8 October.

Warr, T. (2016) 'Book Review: *Willem de Kooning: Nonstop*', *Times Higher Education*, 8 April.

Warr, T. (2017a) 'Book Review: *Bosch and Bruegel*', *Times Higher Education*, 19 January.

Warr, T. (2017b) 'Gazing at future horizons', in *Lake Dolly*. Sydney: Michael Reid Gallery.

Warr, T. (2018a) *The Water Age and Other Fictions*. London: Meanda Books.

Warr, T. (2018b) 'An ecology of words', in *The Water Age: Art and Writing Workshops*. London: Meanda Books.

Warr, T. (2018c) *The Water Age: Children's Art and Writing Workshops*. London: Meanda Books.

Warr, T. (2019) '*Remote Performances* Blog'. Available at https://www.thisisliveart.co.uk/2014/08/05/remote-performances-day-1-what-is-remoteness/.

Watson, G., van Noord, G. and Everall, G. (eds) (2006) *Make Everything New: A Project on Communism*. London: Book Works.

Weibel, P. (1978) 'Statement', *Flash Art*, 80–81, p. 39.

Weiss, J. (2004) 'Language in the vicinity of art: Artists' writings, 1960–1975', *Artforum*, Summer, pp. 212–217.

Wet Sounds (no date). Available at http://www.wetsounds.co.uk.

What, How & for Whom/WHW (2005) *Collective Creativity*. Kassel: Kunsthalle Friedericianum.

Wilkens, A., Jacobi, M. and Schwenk, W. (2005) *Understanding Water: Developments from the Work of Theodor Schwenk*. Translated by D. Auerbach and J. Greene. Edinburgh: Floris Books.

Wilson, S. (2002). *Information Arts: Interfaces of Art, Science and Technology*. London/Cambridge, Mass.: MIT Press.

Worsdale, G. (ed) (1996) *Co-Operators*. Southampton: Southampton City Art Gallery.

Yeazell, R.B. (2015) *Picture Titles: How and Why Western Paintings Acquired Their Names*. New York: Princeton University Press.

Zelevansky, L. (1981–1982) 'Is there life after performance?', *Flash Art*, 105, Dec–Jan, p. 39.

ACKNOWLEDGEMENTS

I am grateful to all the artists, curators, arts funders, publishers and arts organisations I have had the great pleasure of working with over the years.

INDEX

ABOUT THE AUTHOR

Tracey Warr was born in London and lives in southwest France. She worked at the Institute of Contemporary Arts and the Arts Council of England. She was the co-curator of the Edge biennales. She was programme lead in Fine Art at Oxford Brookes University and in Arts Management at Dartington College of Arts. She worked as a senior lecturer at Glasgow School of Art, Scotland; Bauhaus University, Germany; Piet Zwart Institute, Netherlands; and Saint Francis University (US) in France. She established the Arts and Place and Poetics of Imagination MAs at Dartington Arts School.

She is the editor of *The Artist's Body* (Phaidon, 2000), *Setting the Fell on Fire* (Editions North, 2009), *Remote Performances in Nature and Architecture* (Routledge, 2015) and *The Midden* (Garret, 2018). Her essays on contemporary art have been published by Merrell/The Barbican Gallery, Tate, Palgrave Macmillan, Intellect, Manchester University Press and *Performance Research* journal. She has also published five historical novels and a future fiction novella.

See https://traceywarr.substack.com

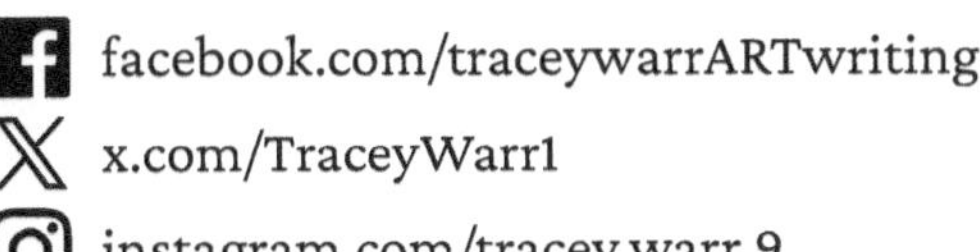

ALSO BY TRACEY WARR

ON CONTEMPORARY ART

The Artist's Body

(Phaidon, 2000)

Setting the Fell on Fire: Allenheads Contemporary Art—Contemporary Art in a Rural Context

(Editions North, 2009)

Remote Performances in Nature and Architecture

(Routledge, 2015)

The Midden

(Garret, 2018)

The Water Age Art and Writing Workshops

(Meanda Books, 2018)

The Water Age Children's Art and Writing Workshops

(Meanda Books, 2018)

FICTION

The Water Age and Other Fictions

(Meanda Books, 2018)

Meanda

(Meanda Books, 2023) [French]

Almodis: The Peaceweaver

(Meanda Books, 2023)

The Viking Hostage

(Meanda Books, 2023)

Daughter of the Last King (Conquest Book I)

(Meanda Books, 2023)

The Drowned Court (Conquest Book 2)

(Meanda Books, 2023)

The Anarchy (Conquest Book 3)

(Meanda Books, 2023)